The Case against Death

The Case against Death

Ingemar Patrick Linden

The MIT Press
Cambridge, Massachusetts
London, England

This book was set in Stone Serif by Westchester Publishing Services. Printed and bound in the United States of America.

Library of Congress Cataloging-in-Publication Data

Names: Linden, Patrick Ingemar, 1968– author.
Title: The case against death / Ingemar Patrick Linden.
Description: Cambridge, Massachusetts : The MIT Press, [2021] |
    Series: Basic bioethics | Includes bibliographical references and index.
Identifiers: LCCN 2021000482 | ISBN 9780262543163 (paperback)
Subjects: LCSH: Death.
Classification: LCC BD444 .L4895 2021 | DDC 128/.5—dc23
LC record available at https://lccn.loc.gov/2021000482

10 9 8 7 6 5 4 3 2 1

To Ingemar Linden and
Else-Marie Linden,
whom I thank for my existence.

Contents

Acknowledgments   xi

1   The Case against Death   1

1.1 The End of Aging and Death   1
1.2 The Wise View: Death's Many Advocates   5
1.3 We Do Not Know What to Think   11
1.4 The Wise View Is Fragile   14
1.5 Can We Reason about Values?   17
1.6 What Is the Point?   18
1.7 Specifying the Case against Death   19

2   The Case against Aging   23

2.1 Aging   23
2.2 Defending the Indefensible   25
2.3 Aging Is Not a Disease, So Medicine Should Leave It Be   34
2.4 Falsified Preferences Concerning Aging and the Morality
of Not Being Antiaging   36

3   Death Is Harmless   39

3.1 What You Don't Know Can't Hurt You   39
3.2 The Deprivation Account of the Badness of Death: What You Don't Know
Can Hurt You   40
3.3 A Timing Challenge to the Deprivation Account   42
3.4 What Kind of Person Can Be Indifferent to Death?   47
3.5 The Mirror Argument   50
3.6 The Differences between Prevital Nonexistence and Posthumous
Nonexistence   51
3.7 We Cannot Diminish the Time That We Do Not Exist   53
3.8 The Folly of Wisdom   54

4   Life Is Overrated   59

4.1 The Case against Life   59
4.2 Suffering and a Dream of a Crystalline State   61
4.2.1 Responding to the Argument from Suffering   63
4.3 Escaping Our Mad Masters   64
4.3.1 In Defense of Our Mad Masters   69
4.4 Meaningless! Meaningless!   71
4.4.1 Responding to Meaninglessness   73

5   Death Is Natural and Therefore Good   77

5.1 Everyone Dies!   77
5.2 Appeals to Nature   78
5.3 Death in the Big Scheme of Things   80
5.4 Responding to Holism   83
5.5 Holism and Collectivism   86
5.6 Defending a Liberal View of Death   90
5.7 Conclusions   93

6   It Would Be Boring to Live Longer   95

6.1 The Spiritual Argument against Life Extension   95
6.2 Losing Interest and Engagement in Life   97
6.3 Not Easily Bored   98
6.4 Motivation and Human Nature   102
6.5 Losing Our Passion for Life: *The Makropulos Case*, a Reflection on the Tedium of Immortality   104
6.5.1 Responding to Williams   106
6.6 A Pill for Interest and Engagement   109
6.7 Conclusions   111

7   We Need a Deadline   113

7.1 We Only Aspire and Take Life Seriously Because We Die   113
7.2 Death and Underdetermination   114
7.3 Death and Procrastination: A Response   115
7.4 Death Makes Life Matter   117
7.5 Death or Senselessness   118
7.6 Death Is Necessary for a Sense of Achievement   121
7.7 Banging Our Heads against Epistemic Walls   125
7.8 The Threat of a Deadline   127
7.9 Life Is Short So . . . What?   131

8   Mortality, Character, Virtue, and Moral Excellence   133

8.1 Immortals Cannot Be Noble   133
8.2 Immortals Can Be Noble   134
8.3 Is Wanting to Live a Character Flaw?   136

9   Death Is the Mother of Beauty   139

9.1 Love and Beauty Depend on Death   139
9.2 Does Beauty Depend on Death?   140
9.3 Mortality and the Motivation to Make Beautiful Objects   143
9.4 Can an Immortal Love an Immortal?   143
9.5 Eight Common Fallacies of Spiritual Arguments in Favor
of Death and Decay   145
9.6 Speaking Nonsense to Desires   147

10   Death Saves Us from Overpopulation   149

10.1 Prolonging Life Would Bring Horrible Social Consequences   149
10.2 The Overpopulation Threat   150
10.3 Why Global Overpopulation Is Unlikely   152
10.4 Are We Running Out of Resources?   157
10.4.1 Water   158
10.4.2 Food   159
10.4.3 Energy   160
10.4.4 The Environment   162
10.5 Alexandra Paul's Tragic Mistake   165
10.6 Conclusions   167

**11   Death Saves Us from Social Consequences Worse
Than Death   171**

11.1 The Graying of the World   171
11.2 The Economy: The Main Challenges   173
11.3 The Economy: Troubles Are Overstated   174
11.4 (Missed) Economic Opportunities of Longevity   177
11.5 Calcified Hierarchies and Stagnation   179
11.6 Immortal Tyrants   186
11.7 Many Other Challenges   187
11.8 The Distribution of Life Extension   189
11.9 A Question of Priorities   194
11.10 The Fog of Future Technology   196

12 The State of the Debate and a Concluding Dialogue Concerning the Badness of Human Mortality   199

12.1 The State of the Debate   199
12.2 A Dialogue Concerning the Badness of Human Mortality   201

Notes   209
Bibliography   239
Index   253

Acknowledgments

The idea for this book can be traced back to a summer a long time ago, sometime in the 1970s, where I counted each day of my summer vacation. I did not want it to end, not so fast, but it did. I spent these summers with my parents and grandparents, and I owe them for nurturing my curiosity and for providing the love and security that gave me the sense that life is a wonderful, beautiful adventure. So firstly, my thanks go out to my family. Then I must thank those who initially encouraged me to write this book, although they are also partly to blame for the pain suffered in writing it. My brother Anders Linden, Douglas Osborne, Andreas Ohlson, Göran Adamson, Kris Kemtrup, Patrik Caesar, Marisa Arpels, and Ignacio Rodriguez are some of the main culprits. Here I should also mention the acquisition editors at MIT Press, Christopher Eyer and Philip Laughlin, who saw the value in my rough prospectus. Next, I must thank those who suffered through some of my drafts: Jeff Stephenson, Pelle Neroth, and most of all Steven Chung, whom I owe a great deal for his careful and comprehensive critique. I thank Kristin Day and the Department of Technology, Culture and Society at NYU Tandon for the opportunity to teach my class "Death, Longevity and Values" and I thank the many students who took the class for the many wonderful conversations we had. My failure to convince them that aging is bad for them, and that death is best avoided, further spurred my efforts. These efforts were rewarded with a grant from the Institute of Human Studies. Finally, I thank my philosophical mentors, in particular Ted Honderich, Jesse Prinz, and Thomas Nagel.

1   The Case against Death

1.1   The End of Aging and Death

Is it bad to die? Or is death after a long, full life a good, fitting end? Our answer to this question matters because it reveals our attitudes about the purpose of our lives and our place in the cosmos. It also matters because science might be on the cusp of introducing a new human condition—one where we will live significantly longer and healthier lives, where aging is addressed as an illness and cured, and where death is not seen as the inevitable consequence of being born. Whether to encourage this research is a significant question.

The last 100 years or so have seen an unprecedented increase in average human life expectancy. A child born in the United States today can expect to live for almost 80 years, nearly 30 more years than one born 100 years ago. By 2100 the United States and the rest of the developed world are expected to achieve a life expectancy at birth of 85 and by 2200 the average person in those countries is expected to reach 90. By 2300, life spans are expected to reach nearly 100.[1] The rest of the world is not far behind and is steadily closing the gap.

Increased longevity is primarily due to better nutrition, improved sanitation, and advances in medicine, such as vaccinations and penicillin. In particular, child mortality has been drastically reduced. In 1900, 63 percent of children in the world survived their first five years; today 96 percent live to see their fifth birthday.[2] However, the increase in life expectancy for older people has not been remotely as drastic as that for the young. The reason for this is that we have a natural limit to our life span that has remained unaltered. We have not raised the ceiling; we have only increased the likelihood that we will reach it.

The United Nations' projections for 2300 rest on the assumption that over the next 280 years we will continue to operate under the constraint of our natural age limit and that therefore increases in life expectancy will slow down until no further gains are possible. There are, however, reasons for questioning this assumption. Not only is 280 years a long time—modern science is not much older than that—but research on aging is experiencing a boom. Such research, in particular if explicitly conducted with life extension as its ultimate goal, was until recently regarded as suspect by the mainstream science community. The taboo, though, is wearing off, and with funding by trillion-dollar companies like Google, we seem to be getting serious about cracking the code of aging and death.

Traditionally, aging and death were seen as determined by God. These were part of the ordained limiting conditions of our earthly existence with which we just had to put up. However, most scientists today take a different view. They see the human life span, like the life span of any species, as nothing but the result of our evolutionary history and, as such, entirely contingent. Conditions being slightly different, we could have had a life span of no more than 50 years, like the mountain gorilla; as much as 200 years, like giant tortoises; or 500 years, like the Greenland shark; or even longer. Recently, it has been discovered that some creatures, such as the immortal jellyfish, hydras, and maybe even ordinary lobsters may have no biological upper limit; they will just keep going as long as no accidents befall them. One explanation for why nature settled on our upper limit of about 120 years is that so few humans survived beyond their youth. Natural selection had no opportunity to remove the genes that cause problems for us as we age. A gene for Alzheimer's disease, for example, could not have been replicated if it expressed itself before reproductive age, as it would have made its bearer unfit to have children. Similarly, blindness afflicts all humans as they hit 90 and 100, but since, in a state of nature, they already would have been dead long before that, it would not have been an obstacle to reproduction and hence it could not have been selected against. The story is the same for all other age-related illnesses that afflict us once we are about age 50.

Evolutionary biology explains why we age and die, but unlike the prescientific, mythological perspective it does not tell us that we must age and die, or that we ought to do so. Fearless and armed with the knowledge of DNA structure, empowered by computers and microscopes that can see and manipulate individual atoms, and advancing on many fronts and on several explanatory levels, scientists now look for ways to break through what they see as the arbitrarily set age limit of human existence. There are already several known ways to significantly prolong the life span of non-human organisms. One of these ways is caloric restriction. Mice given less than their normal calorie intake live 20 to 40 percent longer and are also healthier and more active until they die, an increase that corresponds to adding decades of quality life to a human being. Caloric restriction has also worked for yeasts, worms, rats, cats, dogs, cows, and, most interestingly, for primates. A longitudinal study of 76 rhesus monkeys begun in 1989 by the Wisconsin Primate Research Center shows that monkeys on a 30 percent caloric restriction age slower and have a reduced mortality rate compared to a control group.[3] Four of the monkeys on caloric restriction are the longest living of their kind ever recorded. One of the first scientific studies of the effect of caloric restriction in humans suggests that we too might reap these benefits.[4] Fifty-three healthy, nonobese persons of both sexes between 20 and 50 years of age practiced a 15 percent caloric restriction over two years. The study's main author, Dr. Leanne M. Redman, summarizes the findings as follows: "Restricting calories can slow your basal metabolism, and if by-products of metabolism accelerate aging processes, calorie restriction sustained over several years may help to decrease risk for chronic disease and prolong life."[5] If this conclusion holds up, then we have discovered a way to increase the upper limit of the human life span. Given current baselines and effects comparable to those on mice and monkeys, the calorically restricted human can live 150 years, with an average of 100 years.

Skipping dinner? Salad for lunch? The prospect of going through life half-starved and obsessed about getting enough nutrients is not alluring to many. Even if it were—an extra 10 or 20 years of healthy life is truly a magnificent good—few have the willpower to implement it. However, there is a possible solution to this quandary that seems almost too good to be true: a drug that would make the body believe that it is on caloric restriction even if it is not; that is, a caloric restriction mimetic. This research is still in its infancy, but its promise is tantalizing—a simple pill to postpone death and decay. Genetic modification is another strategy that has already been proven to significantly increase the maximum life span of many species—including a 20 percent increase for mice, who share 92 percent of human DNA. Changes to DNA are permanent and when done to the germline are passed onto the next generation. If successfully applied to humans, the intervention would, therefore, be literally transformative. The human would become an upgraded and more resilient version of her old self. Other scientists approach the issue in the same way one would approach car maintenance. If service is kept up and worn-out parts are replaced, then our bodies will keep running indefinitely.[6] They envision a near future where synthetic biology provides a never-ending supply of spare organs; where nanobots circulate in our bloodstream, repairing and protecting us from all sorts of threats; where computers are literally parts of our brains; and where death is indefinitely postponed. Even more radical thinkers, like Google's chief engineer, the inventor Raymond Kurzweil, explore the possibility of leaving this mortal coil all together, not for heaven, but by uploading our minds to computers in which we could realize ourselves as immortals in silicon and metal.[7]

We are not there yet. There is currently no magic longevity pill in the pharmaceutical pipeline, no elixir of youth ready to be bottled, no software transcription of the human soul, and naysayers further insist that these strategies will never work for humans. Such pessimism seems premature. The last century experienced a never-before-seen rate of technological progress measured by some as equal to all the progress made to that point over thousands of years. And judging by the first decade of this century, progress is only gathering momentum as each new discovery informs and ignites the next, and each new technology can be used to create its successor, triggering an explosion of knowledge and power. It is not only possible but likely that by 2100, and at least by 2300, the upper limits of human life span will have been significantly extended. The seven-year increase in average life expectancy over this century projected by the Life Tables of the US Social Security Administration will likely appear quaintly modest. People—perhaps even you and I—may look back and wonder, "How could they not have seen what was about to happen?"

This book, though, is not about the science and technology of life extension. It is about whether we should want more life. The key question is the following: If we could live in good health to 120 or 200 or 1,000 or indefinitely, would this be good? For me, the answer is clear. My experiences tell me that unless there is a good afterlife, death is a horrific evil and nothing is more important than preventing good people from dying. I am a death abolitionist and a life prolongevist. Clearly there are situations, such as terminal illness and excruciating pain, where death is preferred. However, in most circumstances, life is valuable, and dying—as our irrevocable end—is therefore bad, whether we are 65, 120, 1,000, 5,000, or older. If our life and future is valuable, then dying is one of the worst things that could possibly befall us. I hope there is an afterlife, but if there is not, then death is a personal catastrophe.

Death is evil: this is my central claim. Death, as we will see, has many able defenders, including a star cast of philosophers and artists. We will see that they are simply wrong.

1.2   The Wise View: Death's Many Advocates

The idea is intuitive: It is good to be alive; it is bad to die. Yet many, even most, resist this idea, and not just because they believe in an afterlife. Some of the resistance comes from the worries about what would happen to the world if we lived much longer: Overpopulation! Stagnation! Social security and pension crises! These are reasonable concerns—something that appears to be good for the individual can have such bad effects for society that in the end it is good for no one. But more commonly, people simply appear to accept that death comes after a full life; they do not object to death, only untimely death.

Writer David Ewing Duncan has traveled the United States giving talks on biotechnology and life extension. At each venue, he asked people there if they would want to live 80 years, 120 years, 150 years, or forever.[8] People were allowed to imagine breakthroughs in antiaging medicine. He estimates that out of 30,000 people, 60 percent responded by saying 80 years, 30 percent said 120 years, nearly 10 percent said 150 years, and less than 1 percent said forever. His results were similar to those of a 2013 survey conducted by the Pew Research Center about Americans' opinions on death. When asked how long they would want to live, 69 percent gave a number between 78 and 100. The average ideal life span turned out to be about 90. Only 8 percent said that they would want to live beyond 100, and only 4 percent said they would want to live beyond 120.[9]

People's willingness to die within a natural life span has also been confirmed by my own experience teaching an undergraduate class on the philosophy of death. At the beginning of each semester, I ask my class how long they would want to live, ideally. Contrary to what we might expect, the vast majority are content with a natural life span. They do not worry much about death. Half of the class say that they have never really thought about death. (Of course, this might be because they are young.) As someone who finds death to be a gruesome prospect, I find this easygoing attitude toward death weird. At first, I did not take it seriously. Surely they are only pretending to accept death in order to comfort themselves and each other! But when I pressed people around me on the matter, they too insisted that they were okay with dying. Really. This was not because they, like 80 percent of Americans, believed in an afterlife. People I spoke to were often agnostics, and they did not justify their equanimity by referring to heaven. Rather, they had accepted death and said that they had "made peace" with it. They had the same sentiments with regard to aging. The limiting conditions of our lives are fine to them just the way they are. Gradually it dawned on me: Could it be that what seems obvious (to me), namely, that it is bad to age and die, is actually a countercultural thought?

I began to study ideas about human mortality. What I found was that the acceptance of death is deeply embedded in our cultures. In the literature on death, this view is often referred to as "apologism" and contrasted with prolongevism, but it could also be labeled the "philosophical view" or the "wise view," since all the most important philosophers and teachers of mankind have taught that we should not fear death.[10] Socrates likened earthly existence to a punishment and an illness and understood death to be a relief, something to look forward to. The Buddha similarly taught that life is suffering and saw our final and absolute extinction as the highest good. Stoic philosophers from Zeno to Marcus Aurelius implored us not only to accept death, but to love it as a part of the cosmically just iron laws of nature. The sixteenth-century thinker Montaigne, under the influence of Plato and the Stoics, goes so far as to identify philosophical wisdom with the acceptance of death in the famous title of one of his essays, "To Study Philosophy is to Learn How to Die." Epicureans competed with Platonists and Stoics, but they agreed with these rival schools that death is nothing to fear. In Book III of the Roman epicurean philosopher Lucretius's *On the Nature of Things*, in a section called "On the Folly of Fearing Death," we find nearly all of the main reasons given for not fearing annihilation that we hear to this day: (a) we have no experiences when dead, so it cannot be bad; (b) if we have had a good life, then we should "retire like a guest sated with the banquet"; (c) if we have had a bad life, then "why not make end of life and trouble?"; (d) life will get boring in the end because "all things are ever as they were"; (e) we should "yield" to the younger generation, because "one thing must be restored at the expense of others" in a natural circle of life, whereby "one thing shall never cease to rise up of another, and life is granted to none for freehold, to all on lease"; and (f) we must die to avoid overpopulation since "there must needs be substance that the generations to come may grow."[11]

These are a few examples of death's ardent advocates, and the list could be continued by simply adding the name of any philosopher, or prophet for that matter, who comes to mind. The likelihood that the thinker will be against death is slim. In a recent book on our attitudes toward death, the authors conclude, with some surprise, "[C]ome to think about it, we can't think of a single major philosopher or world religion that subscribes to the position that death is nothing more than a dreadful prospect, the worst possible cheat imaginable."[12] Gerald J. Gruman, author of a classic study on the history of our ideas about death, similarly concludes that "the leading intellectual currents [of the West are] extensively infiltrated by apologism: The belief that prolongevity is neither possible nor desirable."[13]

Many of the stories we tell bring home the apologist message. The human condition seems harsh, since it comes with aging, illness, and death. However, so the message goes, it is actually what is best for us, and if we resist it and try to change it something bad is bound to happen. This is the moral of one of the earliest known pieces of literature from the eighteenth century BC, the *Epic of Gilgamesh*. Gilgamesh, pained and frightened by the death of his companion, sets out to find the secret of eternal life. At one point he finds it in a plant he rescues from the depths of the ocean. When he carelessly leaves the plant on the ground to go bathing, a snake steals it. All his efforts fail in similar ways. He eventually learns that "life, which you look for, you will never find. For when the gods created man, they let death be his share, and life withheld in their own hands." It was also a favorite theme of the Greeks. Man's hubris, his refusal to stay within his proper bounds, is punished: we should not fly too close to the sun. In the tale of Tithonus, Eos—the Goddess of Dawn—falls in love with Tithonus and asks Zeus to make him immortal. Zeus grants Tithonus his wish, but with a catch. While unable to die, Tithonus still ages. In the end, they could do nothing but lock the senile old man in a room where he still lies babbling incoherently. (The moral may be highly relevant today: many fear that the quest for life extension will result in the horrific spectacle of hospital wards with row after row of senile, demented centennials.) We all know how Sisyphus was punished by the gods to push a rock up a hill for all eternity. What, though, did he do to deserve this punishment? The backstory is this: Sisyphus was a king who tricked Death to put on handcuffs. He then locked Death in a wardrobe, with the result that no one died any more. People were still trying to slaughter each other on the battlefield to no avail. Once order was restored and death reinstated, Sisyphus was punished by being given what he wished for—namely, immortality, but again with a catch. This is a fitting punishment thinks the apologist, since in her view life without death is in fact a never-ending, infernal pushing of the rock. Death, more peaceful than the deepest sleep, saves us from sharing Sisyphus's fate. Thank you, Death.

These are, of course, old myths, and we are living in a time which has much less respect for the notion of hubris, but many of our most popular works of imagination continue in the tradition of the acceptance of death. This may not be obvious until one reflects on it. Yet in what popular work of art does a quest for immortality end well? In what work of art does the hero seek immortality but is stopped by the villain? The Lord of the Rings, Narnia, Harry Potter, and Star Wars series, to mention some of our most beloved and widely recognized stories, all reinforce the apologist narrative. Both J. R. R. Tolkien's and C. S. Lewis's fantasy epics were written as responses to what both authors saw as disturbing and dehumanizing science-driven visions for humanity, advanced by writers such as Julian Huxley, J. B. S. Haldane, and Olaf Stapledon.[14] In *The Lord of the Rings*, earthly paradise is a low-tech pastoral old Britain, whereas evil is created in the industrial furnaces of Sauron. The story centers around a magical ring, the One Ring, which can give its bearer great powers, including life extension. But it also corrupts: after having lived five times his natural life span, one of its possessors literally turns into the slimy creep Gollum. Only the Ainur, including wizards, and the elves are immortal. Men, dwarves, hobbits, and most other races cannot live forever and thus are subject to aging and natural death. In Tolkien's universe, despite many having a desire for it, immortality is not desirable for those who are mortal. Every race has a set span; to exceed this span proves to be agony. There are many examples of this. The kings of Numenor lose their minds by clinging to life at all costs. One of the kings starts a war to invade the Blessed Land, believing that conquering it would make him immortal, and he thereby brings ruin to the Kingdom of Numenor. One of the books' main characters, Bilbo, in possession of the One Ring, on his 111th birthday describes himself as feeling stretched too thin, "like butter scraped over too much bread." Peter Jackson, who directed the films based on the books, is not alone in interpreting the One Ring as representing science and technology, as well as their seemingly uncontrollable powers.[15] Even the best, with the best of intentions, cannot control it. We must renounce its powers and return to a more natural way of being in order to save ourselves. In the first two installments of C. S. Lewis's Narnia series, Jadis, a young princess, violates the law of Aslan and eats a magical apple from the Silver Tree, which gives her inexhaustible powers and immortality but also transforms her into the psychopathic, mass-murdering archvillain, the White Witch. In J. K. Rowling's Harry Potter series, the archnemesis is the formidable black magician, Voldemort, who, according to Wikibooks, "apparently believes nothing is worse than death; perhaps his greatest weakness is his inability to love."[16] Taken together, Lewis, Rowling, and Tolkien have sold 600 million copies of their books, far more than any other literature except for a few religious texts, all of which are, of course, also apologist. As movie adaptations— again taken together—they have grossed more than any other franchise, constituting a quarter of the top 40 grossing films of all time.

Speaking of films, while the first three installments of the Star Wars saga did not seem to be concerned with either hubris or death, the prequels showed themselves, at least partly, to be another cautionary tale about what happens if we do not accept death. Darth Vader, we learn, was once a young Jedi Knight whose final turn to the dark side was an effort to save his beloved princess from dying in childbirth. The Jedi Master Yoda, a personification of wisdom, encapsulates the moral: "Death is a natural part of life. Rejoice for those around you who transform into the Force. Mourn them do not. Miss them do not. Attachment leads to jealousy. The shadow of greed, that is."[17]

Moving beyond art, apologism is also the faith of our leading bioethicists. Leon Kass, the former chairman of the President's Council on Bioethics, writes that death "is a blessing for every human individual, whether he knows it or not," and he complains that "the desire to prolong youthfulness [is] an expression of a childish and narcissistic wish incompatible with devotion to posterity."[18] Fellow council member Francis Fukuyama warns that a graying population poses a wide range of threats, from economic collapse to the inability to defend our country. He laments that old people "refuse to get out of the way" and has said in interviews that the government has the right to prevent people from living too long.[19] Daniel Callahan, another leading bioethicist, argues in favor of setting limits to how medicine is used. We should enable people to live well, but we should not seek to prolong their lives. Heart transplants, for example, should be reserved for younger patients, even given relatively ample resources, whereas the priority with older patients is to enable the best quality of life during their remaining years. Callahan believes a full human life is possible to achieve by 65. After 80, one's death is still sad but not a tragedy; it is a tolerable death. Callahan rests his idea of a tolerable death on the concept of a "natural life span," which he bases on "a persistent pattern of judgment in our culture and others of what it means to live out a life."[20] This "persistent pattern of judgment" referred to by Callahan is what I am referring to as the Wise View.

In an echo of Soviet-style psychology, psychologists have even defined acceptance as the only sane, well-adjusted response to death. Thanatophobia, the fear of death, is, according to the mental health profession, no more rational than a fear of spiders, open spaces, or clowns. It is a product of "intrapsychic structural tension," "infantile conflict," or some other pejoratively labeled state. Kübler-Ross's popular grief cycle model of how to face death and other forms of serious loss, by moving through the stages of denial, anger, bargaining, depression, and finally acceptance, was initially intended to be strictly descriptive. However, it is often appropriated as a normative model of a healthy mind: We ought to move from denial to acceptance, and if we do not, then there is something wrong with us.

Should we naively insist that surely death—our own or that of a loved one—is simply gruesome, then philosophers, priests, and psychologists stand ready with their wisdom to tell us not to rage and rebel, but to relax and accept death because

> life has an end because it has a beginning, and it consists of different stages, each one with its particular meaning and charm, not unlike the seasons of the year. The limit of death raises the stakes; it makes each moment significant, each choice important, and it endows life with seriousness and meaning. We should seek a good life, not necessarily a long life. Death is a fitting culmination to a complete life, a well-deserved rest. A fear of death is foolish since either you cease

to exist and can therefore not be harmed in any way (since you are not), or you go to a better place. Immortality should not be sought by greedily hanging on to our own particular existence, by refusing to yield and make space. Immortality should be sought in transcendence, in passing the flame of life on through our children, by contributing to the achievements of man, and through the religious and philosophical appreciation of the fundamental oneness of all being. The fact that many people seek to extend youth and postpone death at any cost is a sign of selfishness and decadence. It is hubristic, promethean, and positivist. Death can be beautiful.[21]

This may sound persuasive, but we should not buy it. Despite its dominance, its distinguished defenders, and its impressive provenance, the Wise View is false. If death is the end then it is simply awful, and it is time we admit it.

1.3   We Do Not Know What to Think

In the above quoted Pew Research study, 96 percent said they wanted to die before 120. We might suspect that this is partly due to their fear of being too decrepit to enjoy life at that point, but this cannot be the whole explanation. When asked whether they "would or would not want medical treatment that slows the aging process and allows the average person to live decades longer, to at least 120 years," a majority answered that they would not want this treatment, and only 38 percent said they would want it. This result has been replicated by other studies.[22] Interestingly, when respondents are asked whether they think that most people would want the imagined medical treatment, the average answer is 68 percent in favor of others wanting such a therapy. Thus, while most respondents do not want the treatment for themselves, they believe others will want it. Could this be because they believe themselves to be wiser than most people? "[F]or such is the nature of men that, howsoever they may acknowledge many others to be more witty or more eloquent or more learned, yet they will hardly believe there be many so wise as themselves."[23] There seems to be this aspect of the Wise View; it tends to make itself out to be more esoteric and elite than it really is. It is not true what apologists always say, that "no one wants to die" or "we all want to live forever." Most people are content with a full life lived within a natural limit. Most people believe in the Wise View, at least judging by what they say.

Yet what we say and what we do are two very different things. The magazine racks at supermarkets and the clickbait ads on the Internet are full of promises of youth. The global market for antiaging products is worth around $250 billion and is expected to grow. If we really do not want to take a pill to slow aging, then why are we buying these products that only falsely promise to do so? Why do we say we want to age and die, while at the same time spend so much on appearing young and staying alive? A straightforward resolution of the cognitive dissonance would be to let go of the Wise View and cease to accept death. Then we could say that we pursue youth and life for the simple reason that youth and life are good and that aging and death are bad. This would be a consistent view, and it is the view defended here.

Philosopher Richard Momeyer characterizes three main responses to death as denial, acceptance, and rebellion.[24] To believe in an afterlife is one way to deny death; it is not the end, only a transition. To accept death is to believe in what we call the Wise View. To rebel against it is to hate death and wage war against it. A rebel does not have to deny that there is an afterlife but would likely be less motivated if she were certain that death is a transition to a better place. Or so one would think. The evidence, however, suggests that believing in an afterlife does not dampen the interest in prolonging this life. Of those who on the aforementioned Pew survey reported a belief in life after death, 39 percent also said that they would want treatment to extend life by decades, compared to 38 percent of the total sample. Belief in a life after death is correlated with a slightly greater interest in prolonging this life. Could it be that some people are simply more interested in staying alive whether in this world or the next? Prolongevism is compatible with a belief in an afterlife and it makes sense for a prolongevist to hope for a good afterlife since even an indefinite life extension will end at some point, at the latest with the heat death of the universe. (It is commonly thought that if we did not age and only died from other causes, we would live to 1,000 on average.) No major religion has an official or univocal stance on life extension in this world and it is hard to imagine that such views will emerge given how diverse the opinions on this topic are also within faiths. (Black Protestants are the most open to slowing their aging and gaining decades of life of all groups in the survey, at 47 percent; white Evangelicals are the least likely at 28 percent.) Religious believers will therefore have to consult their own faith and reason to decide what to think about it. This is one reason why this book will say surprisingly little about religion, despite the fact that religion provides the ideological framework for most people's processing of mortality. The other reason that I will say so little about religion is that I cannot evaluate different religious beliefs about what happens when we die. This means that I have no argument against someone who believes in the Wise View on the basis of a belief in a hereafter. I reject the New Atheists' dismissal of both the possibility and the desirability of a heaven. Christopher Hitchens, for example, compares heaven to a party where a North Korean–style dictator forbids you to ever leave.[25] We have no idea what a continued existence would be like, hence it is impossible to make the case that it would be undesirable. In fact, Hitchens's parody is an application of the Wise View because it says that it is a good thing that death is final and there is no afterlife. It protects from the tragedy of simultaneously yearning for an afterlife and thinking that it is impossible. Religion and theories of the afterlife then will be mostly set aside for the reasons mentioned. I will focus on making a case for what I do know: if death is the irrevocable end, then it is very bad to die. This book is on the side of the rebel.

Why is the rebellion against death such a minority position? What explains the dominance of the Wise View? One reason we have already mentioned is that people are afraid they will be too decrepit to enjoy a longer life. However, as seen, even when presented in conjunction with delayed aging, most still insist that they would prefer to die sooner rather than later. Fear of decrepitude, then, can only explain some of the attraction to the Wise View. Another significant element must be that the Wise View is the traditional and therefore polite view. Faced with death and aging, we are expected to say something comforting, not something upsetting. As Philip Larkin observes in his poem "Aubade," courage in the face of death "means not scaring others."[26] People are not generally philosophers but believe what is considered proper in their social context. The social approval for voicing the Wise View probably causes some to falsify their preferences, saying that they accept aging and death, when in truth they would rather stay young and alive.[27] There is also the feeling that there is no point in wishing for what we cannot have. Is it not at the heart of wisdom to accept what you cannot change? This would explain the paradox of why people both deny that they want to live beyond 100 and also want treatments that would enable them to live to at least 120. They become more interested once a longer life is presented as a real practical possibility.[28] A further reason for the popularity of the Wise View may be that immortality in this world frightens us. How will we cope with an endless life? "Eternity" as they say, "is a long time, especially toward the end." Others are morally motivated to support the Wise View: Is it not greedy and selfish not to want to get out of the way? And how will earth's resources suffice for the immortals?

These are some of the reasons supporting or constituting the Wise View and they will be discussed at length over the course of this book. At bottom, however, I believe there is something else behind our willingness to believe that death is acceptable—namely, the belief that death is inescapable. If death is also very bad, then our situation is tragic, so we reevaluate death from very bad to not bad, or at least to acceptable. We protect ourselves from the awfulness of death by telling a story that makes sense of it as a beautiful and fitting end to a full life. We teach ourselves the Wise View because we do not have the stomach for tragedy. This is what psychologists call preference adaption: we seek to avoid frustration by only wanting what we can have. The fable of the fox and the sour grapes illustrates this psychological strategy of self-protection. The acceptance of aging and death, I will argue, is yet another illustration.

1.4   The Wise View Is Fragile

We find ourselves at a turning point in history where the old stories in praise of human mortality are beginning to lose their grip. We are less willing to see death as a just divine punishment, less certain of an afterlife, less inclined to accept that everything that happens by nature is thereby good, and we are no longer certain that nothing can be done about death. We are beginning to allow ourselves to openly admit what our actions already say: namely, that we want youth and life and that we hate aging and death. A rebellion against death is brewing.

The moral world of our liberal democracy is also asserting a constant erosive pressure on the acceptance of death. Our choices are by its light regarded as sources of value. If someone wants something, then it is seen as her good, and a good society enables people to live lives in accordance with their chosen goods. There are provisos, of course, of which the belief that our desires must not directly injure another is the most important;

but fundamentally, our individual desires are seen as legitimate sources of value. If someone wants to be a Mormon, good for them; if someone wants to be an atheist, good for them; if someone wants to have children, good for them; if they do not, good for them; and so on. We celebrate diversity. Hence, if we one day admit that we do not actually want to age and die, then by liberal logic, aging and death are our evils. And if, despite what people say, it is true that "no one wants to die," then they will become universally recognized evils. And once they are, we can use our money and our votes to support efforts to fight them. This book hopes to contribute to this process.

This ideological dynamic has not escaped bioconservatives. Bioconservatives, though uniformly apologist, can be found both on the left and the right of the political spectrum. They are united by the thought that we ought to respect the natural framing conditions of our lives. Bioconservative ethicist Daniel Callahan writes,

> Individualism, and the classical political liberalism of the eighteenth and nineteenth centuries upon which it is based rests upon the right of the individuals to seek that which in their private judgment brings them happiness. . . . Individual people will look upon aging in different ways, express different tolerances for the burdens of old age, seek different goals and lifestyles in old age, and differ about how long they want to live.[29]

This, Callahan, complains, gives us no common understanding of what it means to age or die. Fellow bioconservative Leon Kass similarly observes that if our desires are taken as the guide, we will, in a liberal society, inevitably end up with prolongevism:

> [L]acking a standard of reasonableness, we fall back on our wants and desires. Under liberal democracy, this means the desires of the majority for whom the attachment to life—or the fear of death—knows no limits. It turns out that the simple answer is the best: We want to live and live, and not to wither and not to die. For most of us, especially under modern secular conditions in which more and more people believe that this is the only life they have, the desire to prolong the life span (even modestly) must be seen as expressing a desire never to grow old and die.[30]

Both Callahan and Kass argue that we should resist the "simple answer" and accept the natural limits to our lives. They are joined in this view by Harvard Professor Michael J. Sandel, who thinks that he has discovered a deficiency in liberal thought that causes a moral blind spot regarding life extension and other bio-enhancements. "[In] liberal societies [we] reach first for the language of autonomy, fairness, and individual rights. However, this part of our moral vocabulary is ill equipped to address the hardest questions posed by genetic engineering. The genomic revolution has induced a kind of moral vertigo."[31] We know, writes Sandel, that there is something wrong with bioengineered enhancements, but we cannot explain to ourselves exactly what. From the point of view of autonomy, the liberal core value, the only thing that could be wrong with engineered life extension would be if someone were forced to undergo it. As long as it is voluntary, it should pass this moral test. Sandel is correct about this. One of the important reasons for why death is bad, is that unless it comes when we want it to come, it contradicts our self-determination and diminishes our space of possibilities. Death is a form of unfreedom. Being a liberal and an apologist are identities in tension with each other. One could perhaps object that our children would not have a choice if we chose a genetic intervention that affected the germline, but Sandel counters that they already do not have a choice with regard to their genetic makeup. Besides, we think that it is permissible to vaccinate children, so we are not in principle against manipulating their genes. Moreover, unlike imagined genetic interventions that would predetermine the child to a particular career or mode of life, having a longer life increases their options and therefore enhances their self-determination. Many would complain that the crux is not so much that it usurps the autonomy of the child but rather that this advantage would be reserved for the rich and be unfair. This objection will be considered in depth in chapter 11, but the quick answer is that so much in life is not available to everyone who wants it, which perhaps is unfair, but it is still much better that some have it than that no one has it. For example, everyone cannot have a heart transplant, but it is a good thing that some can have it. More fundamentally—as recognized by Sandel—the fact that something cannot be distributed equitably does not show that it is not a good thing. Indeed, why would we be worried about the distribution of longevity if we did not think that it is a good thing? Finally, no rights seem to be threatened by voluntary life extension. The right to control what happens to one's own body—what John Locke called self-ownership, including reproductive rights—appears to protect the individual's freedom to undergo any life extension procedure one wants.

Sandel believes that neither autonomy, fairness, nor rights appears capable of explaining to us the presumptive wrongness of enhancement. He proposes that we find a vocabulary outside the mainstream liberal moral world and that we regard what is naturally given as a gift, and not something that we should try to change according to our desires.

As a rebel against death, I agree with Sandel, Kass, and Callahan and other bioconservatives that our liberal moral vocabulary cannot articulate what is wrong about radical life extension, but I do not see this as a shortcoming of liberalism. I take it as evidence that there is in fact nothing morally wrong with using science and technology to extend our lives.

1.5 Can We Reason about Values?

While our liberal political culture seems potentially supportive of the case against death, it must also be noted that, logically and philosophically, the case in no way requires a liberal, subjectivist value theory, certainly not of the simple kind that makes each person the authority over his or her own good. On the contrary, I am defending the claim that anyone who accepts death, in a stronger sense than a mere recognition that it is a reality, is making a mistake, because death—assuming that it is final—is unacceptable. Death is unacceptable whether we accept it or not.

How can this presumption of objectivity be defended? How can it be a fact that death is evil? Facticity is achieved by showing how a negative evaluation of death is congruent with our most deeply held values. Given what we humans normally care about, dying ought to fall in the category of bad things. The objectivity claimed, therefore, is of the same kind as when the physician tells his pregnant patient that she should stop smoking five packs of unfiltered cigarettes a day. The patient may disagree, but she would be wrong. It is a fact that smoking this much in her situation would be bad. However, why would it be a fact? Does this not assume a lot? What if her goal is to become sick, be in terrible pain, damage her baby, and die an early death? Would not smoking then be good for her? This is what a brute subjectivist would have to say. To avoid this appalling conclusion, we can introduce a normative understanding of human nature: as a healthy, sane woman, she should not have these destructive desires.[32] Smoking five packs a day is, therefore, bad for her regardless of her actual desires and her protestations to the contrary. Regardless of this sad woman, the doctor has clearly shown that any sane woman has a reason to quit smoking while pregnant. Similarly, the case against death will assume, all things being equal, that it is good to be healthy, happy, and capable of pursuing one's goals and that it is bad to be sick, suffering, and frustrated. Anyone who shares these values has a reason to think that it is bad for one to age and die. Anyone who does not share them should share them, but this is not an argument that will be made here. If I cannot persuade someone who likes to be sick, in pain, and frustrated to share my view, then this only strengthens the case, because this person is not well. And regardless of the logical possibility of this unfortunate character, anyone who is not like her has a reason to avoid aging and death. While this is not strong objectivity in the sense that our subjective mental states are irrelevant, it is not too different from other branches of knowledge, because every theory (including in mathematics and physics) must have some presuppositions.

My case against death, then, rests on the understanding that truth is different from opinion and that values can therefore be meaningfully discussed. This is also the implicit understanding of anyone who advocates the Wise View. When people say death is acceptable, they mean that it is acceptable also to those who do not accept it. They are saying that insofar as you are sane and rational, the appropriate response to aging and death is acceptance. As Kass puts it, "finitude is a blessing for everyone whether they know it or not."[33] I wish to argue that finitude is a disaster for everyone whether they know it or not.[34]

1.6   What Is the Point?

So, what if the Wise View is nothing but a familiar song we sing to cheer ourselves up and bring a sense of meaning to our existence? Why burst the bubble of the comfort of an acceptance of death?

The first reason is both moral and epistemic. If it is true that death is bad, then we should believe that it is. It is undignified to cling to comforting lies. True courage in the face of mortality is not to pretend that it is a blessing, or in other ways seek to tame death; rather, true courage is to accept that if death is the end then this is a gruesome fact and that therefore the human condition, while wondrous and enjoyable, is fundamentally tragic.

To be clear: the only good reason not to fear death is if there is something good waiting beyond earthly death.

The second reason is, as we have seen, practical and even political. We need to make the right choice between two kinds of attitudes to antiaging research. First, the bioconservative apologist says, "Research on aging seems to me to exemplify the wrong research on the wrong problem."[35] On the other hand, the prolongevist says, "We risk being responsible for the death of 100,000 people every day this technology [antiaging] is not developed if we delay that progress by failing to speak and act to bring it about."[36] As it stands, the medical community does not consider aging an illness. At the same time, it is undeniably the leading cause of cancer, heart disease, stroke, Alzheimer's disease, and all the other familiar killers that make their ghastly appearance after the age of 55. It is, therefore, generally recognized that even a modest gain in antiaging research could have a greater effect on health than any gain made on any particular illness. The reluctance to invest in antiaging research is, therefore, irrational in light of already accepted medical values. The Wise View guides these priorities and therefore actively obstructs efforts to make our lives not only longer but also significantly better.

1.7 Specifying the Case against Death

The case against death developed over the coming chapters is, in brief, the following: It is bad to die because it robs a person of all the goods one would have enjoyed if one had continued to live. Among these goods are the mental skills, valued experiences, and personal relationships built up over the course of a life. Moreover, it is bad to die because it causes grief to those left behind.

To clarify:

1. My argument is against death, on the assumption that death is the irrevocable end of us. Death, as it features in my argument, is synonymous with extinction or annihilation. Either we are dead or we are not dead. I will not discuss borderline cases.

2. The argument is in no way against the possibility of an afterlife. If death is not the irrevocable end, then it might not be bad for us, and it may even be supremely good. That is, I will make no argument against death

acceptance that rests in a belief in an afterlife. Death in the sense here discussed is final. Since I believe that annihilation is bad, I think that it makes sense to hope for a good afterlife.

3. It is not argued that there is anything intrinsically bad about the state of being dead (a corpse does not suffer). The badness of death is explained in terms of what the dead person misses out on by not being alive. This is known as the deprivation account of the badness of death for the person who dies. The badness also follows from our liberal commitment to autonomy. Nothing is a greater infringement on our ability to do what we want than ceasing to exist.

4. The deprivation account implies that we cannot say that an ideal life is 100 or 200 or 2,000 years long, because it depends on what we have to lose by dying. I will, however, argue that it would be good if we could make life worth living significantly longer than what is the norm today. This is why we need to fight aging—the slow and gradual death we experience since birth.

5. The case against death is not an argument in favor of immortality and I doubt that I will want to live forever. Absolute immortality means the inability to die. This is not possible in a physical world. Unless we exist in some separate dimension, we have physical parts, and everything consisting of parts can and will fall apart, if not before then certainly upon contact with a black hole or eventually in the heat death of the universe. And even if—contrary to what we have reason to believe—we could be absolutely immortal in this world, this would be terrifying, since it opens us up to scenarios of eternal misery as bad as hell. Imagine, for example, being stuck under a rock and buried alive, unable to move for tens or hundreds or thousands or millions of years. In a physical world, the only possible kind of immortality is contingent immortality—sometimes referred to as "indefinite life span"—whereby we live on as long as certain conditions are in place. Contingent immortality can be either biological or nonbiological, if we merge with machines. It means that we can die, either by accident (broadly construed) or because we want to, but not because our biology or alternate substrate determines how long we are to live. This is the kind of immortality that we should strive for. I think of this as the liberal view of death, since it gives each individual the freedom to decide when to die, barring accidents. Would

I want to live forever if I were contingently immortal? I can only guess, but I guess not, since the chances are that someday, for some reason, I will find myself in an unfortunate situation worse than death. What I want is this: a life that is good enough that I will continue to want to live and have the ability to do so for as long as possible. The day when death is for me a superior alternative to life is a sad day and I do not foresee it coming any time soon.

6. Radical life extension is one of the four main ambitions of transhumanism. Transhumanists envisage that radical life extension may take not only biological form, but also cybernetic and even entirely algorithmic instantiated in the medium of whatever future computers are made of. What I have in mind when I argue that death is bad because life is good, is a life that is biological. I know of no other life, and I cannot imagine what the nonbiological posthuman states would be like. In fact, I think that the algorithmic mind-uploading scenario is metaphysically impossible. We are not, in my view, exhaustively representable in terms of logical relations. I also doubt that computers can be programmed to have a subjective point of view, and even if they could, we would not be transferable, but only replicable by such programs: it would not be you, only a copy of you. That said, geniuses like Raymond Kurzweil disagree, and if they are right that we can upload and live an amazing life outside our biological bodies, then this would be preferable to death.[37]

7. The other three main ambitions of transhumanism are enhanced cognition, enhanced well-being, and enhanced moral being.[38] At several points in the argument I will hint at these possible enhancements because if realized they would change the equation. For example, the common objection that a longer life would quickly become boring applies to humans with normal, limited psychologies, not their transhuman upgrades. I am skeptical about these ambitions, not, as with mind uploading, because they are fundamentally impossible, but because they are likely to get things wrong: designed well-being may undermine our ambition and dampen our artistic and creative impulses; enhancing cognition risks overriding vital heuristics (often called emotional biases) implanted by nature and without which we become, as they say, too smart for our own good, and moral enhancement opens up the *Brave New World* scenario of turning humans into docile pets and robbing them of the meaningful

activity of self-improvement. I am not against these enhancements because they are unnatural, or because they change who we are, but because I think that they are likely to make us worse off. The case against death, as here presented, is a transhumanist argument only in the limited sense of arguing in favor of transcending the natural human life span. Importantly, it takes off not from a desire to transcend who we are, but from an appreciation for life as it is and a natural wish to preserve it.[39]

8. Finally, the case against death at first glance appears as a negative polemic, which is indeed the case. After all, the thesis is that death and also aging are bad, and that anyone who claims otherwise is simply wrong. At the same time, there is a strong positive side to the argument, since it explains the badness of death as a function of the goodness of life. This optimism will be apparent throughout the book and it will be explicitly defended in chapter 4.

The topic of aging and the topic of death are obviously intertwined. Aging, as I like to think of it, is a drawn out dying. The next chapter will seek to isolate and criticize the Wise View about aging. It will also serve as an introduction that foreshadows several arguments and themes discussed in more detail over the subsequent chapters.

2   The Case against Aging

Just remember, once you're over the hill you begin to pick up speed.
—Charles M. Schulz

2.1   Aging

"Everyone wants to live a long life, and no one wants to grow old." This
is usually said as a joke, poking fun at people's impossible dreams. We are
supposed to mock the wish to stay young forever. We are told to "embrace"
aging as a part of life and not seek to resist it. Aging, they say, is not an illness, and therefore any endeavor to slow it down or arrest it is not a proper
goal of medicine. Biogerontologist Leonard Hayflick, for example, sees "no
value to society or the individual in seeking to slow or stop the aging process."[1] Contrary to the Wise View, I think that a person's dream of eternal
youth expresses a fine ideal. It would be great to have a long life without
growing old.

Aging is defined as a process that makes us more likely to die, as a process
of accumulating damage that results in death, or something along those
lines. We grow and mature, but we age very little up to our twenties, and
thereafter increasingly so. Importantly, for our purposes, growing old is
not the same as aging. If we grow old without damage, then we have not
aged. Or to put it in terms of risk: if our risk of dying does not increase as
a function of age, we have not aged. This is often described as a distinction between chronological aging and biological aging; people of the same
chronological age can be of a different biological age depending on how
much they have been affected by the aging process. The mechanisms of

aging are not fully understood, and they are outside the purview of this book.[2]

Aging reveals itself by the changes it brings to our bodies and minds. Cells become less able to divide and then die; the connective tissue between cells becomes stiffer; the maximum functional capacity of many organs decreases; the wall of the heart gets thicker; the heart muscle becomes less efficient; the aorta becomes thicker, stiffer, and less flexible; many of the body's arteries develop atherosclerosis; it becomes harder for the body to control its temperature (where's my sweater?); the heart rate takes longer to return to normal after exercise; bones become thinner and less strong; joints become stiffer and less flexible; the cartilage and the bones in the joints start to weaken; the muscle tissue becomes less bulky and less strong; the movement of food through the digestive system becomes slower in the stomach, liver, and pancreas; the small intestine makes smaller amounts of digestive juices; the number of nerve cells in the brain and spinal cord decreases; the number of connections between nerve cells decreases; abnormal structures, known as plaques and tangles, may form in the brain; the retinas get thinner and the irises get stiffer; the ocular lenses become less clear; the walls of the ear canal get thinner; the eardrums get thicker; skin gets thinner and becomes less elastic; sweat glands produce less sweat; nails grow more slowly; and some hairs turn gray while some no longer grow. The face is the most visible theater of these changes. The forehead expands as the hairlines retreat; the ears often get a bit longer because the cartilage in them grows; the tip of the nose may droop because the connective tissue supporting nasal cartilage weakens; wrinkles appear; the skin gets blotchy and spots appear; the eyes get smaller as eyelids droop; the fat that gives the face a round appearance loses volume, clumps up, and shifts downwards to create baggy chins and jowly necks; the mouth turns from an upward grin to a downwards frown. One day you look in the mirror and wonder, for a split second, who's that?

As a consequence of these physical changes, we display the following symptoms: increased susceptibility to infection; a greater risk of heat stroke or hypothermia; a slight decrease in height as the bones of our spines get thinner and lose some weight; the bones break more easily; the joints change in ways ranging from minor stiffness to severe arthritis; stooped posture; slowed and limited movement; decrease in overall energy; constipation; urinary incontinence; slowing of memory and thinking; reduced reflexes and coordination; difficulties with balance; decrease in visual acuity; diminished peripheral vision; some degree of hearing loss; wrinkling and sagging of skin; and the whitening or graying of hair. The changes often issue in pathologies such as heart disease, cancer, respiratory diseases, Alzheimer's disease, osteoporosis, diabetes, influenza and pneumonia, and countless other minor and major debilitations. Understanding biological aging in terms of the myriad of adverse effects it has on our functioning and the concomitant increase in risk for pain, illness, and death, makes the popular notion of healthy aging somewhat of an oxymoron.

To approve of aging is to approve of these changes and their terrible consequences. For if we say that we want to grow old *without* these changes and their associated effects, then we are in effect saying that we want to stay young. A clear view of aging in terms of its symptoms is, I think, enough to realize that it is not beneficial. Remember the doctor telling the patient that smoking is bad for her? Well, if we agree with the doctor about smoking, then should we not also say that aging is bad for her? Much worse in fact, since smoking only kills some, while aging, if given the opportunity, kills all. It is baffling that a man of science—a gerontologist, no less—like Hayflick, can be so in the grip of the Wise View that he cannot recognize what he obviously knows: that slowing or stopping aging would be the best thing we can do for the relief of human suffering, at the very least on the individual scale. Such is the mind fog this doctrine causes.

2.2   Defending the Indefensible

> I am appalled that the term we use to talk about aging is "anti." Aging is as natural as a baby's softness and scent. Aging is human evolution in its pure form.
> —Jamie Lee Curtis

When I started writing this book, I thought it would be unnecessary to make an argument against aging, since it is so obviously bad; but this, as we have seen, is not the case. Only 38 percent of the people polled by Pew Research Center would want treatments that would slow their aging process and allow them to live decades longer, perhaps to at least 120.[3] Most people would rather not have the health of someone significantly younger than themselves. They would rather be 80 and look and feel 80 than be 80 and look and feel, say, 50; they prefer more accumulated damage to themselves rather than less, despite the associated risks. Of course, as I said in chapter 1, I do not think these responses should be taken at face value. They are, in many instances, falsified preferences—that is, things people say because they think that it is "the right thing to say." I think the fact that most people think that most *other* people will want antiaging treatment is both accurate and revealing. Whether falsified or not, the professed rejection of treatments that would slow aging reflects that there is an ideology, not just of the acceptance of death, but of the acceptance of aging. Still, sometimes actual arguments are made in favor of aging.

The most common argument is that aging is natural. There is, of course, no denying the naturalness of aging, but there is also no reason to think that this makes it a good thing. Some things, like babies' softness and scent and a mother's love for her child are natural and good. Other things, like AIDS, are natural and bad. The question then becomes, is aging more like motherly love, or is it more like AIDS? I would say that aging is more like AIDS since, in contrast to a mother's love, it undermines health and kills. Only aging makes all people sick and kills more than two-thirds of all people. Consistency therefore requires that we consider aging to be bad. This, I think, is a short, powerful reply. Add to this that whereas a mother's love can be seen as serving the natural function of enabling the survival of her child, aging serves no similar natural purpose, but is rather nothing but the failure of evolution to select against alleles with deleterious effects later in life.[4] Aging obviously does not increase the individual's chances of survival and replication and is therefore, to speak loosely, quite the opposite of "human evolution in its pure form." In the words of the philosopher David Gems, "The evolutionary theory provides the bleak insight that ageing serves no purpose in terms of fitness, but instead is a lethal genetic disease that afflicts all human beings."[5] I will save a more detailed treatment of the argument from nature for chapter 5.

What else do people say in favor of aging?

This book would not have been written had it not been for a dinner I had 10 years ago with a young lady named Susan and her boyfriend, during which, to my outrage, she praised aging. "It would be boring to be the same age," she argued. At the time I responded that I do not find it particularly entertaining to be front row to my rapid physical decline. There are many other things in life keeping me from being bored than watching my hair get thinner and grayer, age spots spreading, skin sagging and wrinkling, muscles atrophying, fat accumulating, and so on. And nothing is more boring than fussing over one's health and listening to others fussing over theirs. These days I think that what she had in mind was not the slow dying per se, but rather the interesting experience of traveling through the stages of life. It brings to mind a ubiquitous nineteenth-century print of the steps of life, depicting a pyramid of a man's life from birth to 100.[6] There are eleven steps, and the first depicts him as an infant in a cradle, the second as a boy playing with a hoop, at the third step he is 20 and married, next he is 30 and he has a family, next he is 40 and successful, next he is 50 and on the top of the pyramid, then he descends to 60 and is carrying a cane, at 70 he is carrying a cane and smoking a pipe, at 80 he looks bent and frail, at 90 he is about to fall over, and at 100 he is sitting, slumped over in a chair, ready to die. What Susan may have meant was that if we did not age, we would be stuck at a certain level of this pyramid of life, and that would eventually be boring: Each step has its own set of priorities, experiences and expectation, and a good, interesting life visits them all. Something along those lines. Similar arguments have been made by philosophers, and other writers, who associate the rejection of aging with the wish to remain a Peter Pan. Bioethicist Gilbert Meilaender writes that although continued health is always tempting, "whatever human flourishing involves, it must include the aging and decline that characterizes bodily organisms."[7] The descending steps of life, are, in his view, essential parts of a good human life.

I want to say two things about the "steps-of-life argument" in favor of aging. First, being against aging does not mean being against growing up to one's physical prime. Developing from an embryo to a fully grown man or woman is not the same as aging, although aging accompanies it to a small degree. It is not the accumulation of damage that takes a man from step one, to step two, to step three; it is growing up. Second, even if we did not age beyond step three, we would still gain experience and learn and develop intellectually rather than be frozen at a particular stage. The wisdom and maturity attained by some is a product of experience and reflection over time, not to mention good luck and intelligent friends; it is not a result of aging. Without aging we would have both the experience necessary for living well and the health and energy to do so. Rather than a pyramid of life where we spend a third of our lives descending, we would be on an open-ended journey whose shape is to a larger degree under our own control. Life without aging would be liberating. There is something oppressive about seeing our life prestructured into distinct steps with adjoint demands and limitations that we must conform to. Indeed, the steps of life model evokes a shopping list view of life, where you have been given a list with stuff that you are supposed to gather. If you have all the items on the list you win, and you are also done; you can check out.

Here, bioconservatives will say that an open-ended life, a life lacking the pyramidal shape, is a shapeless, meandering life and, more seriously, that it is no life at all, at least not a human life. In other words, my wish not to age is, in effect, a wish no longer to be human. This argument—in essence a variation of the argument from nature—is also made about death, and I will therefore save my full answer for later chapters. The shorter answer is this: Aging is not a necessary condition for being a human being. Dictionaries speak of us as bipedal primate mammals. Philosophers usually describe us as essentially rational animals. There is nothing in either definition that suggests that we would cease being humans if we conquered aging. By analogy, when Cynthia Kenyon created the longer living *C. elegans* roundworm by means of genetic mutation, she did not create a new species. These were still roundworms, just longer living. The same, I think, would be true for humans. As modern humans, we have acquired control of the environment around us to a degree that has allowed us to triple the average life expectancy, yet life remains recognizably human. Life without the threat of aging would be even more different, but it would still be a human life, and I argue that it would be overall better. Those who are bothered by the absence of a fixed, preordained pyramidal staircase of life and who think that no other shape is possible for humans may be expressing a merely personal, conservative preference for order as well as for the true and tested.

Many philosophers have argued that there is value in the physical deterioration constitutive of aging. Not just because it is a part of the steps of life model that has so far defined much human existence, but because the deterioration causes us to be, act, and think in ways that we would not otherwise do. Plato makes this argument in book one of *The Republic*. Socrates is introduced to the aging patriarch Cephalus, who mentions how an elderly acquaintance of his always complains, "I cannot eat, I cannot drink; the pleasures of youth and love are fled away: there was good time once, but now that is gone, and life is no longer life."[8] Asked if he is "still the man he used to be" with women (it is implied), Cephalus responds, thank god, no.

He is happy that he has lost his youthful drives, "For certainly old age has a great sense of calm and freedom; when the passions relax their hold, then, as Sophocles says, we are freed from the grasp not of one mad master only, but of many."[9] Aging, he continues, is not to blame for the misery of many older people, but rather, this misery is to be blamed on a person's character and temper, "for he who is of a calm and happy nature will hardly feel the pressure of age, but to him who is of an opposite disposition youth and age are equally a burden."[10]

Research supports the idea that with age comes a measure of calm and a freedom from strong passions. There is also an increase in the frequency of positive feelings as well as an improvement in emotional problem solving.[11] Old people experience less intense negative emotions such as sadness, anger, and fear. There is a gradual diminution of the interest in sex by both men and women. Emotions and passions seem to dull alongside taste and hearing. With less passion, older people become naturally inclined toward more mellow pursuits. This is also mandated by the risk of falling and breaking, for example, the hip, femur, pelvis, or vertebrae. Bridge nights and art history classes replace crowd surfing and skateboarding. The mellowing, the diminished physical and mental capabilities, and the frailty also have the consequence of lowering expectations (a key to happiness) and giving up the often-painful struggle to realize ambitious dreams. It is common for older people to think that "it is what it is," and they focus more on the here and now. A nice walk in the park when it is not too windy, as long as the feet do not ache too much (foot pain afflicts one in four people over 65), may be regarded as good enough for a day's work. As in art, the limits imposed on an artist can sometimes benefit the art; the limits imposed by aging can work in favor of the aged. Perhaps this explains the romanticizing enthusiasm for being old we see all over: "Your 40s are good," says actress Helen Mirren. "Your 50s are great. Your 60s are fab. And 70 is f'ing awesome!"[12]

With some luck, life can be worth living for a long time, even if we age. Some studies on wellbeing show that happiness is a smile-curve with a dip in middle age.[13] Yet, aging is not a good thing. When looking closer at the statistics for those 60 and over, we see that it is those who are the least impaired who are the happiest. That is, it is those who have aged the least over the years, someone like Mirren, who are the most well off. My contention is that her seventies would be even more awesome if she had preserved the youthful robustness of her twenties. Experience allows people to become better at managing stress, including their various ailments, sundry life crises, and even the terror of dying. But being good at managing a threat does not change the fact that it is a threat. Insofar as older people are happy, it is not because of aging, but despite aging.[14] Plato's idea is that as our passions subside, the life of the mind becomes more unencumbered. Unfortunately, while we may escape the passions, the body makes itself felt in many new bad ways as we age. Old people generally speak more about oncology than ontology. Furthermore, while losing one's passions leaves more time for mellower pursuits, including intellectual pursuits, most people are as mellow as they want to be by early middle age. Those who do not share the philosopher's obsession with mental tranquility will therefore reject Plato's idealization of a life without the distraction of passion and, like Cephalus's acquaintance, "bemoan the pleasures of youth and love." Viagra is a popular drug for a reason. Plato would of course respond that common people are ignorant, and they should not want to be passionate. But even if for the sake of the argument we agreed with him, the problem remains that the alleged benefits of mellowing, which a few enlightened souls like Cephalus (but not his acquaintance) experience come at far too high of a cost. The mellowness may be alright for some, but not at the price of an increased risk of some debilitating disease or the humiliation of wearing adult diapers and other indignities of old age.

British guitarist Eric Clapton explains, in an interview for the Telegraph, that he has been in horrific pain the last few years, "You feel like you have electric shocks going down your leg."[15] The condition he has affects nerves in the body's extremities, making it hard for him to play. This might force him to take up some other occupation and adopt a more mellow lifestyle. Still, one can imagine that it would be hard for Clapton, the guitar player, to find something to replace his instrument. Clapton has been abused and robbed by aging; this remains a fact, regardless of whether or not he finds some way to remain content. The case of Clapton reminds us that age-related frailties often prevent us from performing some activity that we take pride in, have developed excellence in, and even see as a part of who we are. I have met a ballet dancer who can no longer dance; a tennis player who can no longer play; a skateboarder who can no longer skate; and recently, a sailor who can no longer sail—and they all are regretting it. Dancers want to dance, not play bridge.

Aging to many is experienced as a wholly external imposition. They still feel mostly like their old self, and they feel that their physical body is hindering and misrepresenting them.

I try hard to avoid my mirror.
There are things I would rather not see,
And even those times when I just catch a glimpse,
I can no longer recognize me

Things I used to do with ease
Can now cause aches and pains,
And the quality of the things I do
Will never be quite the same.

I always compare my older self
To those younger versions of me,
And I know I'm wasting too much time
Missing who I used to be.

But the thing that makes me sad
Is that despite what people see,
Underneath my tattered, worn out shell.
I am still the same old me.[16]

For every visible person like Helen Mirren, there are countless invisible elderly people who are simply destroyed by aging. We pass them in the street every day. I once worked periodically in Swedish elder care and saw sadness and humiliation that I wish I had never seen. I entered gloomy apartments where every blind and curtain were drawn and was met by a musty stench. In the hall and the bedroom were pictures of a client as a young and handsome person, and the comparison to that pitiful, stinking, helpless, and childlike being found half sleeping in a bed with the television blaring was mortifying. The following account written by a son visiting his father hospitalized with pneumonia strikes me as an honest account of the damages of aging:

First, old age is a humiliation, straight up. Because I'm bone-tired, I'll let this example stand for several I observed tonight. I saw an old man crap his pants because he was shuffling to the bathroom and couldn't move fast enough. Later, I could hear a nurse in the patient's holding room sweetly cleaning him up when he made it back, respecting his dignity. I thought about that old man, somebody's grandfather, most likely, maybe a war veteran, reduced to this. Second, whatever we pay nurses, it's not enough. The nurse that cleaned that old man up was also my father's nurse. She and the other nurses who attended him tonight could not possibly have been kinder and more tender to him. I felt so bad for my dad, in his badly weakened state, being poked and prodded and catheterized and all kinds of things. I know what a proud man he is, and how it must have been tearing him up to be reduced to this state of helplessness by his advanced age (he's 80) and the pneumonia. There is no way to compensate for that kind of thing, but the nurses who took care of him tonight and the doctors too made a situation that was very difficult for him, but physically and psychologically, in terms of his dignity, as bearable as it could have been. Listening to and watching the elderly patients on the ward, I knew that this was going to be my fate one day, and though it makes me afraid—afraid not of dying, but of wasting away, and of being humiliated by my body. I don't want a nurse to have to wipe my butt. Nobody does. But it happens every day. I saw a nurse walking down the hall with an adult diaper in her hand, headed into someone's room. The thought that this will be my fate one day is hateful to me. I had better get over it. This is going to be an immense spiritual challenge, aging with dignity when your body does nothing but mock and spite you.[17]

It is not this or that particular illness; it is fact that aging undermines our health and throws us at the mercy of a roll of the dice of maladies: what will it be, stroke, or cancer, or diabetes, or something else? The only way to avoid cancer is to die from some other illness before it gets you. As the philosophers teach, having a great character makes our situation more bearable, but it is still not an ideal situation. There is a grim dimension to the complacency that sometimes settles in on the old. Granted, it is liberating to have one's potential destroyed since it removes the pressure to perform. It is less stressful to sit on the sidelines, observing the game, knowing there is nothing they can do, and nothing they can hope for. But resignation is a sad substitute for real potential and hope. Beautiful dreams are abandoned. There is not enough time, and the energy and health are not there anymore. Aging seems to operate in direct opposition to the ideal life trajectory: We want things to get slowly better and, as long as we have the hope that they will, we find meaning in whatever we do and can endure much more. We are on a cruel path when we gain knowledge of how to live as we lose our ability to live.

And then there is an argument using the very badness of aging as an argument in favor it. French sixteenth-century philosopher Michel de Montaigne observes in his meditations:

> I notice that in proportion as I sink into sickness, I naturally enter into a certain disdain for life. I find that I have much more trouble digesting this resolution

when I am in health than when I have a fever. Inasmuch as I no longer cling so hard to the good things of life when I begin to lose the use and pleasure of them, I come to view death with much less frightened eyes. This makes me hope that the farther I get from life and the nearer to death, the more easily shall I accept the exchange . . .

   If we fell into such a change . . . suddenly, I don't think we would endure it. But when we are led by Nature's hand down a gentle and virtually imperceptible slope, bit by bit, one step at a time, she rolls us in to this wretched state and makes us familiar with it; so that we find no shock when youth dies within us, which in essence and in truth is a harder death than the complete death of a languishing life or the death of old age; inasmuch as the leap is not so cruel from a painful life as from a sweet and flourishing life to a grievous and painful one.[18]

Montaigne's idea is that aging is good because it removes our will to live and, therefore, makes death more palatable. Contemporary conservative bioethicist Leon Kass quotes Montaigne with approval and has gone on to argue that we should not seek scientific ways to compress morbidity. Compressed morbidity, unlike decelerated aging, and the more ambitious arrested aging, as well as the even more ambitious reversed aging, is the modest biogerontological goal of making the last time we have on earth as free of disease and suffering as possible, without significantly delaying, or precipitating, death. Kass's objection to this goal is that it would shorten the time during which we are so diminished that death begins to look attractive: "It is highly likely that even a modest prolongation of life with vigor or even only a preservation of the youthfulness with no increase in longevity would make death less acceptable and exacerbate the desire to keep pushing it away."[19] Meilaender is similarly skeptical of attempts to prolong health, and shorten the time we are mortally ill: "The decline that aging involves is, in a way, a gradual and (at the least sometimes) gentle preparation for the cliff toward which we move. Even now we are especially distressed when someone dies at or near the peak of his powers. If we all died that way, would that be an improvement?"[20] Already only half alive, death may not come as such an icy shock. This is an awful argument. Meilaender, Kass, and Montaigne want people to get frail and sick and stay so for an extended time, rather than a shorter time, so that they get used to dying. Is this not akin to arguing that one of the good things about getting diabetes and necrotic limbs is that it makes it easier to accept having one's limbs amputated? We could praise on the same grounds torture, thirst, and famine; but it is very faint praise to say that something has the virtue of

making life seem less worth continuing. Contrary to what these philosophers hold, aging cannot be seen as a good thing on the ground that it
lowers the opportunity cost of death and makes it seem more acceptable.
Rather, we are dealing with two evils—slow death and death—competing
for being the worst.

2.3   Aging Is Not a Disease, So Medicine Should Leave It Be

Given that aging is the single greatest health risk and cause of death, it is
frustrating that there is a strong resistance to antiaging interventions. Bioethicists and gerontologists still make the argument that medicine should
do nothing about it because aging is natural and normal and therefore
not a disease. Addressing aging would, therefore, they argue, contradict
the meaning or proper purpose of medicine, in the same way that cheek
implants and other spurious plastic surgery should be seen as anathema.

The idea that something that is natural and normal for humans cannot
be seen as a disease—the standard view—has been challenged on the conceptual ground that there exist numerous diseases that afflict a majority
of people and thus might be called the norm. Muscle wastage leading to
sarcopenia, reduction in bone mass and density leading to osteoporosis,
and brain tissue atrophy resulting in dementia are examples of medical
problems that afflict every human if they live long enough—they are perfectly normal—yet they are at the same time classified as diseases in need of
medical intervention. Normality then does not imply that something is not
a disease. As British geneticist and gerontologist Dr. David Gems quips, "to
argue that aging is not a disease by virtue of its universality is as mislead-
ing as it is to argue that the Basenji is not a dog because it does not bark."[21]
The standard view has also been challenged on the ground that what is
considered normal has varied over time and by place and is influenced
by scientific, medical, and technological discoveries. Several currently recognized diseases, such as osteoporosis, isolated systolic hypertension, and
senile Alzheimer's disease, were in the past ascribed to normal aging.[22]

The phenomenon of migrating age-related changes to the category of
disease and the phenomenon of accepting the concept of universal and
quasi-universal diseases signify a stealthy, possibly unstoppable drift toward
a de facto recognition of aging as a disease. If adapting medical practice
toward healing and preventing Alzheimer's disease or osteoporosis, for

example, rather than seeing these as natural aspects of aging, is beneficial, what reason can there be to not regard other similar aspects of aging as diseases, too? For each isolated age-related change, we can ask the same question: is this change for the better and, if not, what can be done about it? Conceptually, it is guaranteed that it is not for the better—aging is never a physical change toward improved functioning—so the answer will be the same for each change, and so there is a rationale in each case to classify the change as a disease and thus as a legitimate subject matter of biogerontology and medical intervention. Such a classification would not require a radical, revisionary understanding of the role of medicine. Aristotle, the grandfather of evidence-based medicine, not only sees aging for the threat to a person that it is, but defines disease as "acquired old age," and, conversely, old age as a natural disease.[23] Nor do we find any explicit or easily derived interdiction against antiaging interventions in the medical ethics of the Hippocratic Oath (formulated between 500 and 300 BC), nor in more recent standards such as the Declaration of Geneva (1948).[24] By signing the Declaration of Geneva, members of the medical profession pledge that "considerations of age" among other factors will not "intervene between my duty and my patient."

The debate over whether aging is or is not a disease is rhetorically and politically important, but it is also a bit exasperating.[25] What does it really matter if a change toward disorder is normal or not, or whether we call it one thing or another? Nosology be damned; if it harms someone, is that not enough to warrant an intervention? Who wants her bones to become more brittle while you debate whether you call that a disease or not? Once at a particularly depressing home visit in Swedish elderly care, I noticed that our client, an elderly man, had a cantaloupe-sized growth on the inside of his leg. I asked what that was, and got the explanation from my colleague, a seasoned nurse, that "he is old." All right then. Relativizing health to age, beyond adulthood, risks serving no other purpose than complacency in the face of suffering in the aged. Because someone was born longer ago, it matters less that their bones are brittle or that their knees are bust. Because it is aging. Thus, we do not have to do anything about it. The refusal to see aging as a decease not only invites complacency but also seems to downplay the preventative role of medicine. We accept, for example, vaccinations, which even may make the patient sick for a short period, in order to prevent sickness. So, even if we grant that aging is not a disease, it could still be a legitimate target for preventative medicine.

I will not take a firm stance on whether or not aging should be regarded as a disease, although I think it makes sense to call it one. My case against aging rests on what it does to the person who ages, regardless of how aging is categorized from the point of view of medicine. Whatever its categorization, preventing aging can be the proper goal of medicine because it causes illness, suffering and death. And to those who persist in arguing that it is not the proper goal of medicine, I say—fine, let us invent a new science and technology, call it medicine+, and get on with the work of keeping people whole.

The debate over whether to think of aging as a disease or not mirrors the debate over whether to think of antiaging as healing or enhancing. This is seen as a crucial distinction by many who think that they can approve of medicine but disapprove of antiaging medicine. However, the distinction between healing and enhancing is hard to maintain for the same reasons as it is difficult to maintain a sharp border between aging and disease. If medicine succeeds in healing every ill and keeping us healthy and whole to 150, then this would be similar to if we had undergone antiaging therapy: in both cases our joints are good, our teeth are fine, our internal organs are working well, and so on. Both cases can be considered as enhanced states, one obtained by the healing paradigm, the other by the antiaging paradigm. That is, the disease-oriented reactive approach of medicine will, if successful, also lead to enhancement, so enhancement cannot be easily contrasted with the "proper" aim of medicine. And if we do not want to call that enhancement but, say, preserving the wholeness of the patient, then on what rational grounds can the preventative approach of antiaging medicine be considered an illegitimate means? How can it be reasonable to, for example, want medicine to cure cancer, but not want medicine to prevent cancer? We need very good reasons for resisting the transformation of medicine toward the preventative antiaging paradigm and I do not think that they can be found in the tradition and meaning of medicine or in the concept of disease.

2.4   Falsified Preferences Concerning Aging and the Morality of Not Being Antiaging

Whatever their reasons are, people like Susan (the young woman at the dinner party) are mistaken if they think that it is literally true that aging is not bad for the one who ages. They are mistaken because, as we have seen, aging threatens their health, their life, their relationships, their acquired abilities, their autonomy, their passion, their beauty, and many other values. Indeed, once we consider the tremendous harm that aging causes, it is hard to avoid the conclusion that it is a moral mistake not to be antiaging. Think of the son visiting his sick and diminished father in the hospital: Is this what he wants for his father? Is this what the father wants for his son? I have argued that the Wise View about aging is built on fallacious arguments and maintained by falsified preferences. Sometimes, when reality imposes itself, a tipping point is reached, and falsified preferences evaporate. The fall of the Berlin Wall was such an imposition of reality. The liberated Germans looked at each other and said, "Me, a communist? I thought you were a communist!" The many who tell themselves and others that they prefer aging over youth will change their tune once the reality of antiaging medicine imposes itself. When they can take a pill that keeps them youthful, they will be free to say what they know in their hearts to be true. "Me, in favor of aging? Don't be ridiculous."

I have said relatively little about the worst thing about aging: its end result. If death is not bad, then it is not to be counted among the things that make aging terrible. The Wise View says that it is not, and it is to this claim we now turn.

3   Death Is Harmless

It's not that I'm afraid to die, I just don't want to be there when it happens.
—Woody Allen, *Without Feathers*

3.1   What You Don't Know Can't Hurt You

The most common philosophical reason that people who are skeptical about an afterlife give for why we should not fear death is that when we are dead, we cannot suffer any harm. The process of dying may be painful and those left behind may be in sorrow, but the troubles are over for the one they mourn. Death, they say, is as innocent as a dreamless sleep. It was one of the two main reasons given by Plato for why death was not to be feared. Either death is the beginning of a better existence or death is the end, in which case we cannot suffer. Plato thought that a better existence awaits the philosopher after death, but the earthier Epicurus favored the second answer.

Epicurus and his followers were atomists who, like Democritus before them, thought that the universe is eternal and infinite and contains nothing but atoms and void. The atoms are indestructible and of infinite number. They constitute all things, like letters constitute all words. What we call the soul is for the materialist a certain configuration of ultrafine fast-moving atoms. The death of a person is nothing but the dispersal of the atoms that constitutes him. The atoms themselves are imperishable and will form new bodies, but the person that they once made up will never exist again.[1] Death is the end. This should not frighten us, argued Epicurus. Rather, it should relieve us. In a letter to one of his younger friends, Menoeceus, Epicurus writes,

Accustom yourself to believe that death is nothing to us, for good and evil imply awareness, and death is privation of all awareness; therefore a right understanding that death is nothing to us makes the mortality of life enjoyable, not by adding to life an unlimited time, but by taking away the yearning after immortality. For life has no terror; for those who thoroughly apprehend that there are no terrors for them in ceasing to live. Foolish, therefore, is the person who says that he fears death, not because it will pain when it comes, but because it pains in the prospect. Whatever causes no annoyance when it is present, causes only a groundless pain in the expectation. Death, therefore, the most awful of evils, is nothing to us, seeing that, when we are, death is not come, and, when death is come, we are not. It is nothing, then, either to the living or to the dead, for with the living it is not and the dead exist no longer.[2]

When I write this sentence, I am alive, and death has therefore not harmed me. One day I am no longer alive, and only my corpse remains. The corpse is not harmed by death. And neither am I, since I do not exist. But I have lost my life! Is that not bad? No, says Epicurus: Why is losing something bad? It is bad because we are experiencing its loss. But death is a loss that cannot be experienced, so how can it be bad? As the Stoic philosopher Seneca wrote several hundred years later, "nothing . . . is lost with less discomfort than that which, when lost, cannot be missed."[3]

Some philosophers dismiss this argument as too implausible to waste one's time on, but this is a mistake. The argument is still with us after 2,000 years for a reason. Its dialectical power flows from the very plausible underlying assumption that for something to be bad for someone, one must, necessarily, exist to experience this harm. This makes sense: after all, there are no headaches without someone who suffers them. If we think that death is the end of awareness, an assumption that will be made throughout our discussion, then it is a fair question to ask how death could possibly be bad for the one who dies.

3.2 The Deprivation Account of the Badness of Death: What You Don't Know Can Hurt You

It will happen to all of us, that at some point you get tapped on the shoulder and told not just that the party is over, but slightly worse: the party's going on—but you have to leave.

—Christopher Hitchens[4]

Epicurus's argument is a perfect example of how philosophy can make us question our basic and unreflective beliefs, such as, in this case, that it can be bad for us to die. As we will see, it is no easy task to counter it in a conclusive and satisfying manner. It is, however, clear what general form the answer must take. Since the Epicurean argument is specifically about the harm to the person who dies, we can set aside harms that his death may cause other people. We can also not argue that death is intrinsically bad because of the way it is experienced, since we are assuming that death is the end of experience. This means that death cannot be bad in the way that, for example, pain is bad. In fact, one of the good things about death is that it prevents us from being in pain. But that immediately brings us to what is so bad about death: the dead cannot suffer, true, and that is good, but they also cannot enjoy their life. This is known as the deprivation account of the badness of death: Death is bad because it deprives the dead of a valuable life. Or to be more precise, the badness of death is a function of the goodness of life. If someone has nothing but hopeless misery ahead of them, death may be a better alternative. But if life is good, death is bad. The evil of death is therefore comparative, rather than intrinsic: we compare living to not living and decide which is the better alternative. This is a familiar way of valuing: Whenever we ask ourselves how to spend our time, we do not look exclusively at how we would experience doing a particular thing, but we also look at what other things we could do instead that may be better. For example, imagine a man who enjoys one of the longest and best naps of his life only to wake up and realize that he missed out on an experience of the greatest joy imaginable.[5] The nap itself was great, but it was still very bad for him in terms of what it excluded. Economists would say that the opportunity cost of that nap was excessive. Death occasions the greatest possible opportunity cost because it excludes all other options.

I believe that the deprivation account captures what many of us hate about death. Today, like every day, someone is given a week or perhaps only a day to live. In her mind, she will imagine all the things about her life whose future enjoyment death soon will destroy: the people that she will never see again, the experiences that she will enjoy no more, the plans and projects that she will leave unfinished, the things that she will never have known or understood, and the story lines that she will leave as they unfold. She feels despair over how much more life she needs to get a grip on the experience of being a human being thrown into this world. She knows that she will die, not ever having reached a fraction of her potential. My life has only begun, she thinks, and now it is over? But I have things to do! I have people to see! I want to feel the wind in my face, and watch snow-flakes slowly drift on a crisp winter's day. She may also feel a deep sadness that her subjective world will be absorbed into the eternal, silent void. No one will know what it was like to be her. How can a unique point of view simply vanish? The British poet Philip Larkin expresses this resentment in "Aubade," a reflection on his existence at 4 a.m., a time too late for night, and too early for morning,

> The mind blanks at the glare
> Not in remorse . . .
> But at the total emptiness forever
> The sure extinction that we travel to
> And shall be lost in always
> Not to be here,
> Not to be anywhere,
> And soon; nothing more terrible, nothing more true.
>
> And specious stuff that says No rational being
> Can fear a thing it will not feel, not seeing
> That this is what we fear—no sight, no sound,
> No touch or taste or smell, nothing to think with,
> Nothing to love or link with,
> The anesthetic from which none come around.[6]

As Larkin writes, the fact (assuming that it is a fact) that once I am dead, my mind is gone—no sight, no sound, no touch, or taste or smell, noth-ing to love or link with—is not a cause for comfort, but rather is precisely how death harms me. It deprives me of the precondition for anything I like doing and experiencing. It is cold comfort that it also cures my headaches.

3.3   A Timing Challenge to the Deprivation Account

The deprivation account is the standard view of what makes death bad for the one who dies. My case against death depends on its truth. Unfor-tunately, the account faces a tough challenge: in all cases but death, we are comparing a living person's actual life to a counterfactual life when we attribute comparative harm or benefits. In the case of the napping man, there is no problem knowing when the deprivation of the greatest bliss occurs; it occurs when he is napping. Contrast this with a case of someone dying. Here there is no actual life to compare the counterfactual life with: Larkin died on December 2, 1985. Before that date he was alive and so he was not deprived of his life. After that date, he was no longer, and therefore could not be deprived of his life. So, when was Larkin harmed by his death? Of course, just after his death, the corpse or the ashes remain, but this is beside the point, because it is not the corpse or the ashes that have lost their life. Neither should we envision some ghostly remnant missing out of a higher degree of reality after death. Ghosts are off the table since we are assuming that death means annihilation. Rather, we are to imagine a world where Larkin used to be alive, but no longer is, and then answer the question of when he is harmed by this lack of existence. This is not an easy question to answer. Apparently, Epicurus's argument still has bite.[7]

One answer is that Larkin was harmed by death before he died. When he was writing his poem, he was harmed by the death that was to happen eight years into his future. But how can that be true? It is not hard to imagine that his thoughts and fears about his impending death sadden him, and are therefore arguably bad, but that is not the issue. Rather, we are to imagine that Larkin is being harmed by something that has not yet happened. Something that is not a fact until eight years later yet is already responsible for depriving Larkin of something—his life—that, in 1977, he has yet to be deprived of. It is hard to imagine. If the harm is deprivation and the deprivation happens in 1985, then how can this deprivation, which has not yet occurred, harm Larkin in 1977? Are we to imagine some kind of backwards time travel of adverse effects? So, it seems the answer cannot be that Larkin is harmed by his future death at the time when he is alive. If, on the other hand, we answer that he is harmed when he is dead, we need to explain how this is possible. Perhaps we could say that after he has died, Larkin is a potential person, because he would have existed had he not died. And this potential Larkin is being deprived of the goods of life he would have enjoyed had he been actual.[8] This seems too fanciful, since a merely potential Larkin is still a nonexistent Larkin and, hence, not a real subject for a comparative harm in the way that the napper is.

A third possible answer rejects the notion that I will no longer exist after I have died. We usually think that the past is no more, and that the future has not yet come, and only the ever-fleeting sliver of the present is real. Present things exist. Nothing else exists. This view is called presentism. Presentism is the commonsense view, and it is implied in the Epicurean argument. Nevertheless, presentism may be incorrect. Some philosophers and theoretical physicists believe that past, present, and future are all real, and that time as we think of it is an illusion. They propose that the universe is a four-dimensional block including all of the tenses. Different times are as real as different places; the 1820s and 2020s are as real as Paris and London. This view is also known as eternalism, and it has been argued that it is implied by special relativity. If there is no absolute perspective, then different events can be differently arranged in time, depending on the frame of reference. This means that there is no objective basis for the commonsense understanding of events being "now." This comes with the implication that the past, present, and future are ontologically irrelevant categories. Everything exists, always. What we think of as the fixed past, real now, and open future, is entirely subjective and psychological.[9]

If eternalism is correct, then the dead person still exists (in the past) and can therefore be the subject of the harm of death. This view has recently been developed by philosopher Ben Bradley, who writes, "If the past is real, there is no difficulty in locating a subject of the evil of death; it is a past person."[10] . . . "The bad thing that happened is that they died. It's bad for them afterwards, because they would have been better off then, but it's not bad because of anything that is happening to them then."[11] To illustrate, Larkin who died in 1985, is real and exists. Of course, not now, in the present, but in the past. This Larkin is deprived (now in 2020) of whatever value his life would have had had he not died in 1985. How great the harm is depends on how good his life would have been. Today Larkin would have been nearly 100, and if he would have been in good shape, he, the Larkin of the past, is missing out; but if he would have been decrepit and suffering, less so.

I obviously do not know if we live in a block universe with an eternalist ontology, but I do know that I do not want to rest my case against death on a view that is esoteric to most people, hard to grasp (I think), and counterintuitive. How strange it would be if one had to deny the reality of the distinction between the past, present, and future in order to defend something as intuitive as the view that it is bad to die. I will therefore set Bradley's answer aside. But are there any more answers out there?

One remaining answer is not so much a straight answer, as a repudiation of the need for a precise answer. This strategy is represented by philosopher

Thomas Nagel who thinks that we have to accept that the goods and ills of a person cannot always be "exactly located in a sequence of places and times."[12] The harm of dying is one such untimable ill. In support of his contention, Nagel describes a case that is a close analogy to a person dying:

> Suppose an intelligent person receives a brain injury that reduces him to the mental condition of a contented infant, and that such desires as remain to him are satisfied by a custodian, so that he is free from care. Such a development would be widely regarded as a severe misfortune, not only for his friends and relations, or for society, but also, and primarily, for the person himself. This does not mean that a contented infant is unfortunate. The intelligent adult who has been reduced to this condition is the subject of the misfortune. He is the one we pity, though of course he does not mind his condition there is some doubt, in fact, whether he can be said to exist any longer. The view that such a man has suffered a misfortune is open to the same objections which have been raised in regard to death. He does not mind his condition. It is in fact the same condition he was in at the age of three months, except that he is bigger. If we did not pity him then, why pity him now; in any case, who is there to pity? The intelligent adult has disappeared, and for a creature like the one before us, happiness consists in a full stomach and a dry diaper.[13]

The man who suffered a brain injury is deprived of the life he could have had, but more than that, we have a case where someone no longer exists or, to put it more carefully, who is no longer who he used to be. As in the case of death, no one minds the debilitation, neither the healthy man before it, nor the man in his reduced state after it. We cannot therefore answer the question of when what happened to the man is bad for him. There is no subject that is both the victim of the severe deprivation and present during the deprivation. This is why the example is such a striking analogy to someone's actual death: it shows that our inability to time the harm does not in the least tempt us to think that there was no harm done and that everything is just fine, or neither good nor bad. And certainly, we do not think that we should be indifferent to whether we suffer such a debilitating accident on the grounds that where the debilitation is, we are not (fully and aware), and where we are (fully and aware) the debilitation has not yet happened! All this is obvious to anyone who has had a family member disappear into childlike dementia. That they are not suffering, or not too much, is good, but that is clearly not enough to dispel the tragedy. We would all rather be an intelligent person dissatisfied than a severely demented person satisfied.

Nagel's argument is strengthened by the fact that there are many examples of untimables. Philosopher Shelley Kagan gives us another vivid example:

> Suppose that on Monday I shoot John. I wound him with the bullet that comes out of my gun. But it's not a wound directly into his heart. He simply starts bleeding. And he bleeds slowly. So he doesn't die on Monday. He's wounded and he's dying, but he doesn't die on Monday. Next, imagine that on Tuesday I have a heart attack and I die. John's still around—bleeding, but still around. On Wednesday, though, the loss of blood finally overtakes him and John dies. . . . I killed him. That's a fact. But when did I kill him? Did I kill him on Monday, the day I shot him? That doesn't seem right. He's not dead on Monday, so how could I have killed him on Monday? And Tuesday is clearly no better: John is still alive on Tuesday as well. John didn't die until Wednesday. So did I kill him on Wednesday? But how could that be? I don't even exist on Wednesday! I died on Tuesday. How can I kill him after I'm dead? So I didn't kill him on Monday, I didn't kill him on Tuesday, and I didn't kill him on Wednesday. So when did I kill him? Maybe the answer is that there's no particular time at all when I killed John. But for all that, it's true that I did kill him.[14]

If we agree that Kagan killed John, and I think we should, then we must recognize that there are facts that are indeterminately timed. The fact that death is bad for the one who dies is one such fact. When Larkin wrote "Aubade," he was anticipating this great harm. Eight years later it occurred. This was bad for him. And that is all we can say. Or, to turn to the first person: I sit here typing and death will deprive me of my life, and this is bad for me. It is bad for me because it means that I cannot continue my worthwhile life. I cannot say at what particular time death is bad for me, but for all that, death is bad for me. To elaborate: I sit here, with possible futures ahead of me that I can rank in terms of desirability. In one I live 50 more years in good health, in another I live only 5 more years in good health, all else being equal. At this point in time, all that I value about being alive, gives me a reason to prefer the first future over the second, and hence to regard it as relatively good; hence, I can truthfully say that if the second future is realized, it would be bad.

I think this is the right answer.

Admittedly, it is hard to feel entirely satisfied. As I said, the puzzle has been around since the ancient Greeks for a reason. The Epicureans can respond by insisting that the harm of death, the deprivation, is given a subject and a time. Nagel says that we do not have to specify a time for the evil; Epicureans insist that we do have to specify a time. Nagel says, we do not exist when we are dead, and this harms us; they say, we do not exist when we are dead so we cannot be harmed. Is this not a draw? Could be. In order to tip the scale further in favor of regarding death as a bad thing, we need to consider the full implications of Epicureanism and similar views.

3.4   What Kind of Person Can Be Indifferent to Death?

Epicureanism presents itself as a recipe for a good life. Epicurus writes, "There is nothing terrible in life for the man who has truly comprehended that there is nothing terrible in not living. . . . Never shall you be disturbed waking or asleep, but you shall live like a god among men."[15] These are bold claims. Live as I say, and you will never be disturbed. You will be a god among men. Closer scrutiny reveals an unattractive and implausible philosophy of life. Consider how first-century Roman Epicurean Lucretius, creator of the important Epicurean thought-poem, *De Rerum Natura* (On the Nature of Things), deals with our complaint that death deprives us of the goods of life:

> Now no more shall thy glad home welcome thee, nor good wife and sweet children run up to snatch the kisses, and touch thy heart with a silent thrill of joy. No more shalt thou have power to prosper in thy ways, or to be a sure defense to thine own. "Pitiful thou art," men say, and "pitifully has one malignant day taken from thee all the many prizes of life." Yet to this they add not: "nor does there abide with thee any longer any yearning for these things." But if they saw this clearly in mind, and followed it out in their words, they would free themselves from great anguish and fear of mind.[16]

Lucretius is making that point that when dead, we no longer yearn for the things that death takes from us. The man is not harmed by never seeing his family again, since he will no longer yearn to see them. If the family man is an Epicurean god, he will therefore be undisturbed by the prospect of dying. I wish to challenge this ideal of the imperturbable wise man.

Epicureans are hedonists, which means that they think that the only thing that is good in itself is pleasure and the only thing that is bad in itself is pain. All other things are only instrumentally good or instrumentally bad, depending on whether they promote or oppose pleasure. Having our desires satisfied, for instance, is only good insofar as it gives us pleasure. My challenge is this: If pleasure is good, then this means that it is worth pursuing, and that there is a reason to pursue it. This follows from the meaning of good. But if there is a reason to pursue the good, then there is a reason to avoid dying. In other words, if we are faced with two possible worlds ahead of us, one containing the good and the other containing something that is neither good nor bad, we should prefer the good. The family man, to illustrate, has reason to prefer the pleasure of seeing his good wife and children over the nonpleasure of nonexistence. And he therefore has a reason to regard death as something to be avoided. Hedonism is therefore incompatible with a neutral evaluation of death. (The same argument can be made in terms of pain. If pain is to be avoided, then, in unfortunate cases, death can be preferred. Therefore, death is not always neutral, but sometimes the lesser of two evils, and therefore a relative good.) To press on, if a hedonist is faced with the choice of a short happy life or a longer happy life, where the longer life contains more happiness, he must prefer the longer life. Hence, he has a reason to prefer not to die; indeed, he has a reason to fear death as a threat to his one and only good. Here the Epicurean will respond: "Yes, but he will not have his preference for a longer life frustrated by dying, because when dead he no longer has the preference! His yearnings disappear with him." The Epicurean god thinks that it would be good to see his family, but at the same time he does not think that it would be bad not to see his family, if he happened to die. In his mind, he cares to see his family, if he happens to be alive, but he does not, somehow, care in a way that makes him prefer being alive to see them. Some desires are conditioned on being alive, in this way. We, for example, breathe if we are alive, but we do not take breathing to be a reason to live. So goes one line of response. The answer to it is that it would be utterly disaffected and alienated to regard all our desires as conditioned on being alive. A drug addict may reasonably want to have his desires canceled rather than satisfied, but a man who yearns to see his family cannot be impartial between having his desires satisfied or having his desires go unfulfilled. What would it mean to yearn to see someone, yet remain indifferent to whether one sees them or not (because one is no longer alive)? "Yes, my love, I am looking forward so much to seeing you! On the other hand, should I die a swift and painless death on my way to see you, then this is just as good, as in that case I will also no longer want to see you. I really don't prefer one scenario over the other; they are equally good to me." It would take a monstrously wise Epicurean god to be indifferent between seeing his wife and children and ceasing to want to see them. The Epicurean god cannot see his yearning as

giving him a reason to live, which, I think, is tantamount to saying that
he cannot really yearn at all. He achieves a tolerance of death by way of
a listless quasi-nihilism, whereby although pleasure is good and nothing
else matters, it is also not worth living for. This awful implication has not
escaped critics. Philosopher Steven Luper writes,

> They [Epicureans] are capable of their indifference to death only because they
> have pared down their concerns to the point that life is now a matter of indiffer-
> ence to them. For in avoiding all aspirations that can be thwarted by death, Epi-
> cureans have had to avoid all desires which are capable of giving them a reason
> for living. In order to maintain their unconcern about dying, they must avoid
> having any reason whatsoever for not dying. However, any reason for living is an
> excellent reason for not dying; so only if they avoid having any reason for living
> can they avoid having any reason for not dying. . . . Epicureans think that death
> is nothing to them only because they think that life is nothing to them.[17]

Just how psychologically and morally implausible this philosophy of
death is becomes clear once we shift to other-regarding desires. The man,
we can assume, has a desire not only to experience the thrill of seeing his
children, but also to raise and protect and teach them. In order to do so, he
certainly must be alive. So how can he remain indifferent to death? Imagine
an Epicurean god thinking, "I care deeply about raising my children and
providing them a safe home, but I am just as happy if I die, because if I do, I
will also stop caring about them. And, sure, my death will cause them grief,
but again, since I am not alive, I will not experience it, so it is nothing to
me." Savor that: his family's grief and the harm his death causes his family
cannot be a reason for him to continue his life because if it were, then he
would have to see it as a reason to fear death. This is not an unfair criticism. In Epicurus's writings and in the writings of his followers, as well as
in other wisdom literature of a similar ilk, the conclusion drawn from the
experiential nothingness of death is that death should be regarded as nothing. Period. They never qualify this conclusion by adding that we can still
hate our death because of what it does to other people. This consideration
is absent. We should be indifferent to death, so apparently, we should be
indifferent to the ill effects that our death may have on others. How else
can we regard death as nothing to us? Caring about others is incompatible
with carelessness regarding death.

Let me conclude the argument by pointing out four implications of
indifference towards death. First, as already touched upon, it would be no

worse to die at 10 than at 100. Second, also as already touched upon, it cannot be better to die than to suffer the greatest possible pain. Euthanasia is never justified in terms of the good of the sufferer. Third, killing an innocent person, if painless, is not to harm him. By taking someone's life, you are taking something that cannot be missed once it is gone, hence there is no harm. Four, the only self-interested reason there is for stepping out of the way of a high-speed freight train is the millisecond of pain at impact. There are no other reasons.

Secular people are fond of citing Epicurus and Lucretius on death—it happens in nearly every piece of writing on the matter—but they rarely go much beyond repeating, in some version, "where I am death is not, and where death is, I am not." Pleased that they have found something to placate their fear of death—indeed, to have found something that makes them invulnerable to its assault—they usually move on to the ad hominem attacks against those of us for whom death is not something of indifference. Unfortunately, what they have found is a placebo. As we have seen, the Epicurean god represents a false ideal to whom few today would subscribe if they saw—if they cared to see—its full implications. Not having a reason to live is a steep price to pay for a personality tolerant of death. This is why, despite admitted perplexities with regard to the timing of the ill of death, it is reasonable to affirm the intuitive belief that death can be something worth avoiding.

3.5   The Mirror Argument

In this section we will consider an argument that is less commonly made, but philosophically intriguing, often referred to as Lucretius's mirror argument. In a section called "On the Folly of the Fear of Death," Lucretius writes,

> Look back again to see how the past ages of everlasting time, before we are born, have been as naught to us. These then nature holds up to us as a mirror of the time that is to come, when we are dead and gone. Is there aught that looks terrible in this, aught that seems gloomy? Is it not a calmer rest than any sleep?[18]

Lucretius's argument is an argument from analogy. It points out that nonexistence is the same state whether it is prevital or posthumous. Since both states are essentially the same, we should have the same attitudes toward them. We already know that prevital existence was not harmful and we do not fear it. To be consistent, we should therefore think that death is not harmful and not fear it.

3.6 The Differences between Prevital Nonexistence and Posthumous Nonexistence

We can begin answering Lucretius by observing that we never fear what has already happened. To fear something that will happen is therefore consistent with not fearing a similar event that has already happened. I can fear going to the dentist next week, but I cannot fear having gone last week. So, too, I can fear posthumous nonexistence, but I cannot fear prevital nonexistence. Where we stand in time matters to how we value something. We fear forward, and we prefer to have bad things to be in the past, just as we hope forward, imagining good things to be in the future.[19] Asymmetrical attitudes toward the past and future are therefore consistent with how we normally make value judgments.

There is also a deeper metaphysical reason for why we care more about not dying than we do about not having come into existence earlier: We cannot come into existence before we actually did. The time before we come into existence is therefore not time that we are deprived of. Many would disagree with this. They would claim to be able to imagine that they lived in an earlier time. "I wished I was born in a different time" is not on its face contradictory, so why think that it expresses a metaphysical impossibility? Suppose there is a woman named Pam, born at 9:15am on Tuesday, May 28, 1959. The question now is, could she have come into existence before she actually did? Could a baby girl named, say, Polly, delivered 10 years earlier in 1949 be Pam? The answer hinges on what we take as necessary conditions for Pam to be Pam. It is a question of personal identity. Personal identity is typically considered as constituted by the body, the personality, or the soul: I am where my body is; I am where my mental content is; or, I am where my soul is.

Could Pam's soul be in Polly? This raises the following questions: In what way would it be Pam's soul, rather than Polly's soul? How could that soul be Pam's if the soul is in Polly, and there is no Pam, and there never will be a Pam? Perhaps the answer is that there is a soul existing in some other dimension, and that soul can be joined with matter at the time of conception, or at a later time in human development. If so, then perhaps it could be possible that a soul that entered the world and was Pam could have entered the world earlier and be Polly. This then would be how it could be true that Pam could have been born 10 years earlier. The question is, is this true in the way imagined by Pam? Depending on the age of her parents, she may have to have different parents. If she has siblings, she would now be the oldest. She would be a child in the 1950s rather than the 1960s. She would look different, think different, listen to different music, watch different films, read different books, eat different, have different friends, and have different teachers, and so on, and so on, and so on. The soul may be the same, but everything else would be different. This is not, I think, what Pam is imagining when she is imagining that she goes back in time to be with the object of her love. (Philosophers who do not believe that there is an immaterial soul, like Epicurus and Lucretius, would add that this is a moot point.)

From the above reasoning, we can also draw the conclusion that if personal identity depends on mental content as stated by the personality view of personal identity, then Polly could not be Pam. Polly does not have any of Pam's mental content and since, ex hypothesis, the mental content is Pam, Polly is not Pam, necessarily. This is different from Pam surviving in the future where she keeps enough of her personality as she grows older: she starts off as Pam and continues as Pam although her personality may gradually change. But in the case of Polly, there is simply no reason to say that she starts off as Pam since she has none of Pam's mental content.

One view of personal identity remains: the bodily view. If we are where our body is, then clearly Polly cannot be Pam. Polly has a completely different body from Pam and therefore cannot be identical to Pam. Even if we assume that she has the same parents, only younger, at most we could say that the baby would be akin to an older sister of Pam. Or think of it like this: The person we call Pam is the person who was born in 1949, was given the name "Pam," and went, say, to middle school together with her best friends Tom and Lisa, and so on. No one who was born in 1959 could possibly be this very same physical person. Of course not. Names for persons, as for objects, attach through a historical process and they cannot be "pulled loose" and simply attached to another object with a completely different history. Proper names are, as some philosophers say, rigid designators.[20] By analogy, the Statue of Liberty replica in Las Vegas, despite its verisimilitude, can never be the Statue of Liberty, the one that greeted hopeful immigrants at Ellis Island. It has the wrong progeny.[21]

I reject backwards time travel because it violates our best theories of personal identity. Contrary to what is commonly believed among philosophers and laymen it is inconceivable that one could have been born before one was born (premature deliveries aside). Only loose thinking makes it seem that way. The time after we are dead is the time that we are deprived of, but the time before we are born is not time that we are deprived of. We therefore cannot regret not having been born earlier in the way that we can regret dying.

Even those who (mistakenly) think that they could have come into existence before they did have a reason to reject the mirror argument. Philosopher Christine Overall remarks that it is quite common for people to wish that they had been born earlier:

> I'm not completely convinced that people feel no regrets about their nonexistence during the time that elapsed before they were born. Although people do not fear or dread their nonexistence before their birth, as they may their nonexistence after death, and probably most people do not lament "the past antiquity of infinite time," some people occasionally feel regrets about the years, decades, or even centuries before their birth. At the level of pop culture, in some songs and stories the narrator expresses sadness about being born too late to love someone who is much older.[22]

Overall's observation provides a surprising way to answer the mirror argument. Rather than correcting our attitudes toward death, we should correct our casual attitudes toward "the past antiquity of infinite time." We should regret the time lost by not having existed in the past, just as we regret the time lost by ceasing to exist. This is enough to counter Lucretius's argument. Nevertheless, I do not believe that this is the right answer. As I argued above, I think that ordinary people and philosophers alike are mistaken when they think that they can imagine having come into existence significantly earlier than they in fact did.

3.7   We Cannot Diminish the Time That We Do Not Exist

Further along in *De Rerum Natura*, Lucretius suggests that the length of time we live is irrelevant. This view is, as we saw above, implied by the Epicurean view that death is harmless at whatever time it strikes. Lucretius offers an independent argument for this highly counterintuitive thesis and it is worth brief consideration mainly for the attitude toward life it manifests. Lucretius writes,

> Nor, by protracting life, do we deduct a single moment from the duration of death; we cannot diminish aught from its reign, or cause that we may be for a less period sunk in non-existence. How many generations so ever, therefore, we may pass in life, nevertheless that same eternal death will still await us.[23]

In short, whether we die at 10 or 100 it is all the same because death is eternal. It is a thought that apparently consoled Marcus Aurelius, who mused that life is a vanishingly small point bookended by an infinite void on both sides; but apart from Aurelius, I do not think that many have found this thought consoling.[24] Sure, eternity is always the same eternity, but so what? We want to lengthen our lives in order to enjoy more existence, not in some vain effort to shorten "eternal death." We should also ask where in Lucretius's metaphysical arguments is the human point of view? Imagine a physician telling grieving parents that by continuing to live, their four-year old child, Amy, would not shorten her time in oblivion. That is, whether little Amy died now or later is all the same. She would gain nothing by living on. The parents should conclude that these words could only come from a cold-hearted person. No doubt, Amy's life is of no importance from the point of view of an infinite universe of nothing but atoms and void. This is the perspective from which nothing matters. It is, therefore, not a helpful starting point for thinking about what matters to us. The relevant perspectives in this case are those of Amy and her parents and from their perspectives it matters whether she will be there to blow out the candles on her fifth birthday cake or not.

3.8 The Folly of Wisdom

> Empty is that philosopher's argument by which no human suffering is therapeutically treated. For just as there is no use in a medical art that does not cast out the sicknesses of bodies, so too there is no use in philosophy, unless it casts out the suffering of the soul.[25]
> —Epicurus

The thought that death is harmless sounds suspiciously like what we would want to be true. I suspect that there is an understandable motivation behind

Epicurean wisdom to not only give a fair assessment of death, but to assess it in a way that makes it less frightening and more acceptable; that is, Epicurus aims to tame death and manage the terror it causes in sensitive minds. Epicureanism and other ancient Hellenistic philosophy aimed at eudaemonia, or the happiness and fulfillment of a good life. This means that it was not merely a theoretical exercise, like so much academic philosophy today is, but practical and even therapeutic.[26] It wanted to communicate a perspective, a truth that would enable the adept to live the best life, a life free of anxiety, a state described as ataraxia. The truth, they thought, would set us free. But what if the truth makes us tremble? What if the truth that philosophy, when properly conducted, reveals is that death opposes nearly all that we care about, including ourselves, our projects, our memories, our relationships to other people, and so on? What if philosophy concludes that death is worthy of fear like almost nothing else?

It is interesting that Epicurus and Lucretius are not only aware that they are going up against the common person's opinion, but that they appear to have a visceral experience of the threat of death beyond what people generally acknowledge. Lucretius writes, "That fear of Acheron must be hurled out headlong. That fear which shakes human life at its very foundations, covering everything over with the blackness of death, and which does not leave any pleasure fluid and pure."[27] If someone has this level of fear, then there is a psychological health imperative to cure it, and hence a job for a medicinal philosophy. The therapeutic mission of these philosophers would arguably not allow them to think that death is simply awful, even if it were true. After all, if "the end all of all our actions is to be free of pain and fear," then believing that death is harmless may be justified even if the opposite is manifestly true. Hedonism holds pleasure as the sole good, not truth, so noble fictions that enable a happy life cannot be ruled out on ethical grounds.

My philosophy aims at truth and thus therapy is accidental to this defining aim. Yes, it may be that if we think a little bit deeper, with the sole aim of believing what is true, that we will understand just how bad it is to go out of existence (if that is what happens when we die), and how much we should tremble. If so, we must side with the common man, the philosopher's fool, who complains, "We poor little humans have only a brief enjoyment here. Soon it has already been, and one cannot call it back."[28] And we should admit to the feeling that we will leave this earth unsatisfied and still wanting more life: we "feed, always, the ungrateful nature of the mind and fill it with good things, but never satisfy it—as the seasons of the year do, when they come round again, bringing their new growth and their varied delights; nor are we ever filled up with the fruits of life."[29] This regret flows naturally from a healthy love of life, a love that rebels against any imposed time limit. Would we not question the state of the mental health of a friend who confesses that she does not care if she lives or dies? Is she depressed? Yet it is this abnormal indifference that is the goal of the Epicurean cure. The therapy offered by the Epicureans is therefore not only in potential conflict with the truth, but may also, if successful, leave the patient significantly worse off.

This is not denying that Epicureans have a lot of good advice about how to live: We should live a simple, honest life and take responsibility for our actions. We should cultivate true friendship, produce meaningful work, and be happy with less. Thoughtful people will agree with this. The problem, as I see it, is their grandiose conception of the power of their philosophy. Epicurus's promise to Menoeceus would make even today's self-help gurus blush. To quote it again: "Exercise yourself in these and kindred precepts day and night . . . then never, either in waking or in dream, will you be disturbed, but will live as a god among people." His dream of a superman-like invulnerability, also found in other philosophies like Stoicism, is a form self-flattering hubris—the philosopher, though dressed in rags, is a demi-god! Nothing ordinary people care about, or love or fear really matters. It is, on the one hand, unrealistic, and on the other unattractive. To not be disturbed by anything is not possible for someone who cares deeply about something or someone. The superman for whom death means nothing, even if it prevents him from realizing his goals and cuts him off from his loved ones, is less attractive, as a type, than the common anxious fool who ardently wants to live. An everyman, like the father in Lucretius's example, who yearns to see his wife and children, and who wants to live to see them, is a better man than a man who "yearns" to see his wife and children, but who also does not care if he dies and never sees them again (because he knows that when dead, he will not miss them). His spouse and his children want him to think that they give him a reason to live. They hope that he would be as disturbed by their death as they would be by theirs. Epicurean supermen and superwomen would find it hard to enter meaningful relationships with mere mortals.

Where death is, we are not, and that is a problem, since it deprives us of all that we value about being alive. The only way to care less about death is to care less about life. It is therefore no surprise that many philosophers have argued that we should have fewer desires that death can thwart. We are taught to deny them, to transcend them, and to observe them with cool detachment. These philosophers also typically add a measure of pessimism: Life is not that great, and we will soon have enough of it. The fear of missing out is therefore unwarranted. It is to this pessimism we now turn.

4   Life Is Overrated

The best thing for all men and women is not to be born. . . . The second best, is, after being born, to die as quickly as possible.

—Silenus

Wherefore I praised the dead which are already dead more than the living which are yet alive. Yea, better is he than both they, which hath not yet been, who hath not seen the evil work that is done under the sun.

—*Ecclesiastes*

[T]he shortness of life, so often lamented, may perhaps be the very best thing about it.

—Arthur Schopenhauer

4.1   The Case against Life

The case against death is really a case for life. Death is bad, I have argued, because life is good. But what if life is not that good? It would seriously weaken my case against death if the life we miss out on by dying is not worth living. Pessimists would have us believe that the human condition is defined by suffering and that the outlook for the future is grim. Their understanding of the trajectory of history is declinist as opposed to progressive. This, they complain, is not a world that one wants to bring children into. The case against death is not complete until such declinist pessimism is answered.[1]

Pessimism is defined as a tendency to think that bad things are more likely to happen and to emphasize the bad part of a situation. Over the next chapters I will discuss many expressions of pessimism. Some forms of pessimism concern our ability to cope with more time. As limited human beings, we would quickly become bored and alienated if we had unlimited time. Another form of pessimism relates to the prognosis about what radical life extension could lead to in terms of demographic challenges to the economy, culture, and society. The worry here is that radical and general life extension would lead to a world that we would not want to live in, and that it is hence a self-defeating project. Some think of it as a tragedy of the commons, where something that benefits the individual cannot be realized if everyone seeks the same benefit. For example, each whaler has a reason to catch as many whales as she can. But if everyone catches as many whales as they can, in the end there would be no more whales and everyone loses. Hence, even if it is good for one person to live to 120, it would be a disaster if everyone lived to 120, and in the end, it would not even be good for that one person. Others worry that radical life extension would lead to overpopulation. Overpopulation means that there would be more people than resources, which would lead to famine, war, and environmental collapse. Yet others think that our society would stagnate, and our economy collapse under the burden of caring for an ever-growing population of the elderly. These and other expressions of pessimism concerning radical life extension as a public choice will be addressed in chapters 10 and 11.

In this chapter, I will address a more profound pessimism that I will refer to as existential pessimism. I call it this because it is not a pessimism about particular aspects of life but about existence as such. Existential pessimism holds that even if we find solutions to many of our social challenges, being human is so hard that death is a blessing, or at least not a vastly inferior alternative to life. This view tells us that our suffering outweighs our happiness and that all our desires and concerns are paltry and pointless. "It would have been better not to have been born" is an ancient idea and the core intuition of existential pessimism. If there is an abundance of pain and all our pursuits are empty and hopeless, then why drag this out? Some existential pessimists go so far as to say that no life is ever worth living and that we have a moral obligation not to have children, so as to end the human race—and that, as an act of mercy, we should euthanize all sentient nonhuman creatures. A measure of pessimism may be beneficial in that it counteracts complacency while also avoiding perfectionism. If we expect the worst, we might be happily surprised. The key to happiness, as they say, is low expectations. Recognizing and emphasizing our flawed nature may engender a benign tolerance. Pessimism can also be prudent. Optimism can fuel foolhardy policies and utopian projects that end in disaster. But when pessimism says that life as such is a curse and an illness, it is excessive.

Existential pessimism, new and old, boils down to three general complaints against life: the abundance of suffering, the hopelessness of desire, and the seeming pointlessness of it all. In what follows, I will argue that none of these complaints justify hating life to the degree that death becomes a preferred alternative.

4.2 Suffering and a Dream of a Crystalline State

> [E]verything in life is certainly calculated to . . . convince us that the purpose of our existence is not to be happy. Indeed, if life is considered more closely and impartially, it presents itself rather as specially intended to show us that we are not to feel happy in it, since by its whole nature it bears the character of something for which we have lost the taste, which must disgust us.[2]
> —Schopenhauer

At this moment there are an estimated 870 million people suffering from chronic undernourishment. Thirty million people are enslaved. A quarter of a billion children aged five to 14 are forced to work, often in sweatshops, in developing countries. Millions around the globe are suffering from painful illnesses. And yet, this is without a doubt the most benign time in history to be alive. Only recently, the world was such a harmful place that the average human could expect to die before the age of 40. Slavery, despotism, public torture, and military conquest were regarded as morally acceptable or good.

Not even middle class people in the developed world are spared from suffering. In his book *Better Never to Have Been: The Harm of Coming into Existence*, South African philosopher David Benatar describes the pain of getting through an average day:

> [U]nless one is eating and drinking so regularly as to prevent hunger and thirst or countering them as they arise, one is likely hungry and thirsty for a few hours a day. Unless one is lying about all day, one is probably tired for a substantial portion of one's waking life. How often does one feel neither too hot nor too cold, but exactly right?[3]

As we get older, the suffering intensifies: "Chronic ailments and advancing age make matters worse. Aches, pains, lethargy, and sometimes frustration from disability become an experiential backdrop for everything else."[4] Benatar continues:

> Now add those discomforts, pains, and sufferings that are experienced either less frequently or only by some (though nonetheless very many) people. These include allergies, headaches, frustration, irritation, colds, menstrual pains, hot flushes, nausea, hypoglycemia, seizures, guilt, shame, boredom, sadness, depression, loneliness, body-image dissatisfaction, the ravages of AIDS, of cancer, and of other such life-threatening diseases, and grief and bereavement. The reach of negative mental states in ordinary lives is extensive.[5]

Life is a painful experience for everyone. So how then can we want more life? Benatar concludes that it would be better never to have been born and that we should spare future generations from suffering by not having children. The German philosopher Arthur Schopenhauer (1788–1860), who arrived at the same conclusion two centuries earlier, invites us to dream of a lifeless world:

> If you try to imagine, as nearly as you can, what an amount of misery, pain and suffering of every kind the sun shines upon in its course, you will admit that it would be much better if, on the earth as little as on the moon, the sun were able to call forth the phenomena of life; and if, here as there, the surface were still in a crystalline state.[6]

Schopenhauer's crystalline state is the logical end point of the pessimist's concern with suffering; only by ending life can suffering be abolished.

The pessimism of Schopenhauer and Benatar has roots that probably stretch back to the first civilizations. The Greek playwright Sophocles (400 BC) encapsulates the case against life, in the following verse from *Oedipus at Colonus*, where the chorus chants,

> Whoever craves the longer length of life, not content to desire a moderate span, him I will judge with no uncertainty: He clings to folly.
>
> For the long years lay in deposit many things nearer to pain than joy; but as for your delights, you will find them nowhere, when someone's life has fallen beyond the fitting period. The Helper comes at last to all alike, when the fate of Hades is suddenly revealed, without marriage-song, or lyre, or dance: Death at the end.
>
> Not to be born is, beyond all estimation, best; but when a man has seen the light of day, this is next best by far, that with utmost speed he should go back from where he came.[7]

The antinatalist, anti-life-cult is not just an extreme theoretical possibility entertained by philosophers concerned with consistency; it is today a global movement. Recently, a young man in India, inspired by Benatar, sued his parents for bringing him into the world without his consent.[8] Perhaps, like Schopenhauer, he was also inspired by the Buddha's teachings that suffering is a central fact of life and that escaping it is our ultimate goal: "Oblivious of the suffering to which life is subject, man begets children, and is thus the cause of old age and death. If he would only realize what suffering he would add to by his act, he would desist from the procreation of children; and so stop the operation of old age and death."[9] The lawsuit is a publicity stunt certainly, but the antinatalist sentiment behind it appears sincere.

4.2.1 Responding to the Argument from Suffering

It is a truism that life contains a balance of both pleasure and pain, and it appears that most people find the balance quite tolerable. A recent poll found that a third of Americans are not only happy, but very happy.[10] This should be enough to refute pessimism, one should think, for if people are happy then life must—despite all the pain—be good enough. I do not know of any more direct and salient evidence of the falsehood of existential pessimism. Benatar disagrees because he dismisses self-reported happiness. He thinks that we are deluding ourselves to think that we are alright by downplaying the bad, by adapting to bad circumstances, and by comparing ourselves to those who are worse off. He points to the phenomenon of someone being the victim of an accident and how often their reported well-being bounces back. In his view, the victim is wrong about his level of well-being. The problem with Benatar's interpretation is that it is hard to draw a firm line between judging ourselves to be alright or happy, and being happy. To remember the good days, to accommodate ourselves to challenging situations, and to remind ourselves how fortunate we are is not to blind ourselves to the "real truth" of our misery. Rather, it is a part of why we are, in fact, not miserable. This is the philosopher's true wisdom, one that I am not attacking: A man's happiness consists largely of attitudes he takes to the world. Moreover, suffering is not always a bad thing. Contrary to philosophies that reduce human psychology to an avoidance of pain, we often seek out painful experiences. Every year there is a New York Marathon where more—and often less—fit individuals voluntarily torture themselves as they run, walk, and stumble through the boroughs. They freely choose this, and many of them willingly return the following year for more punishment. Overcoming the pain makes the run an accomplishment, and something to be proud of. That is why they do it. The pain is essential to the meaning of the marathon and it is just one instance of a wider human experience. Looking back at our lives, we appreciate much of the suffering we have endured, understanding that it plays a part in making us who we are today. Of course, much pain is meaningless, since it is not inextricably connected to any good and is not voluntary; it is just plain, bad pain. Fortunately, as we have seen, we are built to cope with much of it, and it normally does not prevent us from being happy. In fact, the most interesting and worthwhile lives are rarely those with the least suffering. Who wants their gravestone to say that he or she "passed through life with as little discomfort as possible?" The antilife wisdom that sees the escape from suffering as our highest goal is clearly mistaken.

Perhaps the best way to resist antinatalist misanthropy is to picture Schopenhauer's, lifeless universe. Imagine a universe of silent and pointless movements of brute things, a universe existing only in itself. A big show, with no audience, besides perhaps God. This is a horrifying thought. We are ourselves what brings meaning to the world. If we are the only part of the universe, besides perhaps God, and are capable of reflecting on it, we should revel in this privilege. Existential pessimism and its dream of a human-free crystalline state is repulsive in its antihumanism and utter unappreciativeness. The Christian emphasis on life as a gift and each new child a miracle that we should be thankful for, by contrast, strikes me as far more appropriate.[11] Schopenhauer lived a comfortable life and died, for the times, at the impressive age of 72. Apparently, like most of us, he found the balance of pain and pleasure tolerable. David Benatar, 53, is still alive and appears to live a good life, heading the philosophy department at the University of Cape Town and finding purpose in persuading people not to have children. Benatar, like Schopenhauer, believes that suicide is morally permissible, but apparently something keeps him here.

4.3 Escaping Our Mad Masters

Plato believed that we are souls temporarily trapped in bodies. Our bodies prevent us from gaining knowledge, which for Plato is the paramount aim of life, and they lead us astray by imposing their needs and desires on our souls:

> (W)hile the soul is infected with the evils of the body, our desire will not be satisfied and our desire is of the truth. For the body is a source of endless trouble to us by reason of the mere requirement of food; and is liable also to diseases which overtake and impede us in the search after true being: it fills us full of loves, and lusts, and fears, and fancies of all kinds, and endless foolery, and in fact, as men say, takes away from us the power of thinking at all. Whence come wars, and fightings, and factions? whence but from the body and the lusts of the body?[12]

This passage is from Plato's dialogue *Phaedo*, in which he chronicles his friend and teacher Socrates's last hours before he is to be executed by means of drinking a cup of poisonous hemlock. In the *Phaedo*, Socrates tells his friends that he has no fear of death but is looking forward to it. He tells his friends,

> . . . I deem that the true votary of philosophy is likely to be misunderstood by other men; they do not perceive that he is always pursuing death and dying; and if this be so, and he has had the desire of death all his life long, why when his time comes should he repine at that which he has been always pursuing and desiring?[13]

The sooner we can liberate ourselves from our bodies the better. We may not, however, take our own life, but must wait until a time chosen by God or fate. Rather than killing ourselves, we should emulate physical death in life through an ascetic domination of the body. The desire for food, drink, sex, money, power, ambition, and other needs of the body should be ignored as much as possible since they disturb our true essence, our rational selves. Consider as an illustration of this theme the following exchange between Socrates and his friend Simmias, also from the *Phaedo*:

> There is another question, which will probably throw light on our present enquiry if you and I can agree about it. Ought the philosopher to care about the pleasures—if they are to be called pleasures—of eating and drinking?
> Certainly not, answered Simmias.
> And what do you say of the pleasures of love—should he care about them?
> By no means.
> And will he think much of the other ways of indulging the body—for example, the acquisition of costly raiment, or sandals, or other adornments of the body? . . .
> I should say the true philosopher would despise them.

> Would you not say that he is entirely concerned with the soul and not with the body? He would like, as far as he can, to get away from the body and turn to the soul.
> Quite true. [14]

The denial of bodily existence and contempt for the pursuit of satisfying any other desires than those for truth is, for Plato, the defining quest of the philosopher. The desire for death is the soul's longing to be set free. Death is the aim of the philosopher, and he is therefore perfectly tolerant of death.

For Plato, desires drive us to wickedness and blind us toward the truth, and they are therefore a main reason for why this life is not worth prolonging. Another reason for condemning these mad masters is that they will never be satisfied. The Greek myth of Sisyphus tells the story of the king of Corinth who tried to cheat death by tying it up and locking it in a wardrobe. For this act of hubris, he is punished by Zeus to roll a boulder up a hill forever in the depths of Hades. A fitting punishment, since he gets the immortality he seeks. More than that, Sisyphus's rock pushing can, as it was done by French philosopher Albert Camus, be interpreted as an image of the actual life of every man, with the exception that unlike poor Sisyphus we have a way out. Death, the myth teaches us, is our sweet liberator and we should not seek to restrain it. This is also the moral intended by Lucretius when he retells it in the "Folly of the Fear of Death" section of *De Rerum Natura*. The struggle for worldly power, writes Lucretius, is similar "to thrust[ing] uphill with great effort a stone, which after all rolls back from the topmost peak, and headlong makes for the levels of the plain beneath." And the desire for pleasure is equally unfulfilling; we can

> feed the ungrateful nature of the mind, to fill it with good things, yet never satisfy it. . . . so long as we have not what we crave, it seems to surpass all else; afterward, when that is ours, we crave something else, and the same thirst for life besets us ever, openmouthed. [15]

These essentially insatiable desires make us their restless playthings.

> [K]nowing . . . not what he wants, and longing ever for a change of place, as though he could this lay aside the burden. The man who is tired of staying at home, often goes out abroad from his great mansion, and of a sudden returns again, for indeed abroad he feels no better. He races to his country home, furiously driving his ponies, as though he were hurrying to bring help to a burning house; he yawns at once, when he has set foot on the threshold of the villa, or links into a heavy sleep and leeks forgetfulness. or even in hot haste makes for

town, eager to be back. In this way each man struggles to escape himself: yet, despite his will to he clings to the self, which we may be sure, in fact he cannot shun, and hates himself, because in his sickness he knows not the cause of his malady.[16]

As in Plato, the cause of the human malady is existence itself. Whereas Plato expects a more real posthumous existence, Lucretius advises us to overcome our "evil craving for life" and shift our focus toward our eternal nonexistence, where we can forever "lay aside the burden." The philosophical opposition to the treadmill of life is also a central theme of eastern religions, in particular Buddhism. As in the ancient Greek schools of philosophy, the Buddha's philosophy is therapeutic, with the aim of curing suffering. For the Buddha, desires not only keep us on the treadmill of this life, but of many lives, until we find a way to silence these desires. The Buddha's Four Noble Truths are: (1) suffering exists; (2) the origin of suffering is desire, and desire is the cause of the cycle of rebirth and therefore suffering; (3) the cessation of suffering exists in personal annihilation, nirvana; (4) there is a noble eightfold path to the cessation of desire. The reason that desires cause suffering is that the world is impermanent and in constant flux, meaning that all desires are ultimately frustrated, and every attachment is bound to break. Desire in a mutable world is hopeless. We should therefore eradicate desire and detach ourselves from the world. What makes it hard for us to detach ourselves is our illusion that we are excluded from the impermanence surrounding us. In fact, we are nothing; there is no soul, no essence, and no self. We are nothing, because we are mutable, and mutability is, as in Plato, understood as unreal. No physical or mental fact is therefore real. It is all an illusion. Wisdom is the recognition of this truth, and therein lies the key to escape from the cycle of rebirth. Actually, it is not *all* an illusion, as stated in the first noble truth, since suffering is real. Suffering is the only thing that is real and is also the ultimate evil in this philosophy. Buddhism is therefore a pure form of existential pessimism. This pessimism is in some forms of Buddhism combined with an optimism about the afterlife, where there is the possibility of arriving at a heavenly state, rather than total annihilation. My purpose is not to describe the most accurate or most philosophically sound version of Buddhism—that is the work of its many schools and their interpreters. The above outline captures a very common and influential understanding, one that inspired Schopenhauer, and one that you would likely find when researching Buddhism, and my point is that it presents a bleak view of earthly life together with a wish to escape it, and certainly presents no complaint about its brevity.[17]

Some scholars believe that the Buddha and Socrates were contemporaries, and they might both have been influenced by an exchange between Indian and Greek philosophy. Seeing the convergence with existential pessimism, it makes sense that Buddhism, like Christendom, absorbed elements from Plato as it developed over time. It is almost as if ancient wisdom speaks with one voice: Desires and the misperception of appearance for reality are the roots of misery and we should learn to let go of this life. The ideal human being in their minds is not she who complains, rebels, and tries to hold on to that which is by its nature fleeting, but she who sees worldly strivings as a chasing after the wind, and who is reconciled with her fate.

The atheistic pessimism of Schopenhauer, my last example, was directly inspired by Buddhism. Its key texts had just been translated into German and it is easy to see that the Buddha's noble truths would resonate with a misanthrope. For Schopenhauer, the world is the expression of a great Will. Not the will of a benevolent and perfect being, but simply a brute unyielding deterministic and aimless force, pressing forth each living species by allowing the strong to multiply and the weak to die, causing senseless suffering to all living things, and no more so than to humans since we have the added misfortune of being aware of our hopeless predicament. The Will controls us from deep inside: "Its desires are unlimited, its claims are inexhaustible, and every satisfied desire gives birth to a new one. No possible satisfaction in the world would suffice to still its craving, set a goal to its demands, and fill the bottomless pit of its heart."[18] We can temporarily escape suffering by negating the Will to life, "that our heart may be cured of the passion for enjoying and indeed living, and may be turned away from the world."[19] Schopenhauer recommends—as did Plato in his own way—that we transform ourselves into a "pure knowing being, as the undimmed mirror of the world."[20] However, ultimately there is no better cure for our unfortunate condition than death. "Death" writes Schopenhauer "is the great opportunity to no longer be I; to him . . . who embraces it . . . dying is the moment of . . . liberation."[21] Schopenhauer, Plato, and the Buddha, are important examples of thinkers whose philosophies locate the tragedy and suffering of life in our desires. It is noteworthy that they are also by many regarded as near synonymous with profound wisdom.

4.3.1   In Defense of Our Mad Masters

As we have seen, one recurrent complaint is that desires are never conclusively satisfied, but constantly renewed. This is true, but it is not necessarily a problem. The function of desires is to direct us toward what keeps us alive, and since life is a constant struggle against entropy, desires must renew themselves to serve their function. The circle of craving and satisfaction, craving and satisfaction, craving and satisfaction, and so on, is also an important reason that life is enjoyable.

Socrates is contemptuous of the body's needs, such as the need for food and drink, as well as the pleasures we find in their satisfaction. I sometimes ask my students if they would eat a magical meal that would end their need for food as well as their desire and the pleasure they take in eating. It would be a meal to end all meals. So far only a handful out of hundreds of students wanted this magical meal; the rest disagreed with Socrates. Now imagine taking a pill—let's call it the Wisdom Pill—that would remove not only the desire for food, but all cravings: I wake up. I feel hunger, but I simply observe it, and I remain indifferent to whether I eat or not. I see my spouse lying next to me and I have no interest in making love. I might converse with her, but I do not care if I do not. I think about the things I could do during the day, some of which appear pleasant, but that fact leaves me cold. I have no ambitions, and nothing that I want to achieve, so although I do not desire to stay in bed, I do so by default. I observe a discomfort, but I seek not to escape it. I know that if I do not eat, these experiences will cease, but I have no desire that they continue, nor that they do not. I am utterly indifferent. Is this an attractive life?

We do not want permanent satisfaction. We want hunger to precede eating, thirst to precede drinking, yearning to precede sex, fatigue to precede sleep, curiosity to precede learning, struggle to precede victory, and so on. Take the simplest of desires, the appetite for food, and let it stand for desire in general. We wake up and want breakfast, soon we smell the bacon and the coffee, we eat, and we are satisfied. Do we bemoan the fact that this satisfaction is short-lived? On the contrary, we look forward with great relish to tomorrow's breakfast.[22] The treadmill keeps life enjoyable.

The other recurrent complaint is that desire is hopeless in a world in flux. This seems like an overstatement. The world may be changing, but we can still get many of the things we want every day. I desired a cup of coffee this morning and I got what I desired, despite the ongoing flux. There are things that we cannot get—such as, presumably, unfailing health—but we can do our best while accepting occasional failure. We can deal with frustrations. We know that things are often not going to go our way, and when they do not, we seek to improve and move forward. When we lose a hard-fought tennis match, after cursing ourselves out, we go up and shake our opponent's hand. It is not whether you win or lose, it is how you play the game—better to have loved and lost than never to have loved at all, and so on. Rather than wishing that we had no desires, we create stable dispositions that allow us to act on the right impulse at the right time for the right reason. Aristotle's philosophy of finding the golden mean rather than fighting life itself provides a salutary counterbalance to the high-strung other-worldliness/no-worldliness of the just-mentioned philosophers. It is as if they are hypersensitive to defeat and frustration, like certain people who never want to compete because they cannot handle losing. I therefore think we should side with the vulgar (the foolish common man in philosophical literature) who, as described in the *Phaedo*, mock Socrates,

> Though not in a laughing humor, I swear that I cannot help laughing when I think what the wicked world will say when they hear this. They will say that this is very true, and our people will agree with them in saying that the life which philosophers desire is truly death, and that they have found them out to be deserving of the death which they desire.[23]

"The life which philosophers desire is truly death" is a brilliant formulation, for what is left once every physical desire and every bodily pleasure are stripped away? We recognize this critique from our discussion of the Epicurean's claim that death is nothing to us, seeing that it appears to follow from a more general indifference to how things turn out in the world. The family man would enjoy seeing his family, but he does not desire to see them, because then he could no longer be indifferent to death.

Writ large, the call to negate the will to life is simply decadent. Our modern civilization is not built on resignation. It is built on the efforts of often extravagant and willful individuals struggling to master the world around them. The German philosopher Friedrich Nietzsche identified and attacked the resignation of existential pessimism. Opposing Schopenhauer, Nietzsche celebrates the will to life and sees suffering not as the rule of life, but as a weakness: "The struggle for life . . . does occur, but as exception; the general aspect of life is not hunger and distress, but rather wealth, luxury, even absurd prodigality—where there is a struggle it is a struggle for power."[24] Nietzsche went too far in his celebration of the Will to Power (notably in his diatribes against compassion and humility), but this is understandable given that he presents the antithesis to Schopenhauer's equally extreme antilife/death-tolerant philosophy. Clearly there is something weak and unhealthy about wishing away all desires rather than take up the struggle to satisfy them?

In sum, we are built to take frustration and there is no universal imperative to wish away our desires. The philosopher's dream of escaping the demands of our desires is a neurotic's fantasy, a way of dealing with frustration in an uncertain world.

4.4 Meaningless! Meaningless!

The struggles of Sisyphus are not only repetitive and endless, but also seemingly pointless. What is the point of pushing the boulder up the hill? What does it all mean? A human's life is a vanishingly small point on an infinite line, one miniscule flicker among billions of others—and then perhaps nothing. She grows up, moves around the surface of the earth, and is returned to the earth. She thinks that her life is important, and that her projects matter, but why, when all that is built will crumble, and whatever contribution she makes will be forgotten and erased? It is not just the individual human that will disappear as if she never existed, but most likely humankind and the earth she briefly inhabited. And after that, not a trace will remain. Hence, what is the point? It is a timeless question, whose most famous formulation is found in Ecclesiastes of the Old Testament, which is thought to have been written between 450 BC and 180 BC. The teacher tells us the story of his life; he was a king, and he had all the power in the world; all the luxury, all the women, everything, yet he realized that it was all *hebel*, the Hebrew word for vapor:

> "Meaningless! Meaningless!"
>   says the Teacher.
> "Utterly meaningless!
>   Everything is meaningless."
> What do people gain from all their labors
>   at which they toil under the sun?

Generations come and generations go,
    but the earth remains forever.
The sun rises and the sun sets,
    and hurries back to where it rises.
The wind blows to the south
    and turns to the north;
round and round it goes,
    ever returning on its course.
All streams flow into the sea,
    yet the sea is never full.
To the place the streams come from,
    there they return again.
All things are wearisome,
    more than one can say.
The eye never has enough of seeing,
    nor the ear its fill of hearing.
What has been will be again,
    what has been done will be done again;
    there is nothing new under the sun.
Is there anything of which one can say,
    "Look! This is something new"?
It was here already, long ago;
    it was here before our time.
No one remembers the former generations,
    and even those yet to come
will not be remembered
    by those who follow them.
I, the Teacher, was king over Israel in Jerusalem.
I applied my mind to study and to explore by wisdom
all that is done under the heavens. What a heavy burden God has laid on
    mankind!
I have seen all the things that are done under the sun; all of them are meaning-
    less, a chasing after the wind.
What is crooked cannot be straightened;
    what is lacking cannot be counted.
I said to myself, "Look, I have increased in wisdom more than anyone who has
    ruled over Jerusalem before me; I have experienced much of wisdom and
    knowledge."
Then I applied myself to the understanding of wisdom, and also of madness and
    folly, but I learned that this, too, is a chasing after the wind.
For with much wisdom comes much sorrow; the more knowledge, the more
    grief.

The Teacher does not leave us in despair, but points toward a place where meaning can be found. Not, as he has proven by his own experience, in the pleasures, honors, riches, or knowledge of the world, and not in a better life after this life, but in servitude to God:

> Now all has been heard; here is the conclusion of the matter: Fear God and keep His commandments, for this is the whole duty of man. For God will bring every deed into judgment, including every hidden thing, whether it is good or evil.[25]

Theists have this answer, but what about materialists and atheists who think that this world is all there is? It would seem as if they would have to agree with the meaningless part of the teacher's complaint, but not with his answer to it. Their universe is devoid of meaning, like the world described by Bertrand Russell in 1903:

> That Man is the product of causes which had no prevision of the end they were achieving; that his origin, his growth, his hopes and fears, his loves and his beliefs, are but the outcome of accidental collocations of atoms; that no fire, no heroism, no intensity of thought and feeling, can preserve an individual life beyond the grave; that all the labours of the ages, all the devotion, all the inspiration, all the noonday brightness of human genius, are destined to extinction in the vast death of the solar system, and that the whole temple of Man's achievement must inevitably be buried beneath the débris of a universe in ruins—all these things, if not quite beyond dispute, are yet so nearly certain, that no philosophy which rejects them can hope to stand. Only within the scaffolding of these truths, only on the firm foundation of unyielding despair, can the soul's habitation henceforth be safely built.[26]

If "unyielding despair" is the foundation of life, then, well, there seems to be less reason to want to continue existing. The meaninglessness of life can therefore be used as an apology for death. If life is pointless, what is the point of living on?

4.4.1 Responding to Meaninglessness

As I see it, there two main ways of answering this challenge: argue that life is meaningful, or argue that even if life is meaningless, it is still worth continuing.

As we saw, the preacher appears to give the answer that there is a higher meaning to it all, founded in serving God and being rewarded for doing so in the afterlife. There is a point to the rock pushing; if we have pushed it the right way, it leads to a place of bliss. This is the most common answer.

If so, then meaninglessness cannot be used as an argument against life. A variant of this answer finds meaning within a particular religious tradition. Others believe nature itself can give us meaning. Having children and contributing to the biological perpetuation of the species is the meaning of life, they think. The goal is to keep human life going for as long as possible. Yet others find meaning not just in the perpetuation of the species, but in its continual progress. Some transhumanists believe that it is the manifest destiny of the human to advance to the point where she can colonize the entire universe. These were examples of the first strategy.

The second type of response questions the assumption that life needs an ultimate purpose. Jean-Paul Sartre, Albert Camus, and other secular existentialists famously claimed that there is no God, that life is meaningless, and they celebrate this fact, since in their view it gives us the great opportunity and great responsibility to give life meaning. In other words, there is no external meaning, but there can be an internal meaning to life. If one wants to become a doctor and help sick people, then this can be the meaning of one's life. If one wants to have a family, then this can become the meaning of one's life. Planning and preparing a meal for one's friends or playing a game of tennis can be the meaning of a particular day. Activities and pleasures can be engaged in for their own sake, without necessarily serving some larger purpose, like the simple pleasure of watching snow drift on a winter's day. The lack of an ultimate purpose is not treated by existentialists as a reason not to live. The argument that life is not worth living because it is meaningless fails because there may be an objective meaning to life, or we may create our own subjective meaning.

A final thought. Pessimists about meaning appear to ignore the wonder of existence. Everyday life often conceals the fact that our predicament is outrageous. We are inhabiting a temporarily existing round ball with a burning center, spinning 1,675 km an hour, circling another larger gaseous ball of fire that is one of billions in a galaxy inside a universe that we cannot conceive of as having either a temporal or spatial limit (while we also cannot imagine that there are no limits). The likelihood of our existence is next to zero yet here we are, the culmination of everything that has come before us and with a mind that can reflect and grasp these immensities, a mind that is itself the most amazing thing we have encountered so far, a mind so complex and baffling that it cannot grasp itself. All this is a wonderful mystery. It is one reason why despite the pain, the frustration, and the possible lack of final meaning, life is worth living.

We will return to the issue of meaning when considering it in the context of evaluating our spiritual capacity to maintain a sense of meaning over very long time spans.

5   Death Is Natural and Therefore Good

Despise not death, but welcome it, for nature wills it like all else.
—Marcus Aurelius

5.1   Everyone Dies!

The idea that death and the slow death of aging are good because they are natural, universal, and inescapable is in my experience one of the first, if not the first, defense of death that comes to people's minds. When I ask my class if they think it is bad for someone who is 90 years old to die, typically only one or two students think so even when I have specified that the person is in reasonably good health. They believe, like most people, that when we reach the upper limits of our natural life span, then death is no longer a tragedy. "She was old," they say. "Old people die, it's natural."[1] This way of thinking is also the standard view among philosophers. The human, they say, is defined by its mortality, and the fact that there is an end to life is no more tragic than that there is a beginning. The individual dies, but this is necessary for the continued vitality of the species. Aging and the death that it brings about constitute the frame within which a human life plays out—and it is not something that can itself be squarely evaluated. To be human, they argue, is to have a certain life span, hence it makes little sense to question whether it is good or bad. Rather than rage against the dying of the light, we should take comfort in the fact that life continues without us and that better people than ourselves have shared this fate. Rebelling against the framing conditions, from this perspective, is not only futile, but childish in its egotistic wish to escape the very laws that define our existence. So says the Wise View.

5.2 Appeals to Nature

The argument that something is good because it is natural faces some well-known challenges. We have already seen the most obvious, namely that something can be natural and very bad, such as cancer and, as I argued, aging. That is, the appeal to nature faces the challenge of defining the natural in such a way that includes what we think is good and excludes what we think is bad.[2] If, for example, we define the natural as that which is described by the natural sciences, then we would have to say that everything in the physical world is natural, which leads to the absurd normative implication that everything in the world, including earthquakes and genocides, is good. This definition is, therefore, too broad. If, on the other hand, we define the natural as that which is found in nature and is not created by human beings, our definition would be too narrow. It would, for instance, imply that hand axes, shoes, and spectacles are bad because they are not found in nature. To avoid this implication, we could define the natural as that which is normal. If something is normal for humans, then it is good. It is clearly normal for humans to fashion tools, so by this definition the hand axe and other artifacts are acceptable. Unfortunately, this definition is also counterintuitive. Why would something not be natural simply because it is not normal? Are left-handedness, blue eyes, and cleft chins unnatural? And why think that if something is abnormal, it is thereby bad? The musical genius of Mozart as well as the minds of Einstein or Aristotle were abnormal and excellent. For these reasons, it is tempting to think that when "natural" is used in moral arguments, it means nothing more than that we are accustomed to something. We are used to aging and death and therefore see them as natural and somehow beyond criticism.

Does this mean we should dismiss all appeals to human nature? Should we perhaps agree with existentialists like Jean-Paul Sartre that there is no human nature and that "man is nothing but what he makes of himself"?[3] I do not think so. Clearly there is a human nature.[4] After all, we are not beavers or bats. And because we are not, we do not live in ponds and rivers, or chew on wood, or hang upside down in caves when sleeping, or regurgitate blood for each other. We are humans, homo sapiens, and this natural fact determines a range of conditions under which we can flourish. We are a most adaptable species so the range will be wide, but it is not boundless. We can therefore learn what tends to our flourishing and what does not count as a natural good or a natural evil. Love, freedom, and nourishment of the body and mind are good for humans; spending life in slavery or in an isolation cell is bad for humans. The idea belonged to Aristotle, the pupil of Plato, that there is a human essence underlying the diversity we see and that favors certain ways of being over others, while assuming our goal is to flourish in the way humans can flourish. He thought that man was made to live in communities and conduct himself in accordance with reason. This, he thought, was a good fit. To live isolated or for an intelligent man to be treated as a slave; he saw as a bad fit. Some of his judgments we would question today, such as the claim that some men, who are less rational, are natural slaves, but any theory can be misapplied without being fundamentally flawed.

I do not know if the Aristotelian appeal to nature is our best normative theory, but it is, to my knowledge, the best approach to what it could mean for something to be a natural good or bad for man, and I will make the argument that it does not support a positive evaluation of either aging or death. On the contrary, I will argue that appeals to nature, insofar as they are sound, support the case against death. The outline of my argument is simple:

1. We have a natural desire to live.
2. Self-preservation is therefore a natural good.
3. Death negates this good.
4. Death is therefore a natural evil.

The first premise is uncontroversial. Even philosophers who make apologies based on the naturalness of death think that we have a natural instinct to live. *"Intellectus naturaliter desiderat esse semper,"* the mind naturally desires to live forever, Saint Thomas Aquinas writes. The second premise is also nearly uncontroversial for anyone who accepts that there are natural goods. The third premise is true by definition. The conclusion (4) assumes that if something prevents a good from being realized, then it is bad. The way to resist this hidden premise could perhaps be to argue that death is an even greater natural good than life. Such an argument does not seem to be supported by our natural desires. Thus, on what basis could it be argued that death is an even greater good than life, so that even though it thwarts the desire to live, it realizes something even more valuable? Prima facie, it is hard to see what can be said in favor of death being a superior natural good.

What makes it so difficult is that almost all of what we normally would consider to be natural goods are considered as such precisely because they tend toward our preservation. Food, water, shelter, health, love, community, and so on, are goods because they promote life. Generally speaking, once it has been established that something tends to kill us, it is also considered bad for us. In fact, it is hard to make sense of our everyday normative discourse unless it is assumed that our goal is to stay healthy and alive. When someone, for example, says x is dangerous and might kill you, how often do they get the response, "Ok, but explain to me why it is bad?" I therefore do not think that anything persuasive can be said in favor of ranking death above life as a natural good. Death should be seen as a natural evil, together with aging, illness, and all forms of needless suffering imposed by nature. The conclusion (4) stands, and the simple argument that living on is naturally good is sound.

As I said, apologists for death recognize that we have a natural instinct to live, so how then do they make a case for death based on an appeal to what is natural? The answer is that they take a larger view of things.

5.3   Death in the Big Scheme of Things

Those who defend the natural rhythm of life do not deny that we generally desire to live. Indeed, they tend to exaggerate the will to live among people: Their rhetoric always begins with proclamations of how "we all want to live forever" and "no one wants to die," before they proceed to tell us how death and decay is—all things considered—a superior alternative. The way they justify death as a natural good is by insisting that we shift our attention away from the individual's desire for self-preservation and, instead, to consider her place within a larger biological system. If we imagine ourselves as extending beyond our narrowly defined boundaries—our body and its temporal geographical location—and become an aspect of a more permanent thing, such as mankind, all living things, or everything, then our individual death becomes a very small event, not even quite real. I will refer to this idea as holism. This is the perspective taken by Homer when he says, "As is the generation of leaves, so is that of humanity. The wind scatters the leaves to the ground, but the live timber burgeons with leaves again next season of spring returning. So one generation of man will grow while another dies."[5] And it is the perspective taken by Lucretius

when he imagines nature lecturing man about the necessity of his individual death:

> Suppose that the nature of things should of a sudden lift up her voice, and thus
> in these words herself rebuke some one of us: 'Why is death so great a thing
> lamenting to thee, mortal, that thou dost give way overmuch to sickly lamenta-
> tions? Why groan and weep at death? . . .
>
> There must needs be substance that the generations to come may grow; yet
> all of them too will follow thee, when they have had their fill of life; yea, just as
> thyself, these generations have passed away before, and will pass away again. So,
> one thing shall never cease to rise up out of another, and life is granted to none
> for freehold, to all on lease.[6]

The Stoics, one of the major competing schools of philosophy in the
ancient world, made the point of view of nature their ideological funda-
ment. The Stoics taught that there were two fundamental things in the
world, matter and eternal logos or reason, which was sometimes described
as God or designing fire. The logos structures and organizes matter in an
eternally repeating cyclical pattern of birth from fire and return to fire. In
the universe everything happens by causal necessity, not by chance, and
each life has an inescapable fate. We cannot control the world around us;
the only thing we can control is our response to the world, and our response
should be perfectly emotionless. For the Stoics, virtue is the only thing
of importance, and virtue means accepting everything that nature wills.
Roman Emperor and philosopher Marcus Aurelius writes on the power of
his Stoic philosophy:

> Of human life the time is a point, and the substance is in a flux, and the percep-
> tion dull, and the composition of the whole body subject to putrefaction, and
> the soul of a whirl, and fortune hard to divine, and fame a thing devoid of judg-
> ment, And, to say all in a word, everything which belongs to the body is a stream,
> and what belongs to the soul is a dream and vapour, and life is a warfare and a
> stranger's sojourn, and after-fame is oblivion. What, then, is that which is able to
> conduct man? One thing, and only one—philosophy. But this consists in keeping
> the daemon within a man free from violence and unharmed, superior to pains
> and pleasures, doing nothing without a purpose, nor falsely and with hypocrisy,
> not feeling the need of another man's doing or not doing anything; and besides,
> accepting all that happens, and all that is allotted, as coming from thence, wher-
> ever it is, from whence he himself came; and, finally, waiting for death with a
> cheerful mind, as being nothing else than a dissolution of the elements of which
> every living being is compounded. But if there is no harm to the elements them-
> selves in each continually changing into another, why should a man have any

apprehension about the change and dissolution of all the elements? For it is according to nature, and nothing is evil which is according to nature.[7]

Everything is falling apart: here today and gone tomorrow, and alive today and dead tomorrow. And it is all good. What follows from this reality, according to the Stoics, is that we should not attach ourselves to any particular thing or person. Fellow Stoic Epictetus writes,

> With regard to whatever objects give you delight, are useful, or are deeply loved, remember to tell yourself of what general nature they are, beginning from the most insignificant things. If, for example, you are fond of a specific ceramic cup, remind yourself that it is only ceramic cups in general of which you are fond. Then, if it breaks, you will not be disturbed. If you kiss your child, or your wife, say that you only kiss things which are human, and thus you will not be disturbed if either of them dies.[8]

As we saw in Lucretius, there is drift toward nihilism: it doesn't matter if you see your family again because you won't miss them when you are gone, and it doesn't matter if your wife and children die, because it is their nature to die, just like it is in the nature of ceramic cups to break. Besides, there are still women and children around after yours have died. Nothing to worry about; it is what it is. And "nothing is evil which is in accordance with nature."

Today, bioconservatives express similar holistic sentiments. "We are mortal beings," writes John Hardwig, "and death is not only the end result of life, but its telos—the aim and purpose for which we are headed biologically . . . Our natural rhythms are cyclical; we are structured to live and then to die. The question is not if, but when and how."[9] Daniel Callahan, a former member of the President's Council on Bioethics, similarly instructs, "A life marked by a rise in possibilities, followed by a destructive decline—the movement from youth to old age—is surely in one respect fearful and intolerable. Who wants that? Yet at the same time, it is the fate that nature has given us."[10] There is, he continues "in nearly all societies" an understanding that "death at the end of a long and full life is not an evil, that indeed there is something fitting and orderly about it."[11] Bioethicist David Wendler summarizes the underlying principle of bioconservatism as follows:

> Certain natural processes do not merely happen to us, but also define who we are. . . . [T]he fundamental structure of our lives places moral boundaries that we may, ethically speaking, not alter to suit our own aims or desires. . . . [W]e should accept the fundamental structure of our lives as defined by natural processes and live our lives within those boundaries.[12]

Wendler writes in the context of the abortion debate, and the defining natural process he is referring to is the gestation and raising of children. Other allegedly defining processes are aging and dying.

Nowhere has holism been drawn to more radical anti-individualist conclusions than among so-called ecological philosophers (eco-philosophers). "It is impossible," writes eco-philosopher J. Baird Callicot, "to find a clear demarcation between oneself and one's environment ... The world is, indeed, one's extended body."[13] Philosopher Patrick Curry agrees, rejecting the commonsense view that there is a self that is distinct from its environment as a "modernist fantasy."[14] There are no individual human beings; we are all one. Ecological thinking of the more radical "dark green" kind takes this insight to heart and wants to move away from a human-centered ethics to one that recognizes no distinctions between nature and the human and that rejects any hierarchy of beings. "All organisms and entities in the ecosphere, as part of the interrelated whole, are equal in intrinsic worth," pronounces Bill Devall and George Sessions.[15] The similarities to some Eastern religions are obvious. One can picture Jainist monks sweeping the ground in front of them lest they should step on an insect.

> I bequeath myself to the dirt to grow from the grass I love, If you want me again look for me under your boot-soles.[16]

Walt Whitman's famous lines illustrate how our culture has absorbed holist wisdom. Those who share Whitman's sensibility often claim that the fact that their atoms continue to be a part of the circle of life means they are immortal in an important sense. They are not only reconciled to their fate but insist that they are delighted that their life's journey takes them from dust to dust. It is that wonderful circle of life.

5.4   Responding to Holism

Holism may sound enlightened, before one thinks about it. True, we should be good guardians of earth, and we should form strong and supportive communities, but this does not require us to deny the reality of individuals or deny humankind's special status. Contrary to the holists we can easily draw a distinction between a person and one's environment. For instance, I am distinct from the shirt I am wearing. I am not blue; I am not made of cotton; I do not have sleeves and a collar; I am not made by a Malaysian seamstress;

and I do not bathe in the washing machine. There is clearly a demarcation here. I am also distinct from other living things. I am not a beaver, nor am I a bat; I am not Donald Trump. It does not take much "modernist fantasy" to understand this. Moreover, the proposal that we ought to step away from a human-centered morality to one that is neutral between all living things is manifestly unacceptable, perhaps even mad. Should we not, for example, favor a human being over the cancer consuming her? Should we be impartial between the shark and the swimmer? Seeing ourselves as one with all living things and as an insignificant mortal part of an immortal whole, may relieve the anxiety we have concerning mortality, but this anxiety arises only because we are in fact distinct individuals in a way that other living things are not. Plants and, at least lower animals, can without too much sense of tragedy be seen as parts of an evolving creative destruction, where they live, die and become food for each other; but to pretend that, as an aware human being, one considers oneself and one's loved ones as deserving of nothing more elevated than becoming food for microbes and worms, with all one's feelings and memories and ideas ultimately under the boot sole of a farmer, signifies a failure to appreciate the value of individual persons, and is perhaps a sign of self-hatred and misanthropy. Homer's classic comparison between people and leaves is therefore horrendous. No leaf desires to live and no leaf yearns to reunite with his wife and children. Leaves are fully replaceable, people are not.

The death of a child or wife is not a cosmic tragedy, it is one of those things that happens all the time but is nevertheless a personal tragedy and, as a person, it is appropriate to regard it as such, rather than, as recommended by Seneca, to observe that they were just tokens of the types "woman" and "child" that will persist, leaving no reason to be "in the least disturbed." When we think about those we have loved and lost, does it not feel like each one of them is irreplaceable? Whom do we know that is exactly like the ones you lost? And, importantly, once more the question is, do we want to be the kind of person who is not in the least disturbed by the death of our spouse or children? What I describe as inhuman is regarded by Stoics and as we saw in the previous chapter, Epicureans, as supremely human, or ideally human, since in their view it is the way of life of the perfectly rational human, who is invulnerable to life's vagaries, and secure in happiness and virtue. Stoics take the philosophical bulletproof superman, the living god, intimated by Epicureanism and Platonism to its limit. Philosophy, as we saw Aurelius explain above, can secure "the dae-mon [soul/mind] within a man free from violence and unharmed, superior to pains and pleasures . . ." Of course, the price is disengagement with all that we normal people value.

At the heart of the matter lies a conflict between two points of view of our existence. On the one hand we have our subjective point of view, and on the other we have an imagined third-person view from nowhere. This conflict has been the fulcrum of Thomas Nagel's philosophy. In the final paragraph of "Death," Nagel returns to the core,

> Observed from without, human beings obviously have a natural life span and cannot live much longer than a hundred years. A man's sense of his own experi-ence, on the other hand, does not embody this idea of a natural limit. His exis-tence defines for him an essentially open-ended possible future, containing the usual mixture of goods and evils that he has found so tolerable in the past. Having been gratuitously introduced to the world by a collection of natural, historical and social accidents, he finds himself the subject of a life, with an indeterminate and not essentially limited future. Viewed in this way, death, no matter how inevitable, is an abrupt cancellation of indefinitely extensive goods. Normality seems to have nothing to do with it, for the fact that we will all inevitably die in a few score years cannot by itself imply that it would not be good to live longer.[17]

I advocate taking the subjective point of view. If someone is enjoying their life, they should ignore what an imaginary nature is imagined saying. Since we are already committed to regarding an individual's goals of living and flourishing as determining what is good or evil for one, it would be unmo-tivated to suddenly shift to an imagined objective perspective just to be able to argue that death is now one's aim—one's natural good—whether or not it is one's personal aim. Who has dying on their list of life goals? Dying merely happens to us as we are pursuing those goals. Outside Lucretius's anthropomorphizing imagination, there is no Mother Nature who wants us to die. Nature has no aims. Nature wants nothing. More than that, it is not only anthropomorphizing but deifying to think that if nature "intends" death to be our goal that we must, therefore, obey her, even if we desire to live.[18] Whatever we can imagine nature "telling us" to aim at from some external point of view, it is in our nature to aim at self-preservation (and procreation), not death.[19] And this is what matters.

Before turning to the political twin of holism, let me make some points about the apologist claim that *death defines who we are*. First, admittedly we are mortal beings and, barring a supernatural event, nothing will change that. Immortality is, as already explained, not possible in a physical world. As Nuland says, we will die, and it is not a question of if, but when. Setting immortality aside, let me instead address the claim made by apologists, namely that life within the framework set by nature is *defining* of humanity. Is it a necessary truth that homo sapiens is a life form with a maximum life span in the one hundred and twenties? This, after all, is what the claim that our natural life span defines us means. Once disambiguated, we can see that it is an implausible claim. We can clearly imagine humans living 10 times longer than we do today. The Old Testament speaks of humans with a life span of almost 1,000 years, and none of this strikes us as contradictory. Those who doubt that there was a man called Methuselah who lived to 969 years of age, do not do so on *conceptual* grounds.

There is also no reason to think that the current life span "defines" us by being particularly fitting. Anyone with a wish to be properly educated and with an ambitious reading list will find the current life span a painful, narrow fit. Neither does it help to put some kind of evolutionary spin on it. Unlike eyesight, aging and death cannot be understood as adaptions; falling apart and dying obviously does not enhance the chances of survival and reproduction. Life span, it is theorized, most importantly comes down to whether the environment favored those with more offspring earlier in life or those with more surviving offspring due to having longer lives. Built for speed versus built to last.[20] The timer can be manipulated toward a higher life span simply by having only the longest living animals breed, or by changing the environment to one that favors animals "built to last." This has been done in laboratories with fruit flies, worms, rats, and mice. They live longer, but they remain flies, worms, rats, and mice. There has been no discussion concerning whether it is logically or metaphysically impossible to double the lifespan of a mouse or a roundworm because the life span somehow "defines" these creatures. Given how malleable and contingent life spans are, it makes little sense to define us in terms of our life span.

5.5 Holism and Collectivism

Lucretius's thought that we die to make room for the next generation is a perennially popular apology for death. Often death is seen as nature's instrument of progress. Surgeon and influential bioethicist Sherwin B. Nuland writes,

Mankind cannot afford to destroy the balance [of nature]—the economy, if you will—by tinkering with one of its most essential elements, which is the constant renewal within individual species and the invigoration that accomplishes it. For plants and animals renewal requires that death precede it so that the weary may be replaced by the vigorous. This is meant by the cycles of nature. There is nothing pathological or sick about the sequence—in fact, it is the antithesis of sick."[21]

In *The Science of Life*, published in 1934 and written by H. G. Wells and Julian Huxley, the older brother of Aldous Huxley, the author of *Brave New World*, we find a more explicitly Darwinian formulation of the same idea:

Individual death is one of the methods of life . . . Every individual is a biological experiment, and a species progresses and advances by the selection, rejections and multiplication of these individuals. Biologically, life ceases to go forward unless individuals come to an end and are replaced by others. The idea of any sort of individual immortality runs flatly counter to the idea of continuing evolution. . . . Yet these considerations do not abolish the idea of immortality; they only shift it from the personality. In the visible biological world, in the world of fact, life never dies; only the individual it throws up die . . . And our lives do not end with death; they stream on, not merely in direct offspring, but more importantly perhaps in the influence they have had on the rest of life.[22]

Remember what O'Brien tells Winston as he lies stretched out on a torture table, "You are thinking," he said, "that my face is old and tired. You are thinking that I talk of power, and yet I am not even able to prevent the decay of my own body. Can you not understand, Winston, that the individual is only a cell? The weariness of the cell is the vigor of the organism. Do you die when you cut your fingernails?"[23] While George Orwell was primarily satirizing the Soviet Union, the point made by O'Brien is in line with Hermann Göring's pronouncement that "The people are a living community, a great organic, eternal body."[24] In his work on the ideological background of German national socialism, political philosopher Georg Lukács explains the general connection between notions of the organic whole and politics:

Biologism in philosophy and sociology has always been a basis for reactionary philosophical tendencies . . . it cannot permit of any essential change, let alone progress. . . . Oppression, inequality, exploitation and so forth were presented as "facts of nature" or "laws of nature" which, as such, could not be avoided or revoked.[25]

The term "ecological" was minted by German biologist Ernst Haeckel in 1867 as the study of the interrelationship between organisms and the environment. He was a supporter of racial eugenics and social Darwinism. The German national socialists drew on these ideas, translating them into environmentalist policies. French philosopher Luc Ferry writes that,

> The Reichsjagdgesetz (national hunting laws) turns out to be the key pin of the National Socialist ecologist platform: in it, man is no longer positioned as master and possessor of a nature which he humanizes and cultivates, but as responsible for an original wild state endowed with intrinsic rights, the richness and diversity of which it is his responsibility to preserve.[26]

An imaginary biological unit, the German Volk, was seen as a living organism, with its own good that transcended that of its individual parts, and as obeying the laws of nature. The organic whole needs room to live, and it needs to reject everything (everyone) that makes it sick. "There was . . . a widespread feeling . . . that what the National Socialists were saying, many holistic life and mind scientists had been affirming all along as nature's own truths."[27]

Disaffected Germans rejected the liberal democratic system that seemed to have let them down. They welcomed an ideology that would have them exchange their personal failures for a communitarian triumph. The escape from the demands of the capitalist market economy, the unhealth of the cities and the factories, the atomization and mechanism of modernity, the bitter and endless quarrels between the left and the right, and the promise of a return to an imagined state of social wholeness and ecological harmony of blood and soil was the siren song of the National Socialists. They were going to undo the betrayal of nature. This is not merely incidental to the movement. Adolf Hitler's fundamental objection to socialism, liberalism, Christianity, and modern ideas of equality and equal rights was precisely their unnaturalness:

> When Man attempts to rebel against the iron logic of Nature, he comes into struggle with the principles which he himself owes his existence as a man. And so his action against Nature must lead to his own doom . . . Here we encounter the objection [that] "Man's role is to overcome Nature!" . . . But Man has never yet conquered Nature in anything, but at most has caught hold of and tried to lift one corner or another of her immense gigantic veil of eternal riddles and secrets, that in reality he invents nothing but only discovers everything, that he does not dominate Nature, but has only risen on the basis of his knowledge of various laws and secrets to be lord over those other living creatures who lack this knowledge.[28]

The holistic perspective had direct implications for medicine. The national socialist doctors turned away from treating the patient in front of them and toward treating the societal body. From the point of view of society, the patient's death could be more beneficial than its survival. It was the concern with the whole and its wholesomeness that justified the eugenics program. The Volk had to restore its premodern and natural vigor, which had been smothered by liberalism, Christianity, capitalism, and compassion. Cubist depictions of the fragmentation of modern, urban life were out; landscape paintings featuring healthy peasants were in.

The German national socialists present a model that is universally condemned, but dreams of a return to a more primitive, collectivist, and natural way of life still beckon. These dreams find their way into apologism where our "unnatural" confused, modern, liberal, and individualist attitudes to death are decried. Leon Kass writes,

> Though some cultures—such as the Eskimo—can instruct and somewhat moderate the lust for life, liberal Western society gives it free reign, beginning with a liberal political philosophy founded on the fear of violent death, and reaching to our current cult of youth and novelty, the cosmetic replastering of the wrinkles of age, and the widespread anxiety of disease and survival.[29]

Others, like Philippe Ariès, admire medieval attitudes to death: "In death man encountered one of the great laws of the species, and he had no thought of escaping it or glorifying it."[30] But with the advent of the Age of Reason, "a more personal, more inner feeling about death, about the death of the self, [which] betrayed the violent attachment to the things of life but likewise . . . it betrayed the bitter feeling of failure, mingled with mortality: a passion for being, an anxiety at not sufficiently being."[31] Bioethicist Daniel Callahan similarly attacks modern attitudes to death, as well as the "tacit moral premise that sustains the support and celebrity of contemporary medicine: . . . that we are all free under the expansive aegis of medical progress to pursue any personal vision at all of good health and life purposes."[32] Instead of this liberal individualism, we should, he thinks, restrict access to health care for people above a certain age: "Medicine should be used not to further the extension of the life of the aged, but only for the full achievement of a natural and fitting life span and thereafter for the relief of suffering."[33] And who, exactly, is to determine what constitutes a "natural and fitting life span?" "We" are, not as individuals, but as a collective.

5.6 Defending a Liberal View of Death

We have just seen apologists make the case that there is something wrong with our modern, individualistic, liberal attitudes to death. They have argued in favor of a return to the recognition of and humility before our natural limitations. In this section, I will make a case in favor of the modern liberal view.

For a start, we should question the assumption that there is something necessarily "modern" about respecting the individual. The assigning of special status to the human being and to the individual belongs, among other places, to Jewish and Christian thought. Man is made in the image of God, and he is the master of the earth and everything on it belongs to him. Every human life, no matter what its status in society, is a gift from God. This is the reason why suicide is regarded as a sin. Life is something to be grateful for and to venerate in oneself and others. Thus, the appreciation for the individual human life has a religious basis and is not, as some claim, a modern invention. However, it is undeniable that modernity brought with it an increased individualism in thought, religion, politics, and economics, as well as an increased optimism concerning what earthly life could be. The early Renaissance humanist Giovanni Pico della Mirandola writes in the *Oration on the Dignity of Man* (1486):

> We have made you a creature neither of heaven nor of earth, neither mortal nor immortal, in order that you may, as the free and proud shaper of your own being, fashion yourself in the form you may prefer. It will be in your power to descend to the lower, brutish forms of life; you will be able, through your own decision, to rise again to the superior orders whose life is divine.[34]

The humanist vision is that with the help of reason we will be able to wrest power from nature or, as Francis Bacon put it in his infamously violent metaphors, "to conquer and subdue her [nature], to shake her to her foundations."[35] Armed with knowledge and the experimental method, we shall revolt "with united forces against the Nature of Things, to storm and occupy her castles and strongholds, and extend the boundaries of human empire, as far as God Almighty in his goodness may permit."[36] Attending Bacon's call to decipher, to represent, and to intervene in nature bespoke a new kind of confidence in our individual judgment. In the seventeenth century, René Descartes insisted that true knowledge can only begin from absolute certainty; and that certainty was not to be inherited from tradition or (Aristotle's) authority, but from within a person's own perspective. The "I-think-therefore-I-am" is from where knowledge begins. The empiricists in England similarly took one's pure and unfiltered subjective sense data as a starting point of all knowledge.

Part of the project of transformation involved challenging political orders thought to be natural. The egalitarianism inherent in Christianity—we are equal before God—could now express itself in practice. Liberalism, arising in the context of the shift from an agricultural to a commercial culture, demanded a new kind of respect for everyman. Thomas Hobbes and John Locke expressed this respect when they challenged the old paradigm where power was seen as imposed top-down from God through the kings. They proposed a new bottom-up model according to which rulers' authority is ultimately based on what they can do for the individual subject.[37] Locke took this new individualism further by postulating basic individual rights to life, liberty and property, that not even a ruler was allowed to transgress. Locke also argued that religious beliefs should be regarded as a personal matter.

Two new moral philosophies emerged to express the modern point of view: utilitarianism and Kantianism. Utilitarianism postulated that happiness is the ultimate good in life and that moral rules and social arrangements should all be viewed as instruments for furthering the goal of everyone's happiness. This philosophy is more radical than it may at first sound. In effect, it asks us to forget everything we think we know about good and bad, right and wrong, and replace it with the question: How do we become as happy as we can be? In *On Liberty*, J. S. Mill argues that happiness is best served by allowing people to be free individuals. Mill writes, "In this age, the mere example of non-conformity, the mere refusal to bend the knee to custom, is itself a service. Precisely because the tyranny of opinion is such as to make eccentricity a reproach, it is desirable, in order to break through that tyranny, that people should be eccentric."[38] Mill believed that happiness can take many forms and that different individuals can live happily in different ways. What man desires becomes an important determinant of what is good for him. A certain subjectivism and relativism about values belongs to this liberal outlook. The only objective claims are that happiness is the ultimate good and that actions are right in proportion to how much of it they bring about.

Kant's moral philosophy is the clearest expression of the Christian equality of human souls, humanism, and respect for reason. His philosophy denies that happiness is the ultimate good. Instead, it is the rational person and our moral duties that are absolutes. Each human for Kant has reason and freedom and is, therefore, "above all price," and each should be treated accordingly. Our reason enables us to transcend the natural causal flow of things. Humans, unlike animals, can sometimes act against our given impulses, inclinations, and desires, thereby giving us the power to assign value to a world otherwise value neutral, which importantly introduces morality and moral responsibility. The fundamental moral principle recognizes human dignity by commanding that we treat each person as an end in him- or herself, rather than merely useful tools. Reason enables each one of us to know this fundamental principle; there is no need for special authorities here. "Have the courage," implores Kant, "to use your own understanding!"[39]

Politically, this means that people's self-determination must be respected. John Rawls, our most influential political philosopher of the last 50 years, takes this as his starting point. A just society should enable each individual to pursue his or her chosen personal good (within certain moral limits of course) rather than determine what this good should be for them.[40] What is good for a person is allowed by this liberal tradition to be in large part determined by what one personally cares about. Each individual has his or her own individual conception of the good guiding his or her life's hopes.

This is the tradition of modernity and the individual point of view, and we are its fortunate beneficiaries. Its core tenets are taken for granted by most of us. It is because of modern science and technology that newborn babies can expect to survive their first year, and mothers no longer die in the dirt giving birth to their tenth child. This is also the reason that "every year the average person on the planet grows wealthier, healthier, happier, cleverer, cleaner, kinder, freer, safer, more peaceful and more equal."[41] Perhaps it may seem paradoxical on its face, but modernism and the civilized, individualist, high-technological world it has produced is, for all its costs, a more, not a less, human world because we have more power to satisfy our creaturely needs, and therefore more time to pursue distinctly human goods such as knowledge and art.

Liberalism, as recognized by its critics, does imply that individuals are treated as valuable in themselves, and not mere components of a valuable whole, be that nature, society or *das Volk*. Calls for public restrictions on how far we should be allowed to seek health and life are frightening. These calls explicitly contradict the traditional understanding of medicine; namely, that it is for those who are ill, that the patient's wishes should be respected, and that age should be irrelevant. The experience of the German national socialists' turn toward a community-based conception of the aims of medicine is a warning. We should resist reactionary views of any ideological color urging us to reject our human-centered liberal individualism.

5.7   Conclusions

Death, like aging, is natural, inevitable, and universal. It is also very bad. The point of view of nature is irrelevant, because nature has no point of view. What matters is our desire to live. This is a rational desire, since being alive is the foundation for all other natural goods. An appeal to nature therefore, contrary to the apologists, supports life extension and a negative evaluation of death.

Bioconservatives are not mistaken when they recognize that a modern mindset will be more open to the view that a person should be allowed to live as long as she wants, no matter what the natural limits happen to be. However, they are wrong to decry modern individualism, a view that has infinitely more to recommend it than more traditional and holistic alternatives. In fact, the modern mind set and its recognition of the legitimacy of our desire for self-preservation is more in tune with our human nature than death-loving, regressive bioconservatism. If we do not want die, and if we do not want our loved ones to die, then these are perfectly legitimate reasons for regarding death as an evil.

A 90-year-old should not be denied health care on the grounds that death is more natural and fitting. Neither is this person's death necessarily less tragic than the death of someone who is younger. If the ill of death depends on what we miss out on, it is possible that a 90-year-old misses out on more than a younger person. It depends on the individual. If experiences and memories thereof can be enriching, an older subjective world can be a more precious loss than that of a younger subjective world. From the 90-year-old's point of view, death—if death is the end—means the end to all human relationships, memories, actions, and experiences; it is the end of the world as she knows it, not something to trivialize by banal bromides of the "she was old" kind. Only an afterlife can redeem death.

We are not done yet with arguments invoking human nature. Over the next chapters I will investigate whether we are psychologically equipped to handle a significantly longer life. Could it be that death within a natural life span spares us from experiencing existence as a painful burden?

6 It Would Be Boring to Live Longer

6.1 The Spiritual Argument against Life Extension

The first thing people say when they hear about life extension besides "it is unnatural" is, "There would be overpopulation!" Next, they say, "What if only the rich can afford it?" As serious as these and similar concerns are, they are not getting at the heart of the issue. The worry about overpopulation leaves open the idea that life extension could be a good thing for an individual person, or for some people, but not all persons. The equality worry tacitly grants that life extension would be a good thing, for if it were not, then why should we care about whether only the rich could afford it? A pro-death argument that gets at the heart of the issue must rather question the assumption that life extension is good for the individual. It must give us a reason to believe that it is a mistake to wish for more life. The most powerful of such arguments argues that we are psychologically incapable of handling a much longer life and that we need to believe our days are numbered to live well. Thus, while aging and death may seem like an awful prospect, there really is no alternative for us since an indefinitely prolonged life would lack all that makes a human life worth living; we want more of the life we know, but if we have more of it, it will no longer be the life we know: "to imagine a life even remotely recognizable as ours, imbued with the kinds of values that we hold, is to imagine a life that is mortal."[1]

These arguments, like the arguments in the previous chapter, appeal to human nature, but since they focus on our lived experience rather than on the cycle of nature as such, I will call them "spiritual."

A recent example of the spiritual argument can be found in an essay by bioethicist Leon Kass, who writes, "I wish to make the case for the virtues of mortality. Against my own strong love of life, and against my even stronger wish that no more of my loved ones should die, I aspire to speak truth to my desires by showing that the finitude of human life is a blessing for every human individual, whether he knows it or not."[2] Kass thinks that four broad categories of human values and interests would be lost if we conquered death:

1. interest and engagement;
2. seriousness and aspirations;
3. virtue and moral excellence; and
4. beauty and love.

Kass defends mortality and finitude, but his arguments are also supposed to show that any transgression of the natural life span would incur these spiritual costs. This is what makes them a threat to the deprivation account of the badness of death. If we are not spiritually able to live a longer life than we normally do, then death is not depriving us of a valuable life, and hence death is acceptable. That is, although Kass and others speak of what would happen if we did not die/could not die, the intention is to provide an apology not just for death, but also for death within a natural life span or something close to it. The interesting question raised by Kass's arguments is whether we have a reason to think that life exceeding the natural limits would be dehumanizing and spiritually lacking and, if so, how long it would take for these ills to materialize. The less interesting question concerns what it would be like to be immortal in the absolute sense of not being able to die. It is impossible to say that one will want to live, say, a million years from now. The possibility of eternal suffering, such as illustrated by Sisyphus's eternal pointless pushing of the rock, or Prometheus having his liver pecked on by an eagle, makes absolute immortality an excessively risky proposition. Drifting around after the heat death of the universe is probably tedious. Besides, it is not a physically possible alternative. Unless physics is very different from what we now think, we have parts, and everything with parts can and will come apart sooner or later. Contingent immortality/indefinite life span, on the other hand, where we live as long as we want, or as long as we have no fatal accident, is much harder to reject. We can agree that it is important to be able to die and that death plays an important role in our lives without thinking that the natural life span, or any other predetermined life span, is long enough. We want to live on and see what happens. Unfortunately, Kass and other apologists are not always clear on what kind of immortality they assume in their spiritual arguments. They usually proceed by showing death to be important in some way and then, fallaciously, infer that it would not be good to live longer lives. To get the most out of engaging with these arguments, I will sometimes indulge in speculations about absolute immortality and engage in fuzzy, underspecified talk of "immortality," but always with a view to whether we find any persuasive reasons for thinking that radical life extension, or contingent immortality, would be undesirable. This is fair to the apologists, since their arguments are always intended not just to defend death, but death within a natural life span.

6.2   Losing Interest and Engagement in Life

Kass wonders,

> If the human life span were increased even by only twenty years, would the pleasures of life increase proportionately? Would professional tennis players really enjoy playing 25% more games of tennis? Would the Don Juan's of our world feel better for having seduced 1,250 women rather than 1,000? . . . Likewise, those whose satisfaction comes from climbing the career ladder might well ask what there would be to do for fifteen years after one had been CEO of Microsoft, a member of Congress, or the President of Harvard for a quarter of a century? Even less clear are the additions to personal happiness from more of the same of the less pleasant and less fulfilling activities in which so many of us are engaged so much of the time.[3]

For Kass, the answer in all three imagined cases is the same: No. Adding more time would not add anything of significance and, therefore, more time would not benefit them. It is clear that Kass intends the tennis player, the Don Juan, and the ladder climber to represent areas of human striving so that if we agree with his judgments in these cases then we would also have to accept the more general conclusion that life would not gain much value by being lengthened. Kass's argument is reminiscent of Lucretius's personified Nature, which tells us to be satisfied with the life we have.

> For there is naught more, which I can contrive and discover to please thee; all things are ever as they were. If thy body is not yet wasted with years, nor thy limbs worn and decayed, yet all things remain as they were, even if thou shouldst go on to overpass all generations, nay rather, if thou shouldst never die.[4]

Perhaps more than anything, the argument brings to mind the common objection that it would be boring to live beyond our natural life span.

6.3 Not Easily Bored

Would a professional tennis player, given an increased health span, enjoy to a proportional degree playing 25 percent more matches on the professional tour? It would seem that for many or most, the answer is yes, they would enjoy playing more matches. The increased use of physical coaches is motivated by precisely the wish to prolong their careers. As a result, the average age of players ranked in the top 100 is higher than ever. We could say that today's players are in fact enjoying 25 percent more matches than previous generations. Björn Borg retired at 26 in 1983 and Roger Federer has yet to retire at the age of 39 (as of 2021). However, does 25 percent add up proportionally to the pleasure of playing? Or is there a diminishing return, so that the first 75 percent of matches represents, say, 90 percent of the pleasure, while the last 25 percent represents only 10 percent of the pleasure? There is probably no general answer here. The amount of pleasure derived will vary with the individual and be dependent on a host of factors, such as one's success on the court, life projects outside the court, and so on. For some, the latter 25 percent may be on average worse than the earlier 75 percent, yet for others the latter part of their career could bring them more pleasure than the earlier parts of their career. In many cases in professional tennis, the last 25 percent—roughly 200 matches, considering an average top 100 play schedule—are career defining. When we speak of Jimmy Connors and Andre Agassi, we always mention how well they did even in their thirties. We could also consider Roger Federer's last 200 matches. In 2017, he came back after a six-month layoff due to a back injury and miraculously won not just the Australian Open but also thereafter Wimbledon, ending a five-year dry spell. These were his eighteenth and nineteenth grand slam tournament wins. In 2018, he defended his Australian Open title, his twentieth grand slam, and went on a historic 18-match winning streak. He certainly did not look bored with tennis. In his loss to Del Potro in the final of the 2018 Palm Springs Paribas Open, he displayed a frightening, maniacal will to win, including berating the umpire and striking a ball hard at Juan Martin del Potro.[5]

Contrary to Kass's conjecture, there are many tennis players who pine to extend their careers. There are, for example, the late bloomers who only find their game in their late twenties or early thirties. Then there are all those who have lost time in their twenties due to injuries, like Robin Söderling, the big Swede, who after many years on the tour broke through, beat Nadal "the King of Clay" at the 2010 French Open, and then smashed the mighty Federer on grass, allowing him to rank number four in the world. After his hard-earned success, he then contracted mononucleosis and had to stop playing. Now aged 36, he has given up tennis and pines that he does not have enough time left. This is a further sign that the youthfulness to play more professional tennis matches would be near universally desired by the many pros who keep playing even when they are well past their prime and financially secure. When they can no longer compete in the singles, they shift to the doubles, and when they cannot compete in the doubles, they shift to the senior tour. They never want to quit because they enjoy playing. One example is John McEnroe, who played his first major tournament in 1977 and who is still playing on the senior tour, where occasionally he will show his old self in vituperative abuses of racquets and referees. If we consider not just pros but also amateur players, it is certain that most of them would benefit from 25 percent more healthy years to play. Many amateurs have come late to the game, because their lives have not permitted them time or perhaps resources to play. For this category of players, the additional years would offer a disproportionate amount of pleasure because, *ceteris paribus*, the better you play, the more fun it is to play. The short window of health disproportionately favors those who were fortunate to receive instruction when young, since it is difficult—but not impossible—to make up for starting late. Besides, even if an activity does not bring a proportional gain in pleasure, it may still bring enough enjoyment to be worth pursuing.

What about Don Juan? Would he "feel better" if he was healthy enough to enjoy another 250 conquests? Again, the answer is yes. Would he not feel better if given an elixir restoring his vitality for another 250 escapades? He would want nothing more than that. Or are we to interpret this as a comparison between making 250 more conquests or dying? If so, then he is likely to feel better making the conquests, since he would feel nothing if he were dead. Someone may object that serial seduction is not a life project that can make a man feel good, but if so, then this would be true at any point in Don Juan's life, and it would not be relevant to the issue of life extension.

As for the third of Kass's cases, the ladder-climber would probably be able to figure out what to do with another 15 years after having reached some top. She could find some other ladder to climb, or mentor, or cultivate some other side of her. This brings us to the following point: the tennis professional, the Don Juan, and the ladder-climber are meant to represent different broad types of personalities and their different interests. However, they fail to represent real humans. Real humans are not obliged or restricted to keep pursuing one single interest. No one would be surprised to hear of a tennis professional who is also an ambitious businessman or of a businessman who is also an avid tennis player and a Don Juan. Moreover, our interests constantly evolve, some become deeper, others fall away, some are things that we sometimes return to, and new ones regularly introduce themselves. Hence, even if it were true that we would not enjoy more time doing one single particular thing, we could still want that time to pursue a plurality of interests, either new or old.

Prolongevist Christine Overall reminds us of just how much persons of any age have in front of them:

> Just consider all the areas of the world you have not yet explored; the people whom you have not yet encountered; the capacities, talents, and interests you have not yet developed; the hours you have not yet passed with your parents, siblings, children, or grandchildren, your lovers and your friends; the music and art you have not yet created or experienced; the books you have not yet read; the films or plays you have not yet seen; the sports, games, hobbies, and leisure activities you have not yet indulged in; and the new projects you have not yet undertaken.[6]

Even conservative bioethicist Daniel Callahan, who thinks that we should deny care to people over 65 that would lengthen their lives, points out that,

> For the lifelong reader there will still be many old books not read, and a constant stream of new books to be read. For the painter, there will be an infinite number of further possibilities, as there will be for one who enjoys investing in the stock market, understanding nature, watching scientific and other knowledge being discovered, growing a garden, observing the sunset, enjoying music, and taking walks. In that sense, however, life's possibilities, will never be exhausted; death at any time, at age 90, or 100, or 110, will frustrate those further possibilities, which are endless and likely never to be satisfied for one who has remained lively and inquiring.[7]

Callahan is right to point out that if we remain "lively and inquiring," life will be interesting. There must, I think, be something wrong with someone who cannot imagine anything they would rather do after 90 or 100 or 110, if in decent health, than be dead. If they are not dull or unimaginative, then they must be severely depressed. A much longer life would for many involve recurrent episodes of depression and loss of interest, but given how intrinsically intriguing life is—remember, we are standing on a rock with a fiery molten core floating in a place we call the universe, and our minds may be the most miraculous thing in it!—why think that we are determined to become irrevocably and permanently bored and apathetic? And why would it not be better to live to find out, rather than to simply guess that the grapes of a longer life are sour? There is, after all, no a priori warrant for believing that a longer life would be tedious, as the bioconservatives claim.

The ancient complaint that there is nothing new under the sun and that we, therefore, have little to look forward to by prolonging our life may have had some faint validity when it first was brought up. Clearly life was tough and monotonous for many in the past, perhaps in particular after the agricultural revolution. The men would toil in fields like their fathers had done, while the women would be pregnant or engaged in domestic work. Each generation would live more or less like the previous one and there would be no idea of history as progress. That, though, is the past. Today, our lives are much more varied and there is always something new and interesting to discover. Life in 2020 is very different from 1920 or 1820—and even quite different from 2010. We can expect an accelerated plentitude of new things under the sun.

But are these answers failing to appreciate the meaning of endlessness? A few hundred years may be easy to fill without vicious repetition, but what about 300 million years? Might we not ultimately simply tire of our limited repertoire of thoughts and feelings. We may eventually become like an old cinema, running the same limited number of films over and over and over. This is a possible scenario, but I am not convinced that it is inevitable, partly because of the reasons already mentioned and partly because of a feature of our limited mind, namely our limited memory and our limited foresight. Our sense of repetition is constrained by what we can recall. This we know is already the case in our short lives. We discover that we have already seen a film when half-way through it, and if we do not remember how it ended, but do remember that we liked it, we may want to see it again. Hence, even if we become like an old cinema, we will not mind the limited repertoire playing before our mind's eye. Rediscovered delights are delights all the same.

Moreover, interest and engagement do not necessarily require a constant stream of novelty. Many things in life gain by repetition and experience.

Re-watching a film or rereading a book can be a better experience than the first time; ceremonies owe their impact to repetition. For example, we do not think the national anthem, the "Star-Spangled Banner," has lost its force because we have heard it before. And friendships and companionships are to a large extent constituted by having a past of repeated contacts. Some of the best things in life become better with age; complex art and science bear revisiting and often reveal more every time they are approached; expertise is a function of repetition and it is often not until the technique has become second nature that exercising an art becomes maximally enjoyable. Finally, even the simplest pleasures bear seemingly endless repeating, like drinking when thirsty, eating when hungry, having a good sleep after a long day, or watching snowflakes drift on a winter's day. Novelty has its charm, but so does the familiar.

Reality offers up a never-ending stream of unique combinations. The longer we live, the more there is for us to discover and enjoy, as history and human activity adds to the number of possible constellations. There is, for example, even after a lifetime of reading, more books we have not read than when we began reading. If we are bored to the point of preferring death, we should seek out people who can help us appreciate life. With some ingenuity we can get used to leading longer, healthier lives. Perhaps some people, or even many people, would not be able to cope with more life but will lose interest and engagement and find it all unutterably boring, but I do not think that there are good reasons for thinking that such ennui is inevitable, which is the claim of the bioconservatives. While they are putting forth reasons for denying everyone life extension on the ground that it is not good for anyone, I am arguing that life extension can be good for many, and for the liberal view that one should be free to accept or reject life-extending medicine.

6.4   Motivation and Human Nature

Reflecting on how we would react to extreme life extension requires imagination, which is why speculations by ancient philosophers and works of fiction—ancient myths, literary characters, even poetry—are legitimate tools. However, our predictions should also be compatible with our best psychological and neurological theories. Most fundamentally, we do things either instinctively, out of habit, or because we think that they will satisfy some desire. This desire is ultimately connected to the avoidance of pain or the realization of pleasure, the mechanism of attraction and repulsion. What then, in general, do we desire? Psychologist Steven Reiss asked 7,000 participants and concluded that there are 16 life motives:

1. The need for food and water and other basic necessities;
2. the need to be appreciated;
3. curiosity, the need to gain knowledge;
4. romance, the need for mating or sex;
5. family, the need to take care of one's offspring;
6. honor, the need to be faithful to the customary values of an individual's ethnic group, community, family, or clan;
7. idealism, the need for social justice;
8. independence, the need to be distinct and self-reliant;
9. order, the need for prepared, established, and conventional environments;
10. physical activity, the need for physical exercise;
11. power, the need for control of will;
12. saving, the need to accumulate something;
13. social contact, the need for relationships with others;
14. social status, the need for social significance;
15. tranquility, the need to be secure and protected; and
16. vengeance, the need to strike back against another person.

These 16 drives are genetically hardwired, and experience—including cultural experience—gives shape to their particular expression. A monogamous society will, for example, shape sexual desire to be directed toward one mate. The relative importance we assign these motivations define our personality, our personal Reiss profile. With this brief sketch of motivation psychology in mind, we can ask whether we have a reason to predict that a healthy person would necessarily lose all or some of these desires if they lived beyond the natural life span and as a result became bored and disengaged.[8] I think that the answer is no. Given how deep-seated our basic desires are, we have no good reason to think that they would abate in an otherwise healthy individual as a function of chronological age. Consider, for instance, the basic drive of curiosity. A recent article in *Neuro*, a neuroscientific journal, describes it as follows:

Curiosity is such a basic component of our nature that we are nearly oblivious to its pervasiveness in our lives. Consider, though, how much of our time we spend seeking and consuming information, whether listening to the news or music; browsing the internet; reading books or magazines; watching television, movies, and sports; or otherwise engaging in activities not directly related to eating, reproduction, and basic survival. Our insatiable demand for information drives a much of the global economy and, on a micro-scale, motivates learning and drives patterns of foraging in animals. Its diminution is a symptom of depression . . . Curiosity is thought of as the noblest of human drives.[9]

Think about that wide-eyed response with which a toddler greets an unfamiliar object and begins to stare, touch, and taste. Other animals can be curious, but it is merely directed toward solving immediate problems. The desire to find out how things work in general is distinctly human. Psychologist Daniel Berlyne calls this curiosity "epistemic" as opposed to a more present-directed "perceptual" kind that we share with animals.[10] The neural mechanisms of curiosity are not yet well understood; but the details are not pertinent to our purpose. Whichever theory physiologists ultimately settle on, they agree that curiosity is built into the human brain. And since it is, we have reason to believe that it is not easily extinguished in a healthy human. We could draw an analogy here to taste: no matter how long we live, as long as we are physically healthy, sugar will taste sweet and lemons will taste sour. The same would probably be true about all the other basic drives. People would still be hungry and thirsty, still need to be loved and appreciated, still want sex and romance, still seek power and status, still thirst for revenge, and so on, even if they lived for 120 years and beyond, and as long as they do, we should not expect them to be bored and disengaged.

6.5 Losing Our Passion for Life: *The Makropulos Case,* a Reflection on the Tedium of Immortality

British philosopher Bernard Williams believes that life can be too long.[11] Even if we may still have our natural desires, we will grow tired of having to satisfy them. That is, we may still desire knowledge, for example, but we will lose our interest in desiring knowledge and become indifferent between further satisfaction and its cancellation through death. And then perhaps this lack of interest and sense will ooze down and poison our entire motivational nature, leaving us cold and apathetic. After all, we are humans and not, say, dogs, who seem to be equally happy chasing things, chewing on toys, and eating the same dogfood day after day forever. A dog does not get *Weltschmertz*, anguish, or ennui. However, we do. We need a sense that there is more to life—something more at stake—and perhaps death can give us this.

Williams uses *The Makropulos Case*, a play by Czech playwright Karel Capek that was later made into an opera by Leos Janacek, as his point of departure.[12] It tells the story of a 42-year-old woman called Elina Makropulos, E. M., who was given an elixir of life by her father, a court physician to a sixteenth-century emperor. The elixir gives her 300 years of life. After that, she can decide if she wants to imbibe another draught or age and die naturally. The story picks up 300 years later. To hide her condition, she has assumed a series of identities all with the initials E. M. At 342, she is unable to hide that she has become, as one protagonist says, "cold as a knife." Her life, writes Williams, "has come to a state of boredom, indifference, and coldness." Elina complains,

> Boredom. No, it isn't even boredom. It is . . . it is . . . oh, you people, you people, you have no name for it. . . . Everything is so pointless, so empty, so meaning-less . . . One finds out that one cannot believe in anything. Anything. And from that comes this cold emptiness . . . And no one can love for 300 years—it cannot last. And then everything tires one. It tires one to be good, it tires one to be bad. The earth itself tires one.[13]

She decides to not take the elixir and she begins to age rapidly before our eyes. Before she dies, she offers the elixir to her friend Christina, who rejects it and sets it alight by a candle, exclaiming, "Ha, ha, the end of immortality."[14] Williams believes that Elina's ennui is not merely a reflection of her personal inability to cope with more time. We would all become like her if our deadline was moved up. The only way we can escape this state of utter apathy, says Williams, is to evolve constantly. Each of us would have to change continuously into different persons. However, this strategy, argues Williams, faces the following serious challenge, "The state in which I survive should be one which, to me looking forward, will be adequately related, in the life it presents, to those aims which I now have in wanting to survive at all . . . It should clearly be me who lives forever."[15] According to Williams, we are faced with a tragic dilemma: either we do not change and, therefore, suffer a deep ennui, or we do change and thereby lose ourselves. In either case, our life ceases to matter to us.

6.5.1 Responding to Williams

In Williams's scenario, we have various first order desires, but we do not care if they are satisfied or if they are canceled. In fact, as Elina's choice reveals, we would prefer to have them canceled. We would see all our desires as dependent on us being alive, but none of them as a reason to be alive. Thus, after 300 years, we would rather not be hungry in the first place than have a delicious meal to satisfy our hunger; we would rather not be sexually aroused than to have our arousal satisfied; we would rather not want to see our friends and family for Christmas than to have our wish to see them satisfied; we would rather not be curious than learn something new; and so on. We would in short be terribly in a state of ennui, or perhaps alienated is the right word. The question then is if we have good reasons for thinking that this is what would happen to us once we live hundreds of years.

Prima facie, it seems unlikely. The Argentine writer Luis Borges had reached Elina's state of ennui already in his seventies. He complained about having outlived his biblical threescore years and ten and he was tired of himself. But the fact that some are tired of their existence does not prove that this state is an inevitable function of time. Time goes by quickly and judging by the attitudes of most older people, boredom and existential fatigue is not generally experienced to the level that death is a superior alternative. Williams's idea that, although we would still have desires, we would be indifferent to whether they are satisfied or canceled, also seems implausible. If at age 300, we are excited about having dinner with an old friend, why would we not want to have dinner with an old friend, rather than having this desire canceled? Or if we really want to travel to Mars, why would we be indifferent to whether we go to Mars or have this desire canceled? And so on. It is interesting that the state of indifference to whether desires are satisfied or canceled (and therefore thwarted) is described as ennui by Williams and as wisdom by the Epicureans and Stoics. It once more reveals the unattractiveness of their ideal. The man who is indifferent to whether he sees his family or whether he dies, and the man who is not in the least disturbed if his wife and children die, both probably can be described as in a state of ennui, or as depressed, or as suffering some type of affective disorder. This is what I puckishly call the folly of wisdom.

Williams wants us to think that this is indeed how we must turn out because unless we deny ourselves a kind of natural and dynamic progress, we will lose our personal identity. This was the second lemma. It is not particularly persuasive. Desires associated with our creaturely needs either will not change much, or their change will not necessarily destroy our identity. I will probably still like to drink coffee in the year 2500, but if I do not, it is not a great threat to my personality. More complex goals can also be expected to either stay the same or, if abandoned, their loss will not necessarily destroy my identity. I will probably still care about philosophy in the year 2500, but if I do not, then I assume that I have simply changed. It would still be me, just with a different mindset. My views on things have changed in the past and I expect them to continue to evolve; I have evolved over time; I have not gone out of existence. Someone in the position of Capek's Elina does not have to be "cold as a knife" in order to preserve her identity, and neither do we.[16] She should relax and allow herself to evolve, rather than clinging onto the bizarre belief that her future self must have the same goals and priorities as her present self. Contrary to what Williams argues, our future state does not have to be related to our present reasons for wanting to live. Just as we can desire to go to Tokyo without any precise idea of what we will do once there, we can reasonably want to get to our 342nd birthday without having any precise idea of how to celebrate it.

Is this answer too quick? What if we gradually changed in profound ways, and became in significant aspects the opposite of how we are today? Yale philosopher Shelly Kagan describes just such a scenario of transformation:

> Suppose that somewhere around 200, my friends give me a new nickname. They call me Jo-Jo. . . . By the time I'm 300, 350, 400, I've forgotten that anybody ever called me Shelly. . . . And imagine that while all this is going on, while I'm getting older and older, my personality is changing as well. Along the way I lose all interest in philosophy and take up an interest in something I've never cared about before at all, perhaps organic chemistry. . . . And my values change too. Right now, today, I'm a kind, compassionate, warm individual who cares about the down-trodden. But around 300 I start to lose my compassion. At 400 I start saying things like, "The downtrodden, who needs them?" and by the time I'm 500, I'm completely self-absorbed: I'm a cruel vindictive person.[17]

Kagan thinks that this is not the kind of survival he would be interested in:

> I find myself wanting to say, "it's me, but so what? This does not give me what I want. It does not give me what matters." . . . When I think about what I want, it's not just surviving. And it is not just surviving with the same evolving-through-time personality. Roughly speaking, what I want is survival with a *similar* personality [emphasis is Kagan's own].[18]

Could we benefit from living if we change into a very different person? This is an important question since if we are bound to change significantly over time, then perhaps at some point, perhaps already after a couple of hundred years, we would no longer benefit from living. This would weaken the case against death. As it happens, though, Kagan's argument is unpersuasive. Kagan is wrong to claim that we would not be interested in surviving to become someone very different from who we are. Contrary to Williams and Kagan, becoming a different personality is not necessarily undesirable. The problem with Jo-Jo is not that he is dissimilar from Kagan. The problem is rather that Jo-Jo is dissimilar in a bad way. If we changed the story so that Jo-Jo is wiser and nobler than Kagan, then why would he not want to gradually become Jo-Jo? Is it not rather narcissistic of his present personality to insist that his current time-slice must be preferred and preserved? Why not think that he would be in a better position to judge how he should be after having lived another 100 years or so? Certainly, few of us would give the authority to our 16-year-old selves to determine how we should be, for as long as we live.

Returning to Williams's case, there are some specific features of Elina's personality, as well as her situation, that contribute to her suffering. First, in Capek's story Elina is the only one who lives longer. Her situation is unique. This obviously introduces the problem of how to deal with mere mortals, in particular with forming bonds of love and friendship. But why think that an extreme life extension scenario would involve only one person?[19]

Second, judging by what we are told, Elina has no interest in science, the arts, philosophy, politics, religion, philanthropy, or any such self-transcendent domains. She also does not seem to have to work for a living. Such a socially disconnected, narrow, and self-centered personality would likely be bored and alienated already within a normal life span. The lesson could therefore be not that 300 years would be unbearable, but that we should interest ourselves in the world and people around us if we want to enjoy our added years.

Third, Capek has Elina explain one source of her ennui as having to do with a kind of global skepticism. "[O]ne cannot believe in anything," she says. Perhaps the thought is that since over time we are prone to have our beliefs turn out to be false, that after having experienced that for long enough, we will end up not wanting to believe anything. This does not seem impossible, but it would be an utterly irrational response. In terms of our beliefs about the world, the last 300 years have experienced an enormous amount of progress, and this is likely to continue. Why would experiencing a progress of shedding false beliefs for true lead one to a state of complete skepticism? And in any case, most of our beliefs have remained the same. Ice is cold and fire is hot, $2+2=4$, and so on. Why think that we must end up doubting such basic truths? The same goes for our moral beliefs. The Golden Rule has stood the test of time, and the same is true for virtues such as courage and honesty. Of course, some moral beliefs have been revised: We used to believe that slavery was justifiable and now we do not, but why can we not see this as progress, rather than draw the nihilistic conclusion that we can no longer believe in anything? Epistemic nihilism is a very unlikely and completely unmotivated reaction to super-longevity. In fact, it is contradictory if longevity is produced by science, since it would prove that our knowledge increases over time.

Fourth, is not Elina's immortality of a very unusual type? It is clearly contingent on taking the potion. But, on the other hand, Elina cannot commit suicide (I assume) so it is also absolute, for as long as it lasts. Elina could throw herself into a volcano and not die, so she must endure the time it takes for the potion to wear off. This esoteric understanding severely limits the lessons that can be drawn from her case. Importantly, it gives us no reason not to seek contingent immortality, since it does not confer a temporary inability to die, and since if boredom becomes insufferable, we can commit suicide.

In sum, there are plenty of reasons for denying Williams's conclusion. If we are not like Elina, we will not be easily bored, and part of the reason is that we will evolve over time. This evolution is not a threat to our identity. We have no more reason to think that we would lose our identity by living to 300 than we have for thinking that we lose our identity by growing up. In fact, our gradual evolution is one of the exciting aspects of living on. Anyone who has the same personality after 300 years has probably been wasting their time.

6.6 A Pill for Interest and Engagement

There is a further complication that may turn out to be crucial. The spiritual complications are not seen as an effect of physical deterioration and illness, but as purely mental. But this distinction may be illusory; if the mental is constituted or determined by the physical, then assuming physical health is *eo ipso* to assume mental health. Body and spirit is one. To simplify, if all is well with the brain, then all is well with the mind. As neuropsychology evolves and the boundaries between what we consider physical and mental health become harder to draw, there might come a time when lacking normal interests in life is regarded as a state of physical unhealth to be cured. We already have medicines like Prozac and Zoloft that work for some; why not think that these could improve? Why not think that we would find ways to restore interest in life if we lost it over time? This will mean that the assumption that someone like Elina can be in physical health, yet in so much mental pain, becomes incoherent: If she is psychologically unwell, then she cannot be physiologically well, and if she is physiologically well, she cannot be psychologically unwell.

At this point in the argument we are back to the issue of the previous chapter. Are there some natural limits that we should not transgress? Would manipulating our psychology into feeling an interest and engagement in life be a violation of something sacred? Would a pill that made us interested and engaged in life perhaps mask and destroy our identity? Is it better to be authentically mortally bored than to be artificially enjoying life? The specter of *Brave New World* haunts psychotropic drugs, and there is something eerie about the chemical manipulation of our minds. On the other hand, even the staunchest bioconservatives allow for medicine. They disagree with medicine used for human enhancement, but they believe in its restorative use. Hence, our imagined pill, if not abused or used in the first resort, would seem to pass muster, since it merely restores or maintains an individual's natural interest in life. It would be akin to eyeglasses for faltering eyes, eyeglasses that would enable us to see the way we are naturally supposed to. If one marvels at the universe and finds interest in people and things around oneself as one did when one was young and healthy, does it matter that it is enabled by medicine? After all, the universe merits interest. Aldous Huxley warned about numbing and distracting drugs like the imaginary soma of *Brave New World*, but in real life he was advocating for what he regarded as mind-expanding drugs like mescaline and LSD. If there were a drug that would open closed minds to the truly mysterious and amazing nature of existence, then it is less obvious to see what is wrong with it when the alternative is that we are so depressed that death is a preferred alternative. Few today complain when someone is saved from the brink of suicide by their psychotropic medication. Why complain if occasionally some would have to medicate to deal with the challenging benefit of a longer life? The psychopharmacological option should always be kept in mind when speculating how we would cope mentally with a much longer life.

That said, I am myself a pharmacological near-teetotaler and would prefer to live on without chemical crutches for the reasons explored by Huxley in *Brave New World*. I am also fairly confident that most of us could live on without psychotropics. Diet, exercise, social activities, vocation, meditation, prayer, routines, goal setting, sleeping, mindfulness of negative thoughts, music and dancing, having pets, visiting nature, and taking on more responsibilities are some activities that counter depression. And if, despite all these salutary activities, lack of interest and engagement still haunt us, we will probably discover new ways of dealing with it.

6.7   Conclusions

Given how deeply anchored our interests are in our nature, we have reason to think that they would last far beyond our natural life span.

Still, philosophers may wonder if we would not sooner rather than later simply not want to retain our interests and desires. They recognize that we have all these innate interests that perhaps will always be there, but they believe we will sooner rather than later lose a sense of meaning; without meaning we would lose interest in satisfying our innate interests and become apathetic. Even if we knew that we could restore our interests naturally or via medicine, we would not want to, because we would ultimately regard it all as pointless. So we are returning to the question of the meaning of life. In chapter four we discussed the claim that life is not worth living because there is no objective meaning to it; here the claim is rather that death is essential to meaning, and that without death, life would be an unrewarding and aimless drift. It is to this argument we now turn.

7   We Need a Deadline

When a man knows he is to be hanged . . . it concentrates his mind wonderfully.
—Samuel Johnson

7.1   We Only Aspire and Take Life Seriously Because We Die

"Could life be serious or meaningful without the limit of mortality? Is not the limit on our time the ground of our taking life seriously and living it passionately?" Kass asks. He answers his own questions "no," life could not be serious and meaningful without the limit of mortality, and "yes," the limit on our time is the ground for our taking life seriously and living it passionately:

> To know and to feel that one goes around only once, and that the deadline is not out of sight, is for many people the necessary spur to the pursuit of something worthwhile. "Teach us to number our days," says the Psalmist, "that we may get a heart of wisdom." To number our days is the condition for making them count. . . . Mortality makes life matter.[1]

The thought that death makes life matter and that without the grim reaper breathing down our necks we would lack any reason for doing something now, rather than later, is familiar. "If we were immortal," writes Austrian psychiatrist Victor Frankl, "we could legitimately postpone every action forever. It would be of no consequence whether we did a thing now; every act might as well be done tomorrow or the day after or a year from now or ten years hence."[2] Death, the argument goes, not only serves as a spur but provides life with the end point necessary for it to be meaningful. Others worry that we would run out of worthwhile things to do and life would become unbearable. Another concern is that given infinite time, everyone would do everything so nothing could count as a distinguishing accomplishment. And then there is the frustration of unanswerable questions, how would we bear that?

All these arguments can be put in the category of worries about meaning and sense in the absence of death. While the authors of these arguments often speak of what would happen to us if we were immortal, presumably, in an absolute sense, it is usually meant to apply equally to cases of mere life extension. We are supposed to need the thought that we will die relatively soon, rather than say hundreds, thousands, or millions of years from now. It is, Kass writes, important that "the deadline is not out of sight."[3] For Kass, the deadline we are currently under is a fitting one. Any extension, he thinks, would attenuate the intensity of life and invite a state of despondent procrastination and senselessness. I will consider various versions of this complaint, but first I will make a more general point about the dialectic.

7.2   Death and Underdetermination

We should be skeptical toward categorical claims about the psychological role of thoughts about death. First, in the previous chapter, I argued that different people probably would react in different ways to the thought that their lives are radically extended, or that they are immortal in some sense. This underdetermination is a particular instance of a more general phenomenon of facts underdetermining representations, and representations underdetermining our responses to these representations.[4] In other words, the same event can be described differently when coming from different points of view, and even if we agree upon a description of an event, we might feel differently about it, and it might mean different things to different people. This is the reason for why, as the joke goes, if you put two economists in a room, you will get at least three completely different opinions (even if they are given the same set of data). It can also be confirmed every day by switching between CNN and FOX News. Prima facie, it would be surprising if beliefs about death would be exceptions to this underdetermination. Why think that there are varied responses to all kinds of facts, but one uniform response to death? Second, people rarely have their own death in mind and when they do, they have a rather hazy view of it. We often hear that people discover their mortality when their parents die or after a brush with death such as a serious accident. Without these reminders, it appears that for most people their mortality is a rather vague notion. This is why the philosophers' advice of keeping a memento mori makes sense. Sigmund Freud, the father of psychoanalysis, thought that none of us can ever fully grasp it: while we might say that all humans are mortal, we all think of ourselves as immortal:

> We have shown an unmistakable tendency to put death aside, to eliminate it from life. We attempted to hush it up, in fact, we have the proverb: to think of something as of death. Of course, we meant our own death. We cannot, indeed, imagine our own death; whenever we try to do so we find that we survive ourselves as spectators. The school of psychoanalysis could thus assert that at bottom no one believes in his own death, which amounts to saying: in the unconscious every one of us is convinced of his immortality.[5]

Freud's view is reminiscent of Thomas Nagel's observation that we simultaneously hold two contrary views of our mortality (also quoted in chapter 4):

> Observed from without, human beings obviously have a natural lifespan and cannot live much longer than a hundred years. A man's sense of his own experience, on the other hand, does not embody this idea of a natural limit. His existence defines for him an essentially open-ended possible future.[6]

If Nagel and Freud are correct, then we have a complicated psychological relationship to our mortality. We both affirm it and deny it. We know that we are going to die, but we also cannot fully imagine it. This suggests that the belief in our mortality is simply too foggy in most minds for us to expect that it serves a necessary role in our motivational psychology.

With these two points in mind—the underdetermination and the fogginess—let us now consider the reasons given for the claim that death is a necessary spur for action, and thereafter evaluate various formulations of the claim that there is no sense to life without death.

7.3   Death and Procrastination: A Response

Almost everyone is a procrastinator to a greater or lesser degree. Hence, perhaps every advance in life expectancy would lead to more postponement, and perhaps without death everything would be postponed. There seems to be some evidence in favor of thinking so. We have gained 30 years in life expectancy over the last 100 years or so, and this is reflected in some of our choices. We marry later and we have children later. Each generation since the Greatest Generation, born in the 1920s, seems more and more to stretch out its adolescence and postpone adulthood. Adult children live at home longer than during past generations. Failure to launch is a cultural meme. Perhaps only the limited window of a woman's fertility puts pressure on her to marry before it is too late for her to have children. Desperation sets in due to this partial death, and perhaps without it the choice to marry and have children would be indefinitely postponed. Others are anxious to leave their mark on the world and, knowing how little time they have, apply themselves intensely. Yet others try to cram in as many interesting or exciting experiences as possible, knowing that their time is short.

Notwithstanding the ways in which the thought of death appears to motivate us, it is clearly not a sufficient condition. Everyone is aware of his/her mortality to some degree, but not everyone takes life seriously and aspires to great things. One's personality type and life circumstances importantly influence how much passion and purpose one brings to one's life. The real question is whether thoughts of death are necessary for motivating one to act sooner rather than later. I think this question can in part be answered by considering again the 16 categories of life goals of the Reiss profile mentioned in the previous chapter. There are several goals that intuitively would have traction even for someone unaware of their mortality. Would we not, for example, want social contact and love if we thought of ourselves as immortal? Would we legitimately postpone getting hugs and affection? I cannot see why we would. Surprisingly, Kass admits that there are exceptions to his thesis,

> There may be some activities, especially in some human beings, that do not require finitude as a spur. A powerful desire for understanding can do without external prodding, let alone one related to mortality; and as there is never too much time to learn and to understand, longer, more vigorous life might be simply a boon. The best sorts of friendship, too, seem capable of indefinite growth, especially where growth is somehow tied to learning.[7]

This is not a minor concession; it is a complete surrender. A longer life of learning and friendship already begins to sound attractive. And if we can care about friendship and knowledge without "finitude as a spur," then we can probably care about health, virtue, justice, excellence, art, and so on, and so on. And if we care about these things, then why would we not care about basic things like experiencing pleasure and avoiding pain? Imagine someone reasoning as follows: "I still care about exploring the world, and cultivating friendships, but since there is no end in sight, I don't mind this throbbing toothache." I cannot see how the thought that one is immortal, or the absence of a thought that one is mortal, or the thought that one's life is indefinitely long would necessarily make one careless about experiencing pain and suffering. Imagine that the person with the toothache finds herself in the dentist chair. Will she say, "Take your time with the root canal and there is no need for anesthetics because I will live forever"? If not, then the conclusion is that pain, suffering, and discomfort—a repellent state—would continue to be a spur in a state of infinitude. And if she wants to avoid pain, then she would also have a reason to get to work on time, develop her skills, cultivate friendships, exercise, eat well, pay her taxes, avoid ostracism, and so on.

We actually know that a sentient being can be active and engaged without thoughts of mortality: animals and young children have no thoughts of death yet suffer no procrastination and despondency. Given that most of us do not think that much about death, it is probable that we could likewise maintain an interest in various worthwhile activities even in the absence of such thoughts. In sum, granted, the thought that death is rapidly approaching sometimes acts as a spur, but besides arranging for one's own funeral, or taking out a life insurance policy, I am not sure that any activity strictly speaking needs this thought.[8]

7.4 Death Makes Life Matter

Kass argues that like a precious metal, our days can only matter if they are not in infinite supply. "To number our days is the condition for making them count. . . . Mortality makes life matter." American philosopher Martha Nussbaum agrees:

> The intensity and dedication with which very many human activities are pursued cannot be explained without reference to the awareness that our opportunities are finite, that we cannot choose those activities indefinitely many times. In raising a child, in cherishing a lover, in performing a demanding task of work or thought or artistic creation, we are aware, at some level, of the thought that each of these efforts is structured and constrained by finite time.[9]

Nothing is at stake, thinks Nussbaum, when you have an eternity to do certain things and redo them again and again. It is like playing poker with an unlimited amount of poker chips. Who can take such a game seriously?

As common as this argument is, it fails because it gets valuing backwards. If we do one thing rather than another, then it means we value this thing over the other, at least at the moment of choice. However, this does not mean the value of what we choose resides in the fact that we choose it over something else. If this were so, then we could never choose to do something lacking in value! To illustrate, the value of this book is unrelated to the time spent writing it. Its value is determined by how well it accomplishes what it is intended to accomplish. Whether I spent five weeks or five years on it is irrelevant. I could have spent ten years on it, and it could still be worthless. Or, to take Nussbaum's own example, the value of raising children is not constituted by the valuable things it prevents me from doing. Would it not be preferable to be able to enjoy parenthood without the nagging thought that time spent with your children is time when we are not, for example, developing our mind, cultivating our adult friendships, or working on our long-neglected book—or other life projects? Or, if the life choice is the reverse: The value of having a great career is not constituted by the fact that we did not have children, or if we did, by the fact that we failed to spend time with them. Contrary to common wisdom, not having time enough to pursue a valued activity detracts rather than adds value to our life.

So what does bring value to life? In her brilliant book on the good life, philosopher Jean Kazez proposes a number of things that add value to a life.[10] They include self-determination, self-expression, pleasure derived from worthwhile activities, and an increase rather than a decrease in good things over time. None of these good things appear dependent on death, but rather appear to be threatened by it: death is a threat to self-determination because it imposes itself on us whether we want it or not; it is a threat to self-expression since it ends the self; it is a threat to our pleasures since they die with us; it is a threat to our progress since it curtails it; and it is—via the slow death of aging—decreasing access to many good things over time.

7.5   Death or Senselessness

In his article, "Death Is Good for You," British writer Hadrian Wise expresses eloquently the worry that endless lives are senseless lives:

> The real problem isn't boredom, but this: what should we think of a novel that went on and on without ending? It couldn't really be a work of art, because it couldn't really have a point. Physically, the point of something—a pencil,

say—comes at the end, and the rest of the object in a sense leads up to it. In the same way, the point of a work of art is in its overall organization, in how each part relates to every other, and no limited being, no being below God, can organize anything overall or divide a whole thing into parts unless that thing is finite too. A human life is no work of art, but it does have to have a point, an overall purpose, to be satisfying, or in the long run bearable. And it can't have an overall purpose if it never ends. Immortality is an infinity of purposelessness. If this is too dry and abstract to worry you, bring back to your minds the nagging question, ever more insistent in this age of luxury and longevity, "Why am I here?" Can you imagine how that question would scream inside your head after 2,000 years? 10,000? A million? Why am I still here? What else do you want with me? It would drive you completely and utterly insane.[11]

Wise echoes Hardwig's claim that "death is the point and purpose" that nature intended with our lives, which we discussed in chapter 4 when concerned with arguments from nature. There I argued that nature has no purpose for us, but if you like to think so, then survival and reproduction are more reasonable candidates for natural meaning. Wise is worried that questions about the meaning of life would drive us insane after a couple of thousand or a million years, but this is probably an idiosyncrasy. Many have found meaning in God, in nature, or are satisfied with the internal meaning they derive from their projects and commitments. There is no screaming for sense inside of their heads. Extrapolating from this fact gives us a reason to think that it is possible to find life bereft of an overall purpose bearable even in the long run. In fact, thoughtful people, in my experience, usually admit to a certain easygoing agnosticism, and they go on with their lives regardless. They don't know what the ultimate meaning of life is, or whether there is such a thing, but they know what they want to do next weekend. Perhaps on some level they agree with the influential Austrian philosopher Ludwig Wittgenstein when he says that there really is no question of the meaning of life and that it is a mistake to think that the question makes sense:

> For an answer which cannot be expressed the question too cannot be expressed. The riddle does not exist. If a question can be put at all, then it can also be answered. Skepticism is not irrefutable, but palpably senseless, if it would doubt where a question cannot be asked. For doubt can only exist where there is a question; a question only where there is an answer, and this only where something can be said. We feel that even if all possible scientific questions be answered, the problems of life have still not been touched at all. Of course, there is then no question left, and just this is the answer. The solution of the problem of life is

seen in the vanishing of this problem. (Is not this the reason why men to whom after long doubting the sense of life became clear, could not then say wherein this sense consisted?) There is indeed the inexpressible. This shows itself; it is the mystical . . . Whereof one cannot speak, thereof one must be silent.[12]

If Wittgenstein is correct, then this means that an indefinite life, or an eternal life would have no more and no less of an issue with meaning. It is not something to ponder in the propositional language of thought but is mystical. That is, Wise's question is a nonquestion, and the answer lies in not asking it. If it starts screaming inside his head, then it calls for philosophical therapy.

I mention this answer because many philosophers and nonphilosophers have the feeling that there is something hopeless about asking for *the* overarching objective meaning of life. There is, in our culture, a certain light mockery of those who are "searching for the meaning of life" rather than attending to more tangible concerns. That said, I do not agree with this mockery, and I do not agree with Wittgenstein. For me, the question of whether there is an ultimate purpose to our lives as individuals and as a race makes sense, but the fact that there is this common skepticism about raising the big question and about being a "searcher" shows that many of us will not be particularly fazed by the prospect of living on without a clear answer to "why are we here." They are thinking about other things. And, as said before, many will probably continue to have answers, or make do with internal meaning. In any case, the question is not going to drive all of us insane.

Then there is the comparison between a human life and a novel. The novel must have an end to be a work of art, Wise writes. Analogously, therefore, our lives must have an end, too. This is, in essence, the same argument that ancient philosophers liked to make when comparing a human life to a play, arguing that both should be a proper length and no more. The analogy fails. First of all, it is easy to imagine a novel that is serialized with no definite end, like a Netflix series that may continue with a new installation each season, or each century, or forever. When we find unfinished novels, we do not think that they are not novels; we think that they are just not finished. Secondly, as Wise himself points out, a human life is not a work of art, and hence this is a flawed analogy. A novel, unlike a person, is not removed from this world when it ends, and neither is it missing out on all the good things it would have had were it not completed. And so forth. We may or may not want our novels and television series to end, but we can still prefer our own story to keep going.

7.6   Death Is Necessary for a Sense of Achievement

In a related "death or senselessness" type of argument, philosopher Aaron Smuts argues that we need a deadline in order to maintain a sense of achievement. Once more, we are asked to consider a work of fiction, this time a short story by Argentinian writer Borges titled "The Immortal."[13] In the story we are told of a man who accidentally drinks from the stream of eternal life outside the City of the Immortals. After he ventures through a labyrinthine passage leading to the fabled city, he enters it and is appalled by what he sees:

> To the impression of enormous antiquity others were added: that of the interminable, that of the atrocious, that of the completely senseless. A labyrinth is a structure compounded to confuse men; its architecture, rich in symmetries, is subordinated to that end. In the palace I imperfectly explored, the architecture lacked any such finality. It abounded in dead end corridors, high unattainable windows, portentous doors which led to a cell or a pit, incredible inverted stairways whose steps and balustrades hung downwards. Other stairways, clinging airily to the side of a monumental wall, would die without leading anywhere, after making two or three turns in the lofty darkness of the cupolas.[14]

The grotesqueness of the architecture holds up a mirror to that of its immortal inhabitants. Having exhausted and fulfilled every aspiration and then finding their mundane desires insufficient reasons for life, they linger on as sad, apathetic shadow beings:

> They knew that over an infinitely long span of time, all things happen to all men. As reward for his past and future virtues, every man merited every kindness—yet also every betrayal, as reward for his past and future iniquities. Much as the way in games of chance, heads and tails tend to even out, so cleverness and dullness cancel and correct each other. There are no spiritual or intellectual merits. . . . Homer composed the Odyssey; given infinite time, with infinite circumstances and changes, it is impossible that the Odyssey should not be composed at least once. No one is someone; a single immortal man is all men.[15]

Smuts's worry is that Borges's immortals have been robbed of the possibility of achievement because everything can be achieved by everyone by sheer perseverance. This implies the impossibility of personal, individuating achievements. Everyone, given enough time, can do and be everything.

"No one is someone; a single immortal man is all men." Smuts concludes that,

> Immortality would be motivationally devastating, since our decisions would carry little weight, our achievements would be hollow victories of mere diligence, and the prospect of eternal frustration would haunt our every effort. An immortal life for those of limited ability will inevitably result in endless frustration, since the number of significant projects that one is capable of completing is finite, but the span of time is infinite. . . . we would lose reason to go on if we were to live forever.[16]

Our immortal lives would be like Borges's labyrinth: interminable, atrocious, and completely senseless.

In what follows I will respond to Borges and Smuts that

1. an eternal life is not sufficient for achievement;
2. an eternal life is not incompatible with achievements;
3. some of these achievements may be distinguishing;
4. perseverance is a fine ground for achievement;
5. we do not necessarily need distinguishing achievements; and
6. we would probably be able to accept that we cannot solve all the riddles of the universe.

Before making these points, it is worth reminding ourselves, once more, that we are playing along with the notion of immortality of perhaps an absolute kind, or nearly so. Nothing that Williams, Kass, Smuts, and Borges say necessarily bears on the issue of more moderate life extension or even contingent immortality. Now, on to the argument.

It has been suggested that if one gave a bunch of monkeys a typewriter and an eternity, they would produce *Hamlet* as a matter of coincidence. Neither talent nor intelligence is required, just persistence and mindless hammering on the typewriter. This is analogous to Borges's idea that everyone is destined to write the *Iliad* or *Hamlet* given an eternity. Neither of these claims hold up to closer scrutiny, for while it may be theoretically true that generating random letters within a computer program would at some point end up producing a series of letters accidentally mimicking all the great works ever written, including Hamlet, this is insufficient grounds for thinking that, given an eternity, real monkeys in the real world would somehow accidentally write every masterpiece. The world and our actions in it are not equivalent to a computer randomly generating strings of letters. For starters, from where would the monkeys get the typewriter, the paper, and the ink? How will they know how to change the page, replace the ink, and so on? There are simply too many contingent reasons pertaining to the monkeys and their environment to think that they would ever pound out even a short poem like "Rage Against the Night," let alone *Hamlet* or the *Iliad*. It is even less likely that every single eternal chimp would accidentally find a typewriter and happen to hammer out every single masterpiece. Similarly, without a certain intellectual talent, there is no reason to think that a person would discover calculus, and without certain physical attributes and an interest in sports, there is no reason to think that someone would necessarily, given an eternity, become the strongest man in the world or win Wimbledon eight times. Similarly, the particular circumstances surrounding Homer's creation of the *Odyssey* will never be reproduced. An illiterate Bushman or a college professor in Park Slope, Brooklyn, could never have written it. Only a few contemporary Bronze Age Greeks could have written it, and only one (or a few) actually did. There are seven billion people in the world. Over one year, that is a combined seven billion years of life. Despite this, the number of true achievements on the level of Newton's physics and Leibniz's development of modern calculus are rare. They certainly do not happen every year. Why think that one person's seven-billion-year life would be more scientifically fecund?

Even if we suppose that Smuts is right (he is not) and we all ultimately do everything, this would not necessarily mean that we would lose our motivation. First, not everyone would believe that they would "do everything," even if it were true. Many would probably reason like I just did and conclude that no matter how long they live there may be things that only some can do, or will want to do, or will be able to do, or will have the right opportunity to do. Many will not be able to see that far and, even if they do, their emotional response may not be uniformly one of senselessness. Second, many achievements would probably be forgotten, so we would have the pleasure of achieving them again as if for the first time. And is there not some glory in rediscovering something great? Third, the fact that others may also one day achieve what we have achieved does not usually cause apathy. Elite mathematicians do not feel discouraged by the belief that if they do not discover some particular mathematical truth then someone else will. In many cases this belief seems instead to spur them on. They want to be the first, just as the first man on the moon will always be the first man on the moon and the first human on Mars will always be the first human on Mars. Or less egotistically, they just want it done and they happen to be good at it, whatever "it" is.

Not that we normally care about being the first or the only one to achieve something. Most of us do not dream of discovering the next level of modern calculus or of accomplishing anything else on the scale of Newton, Leibniz, or Einstein. We are content with achieving more common things whose universality does not take away from the fact that they are achievements. Finishing high school is an achievement even though all reasonably intelligent people can do it. Being reliable, trustworthy, patient, and loving is an achievement no matter how ordinary. Maintaining a good relationship with one's family and loved ones is another example. All of these achievements remain as challenges, even if one is given an eternity.

If we were immortal would that not make "our achievements . . . hollow victories of mere diligence"? Probably not. What does this even mean in relation to the goal of being a good friend? How can this achievement be "hollow" because it is achieved by diligence? Moreover, it is hard to see how diligence can make up for the lack of other powers. If we equipped our imaginary chimps with an unlimited reservoir of persistence, they would still not compose epic poetry in ancient Greek hexameter. And neither would most of us if similarly enhanced. Nor can we survive on persistence alone in more mundane accomplishments such as maintaining friendships or competing for some good. And why think that an achievement is only a proper achievement if it is a consequence of talent or intelligence and not diligence? Do we not celebrate those who overcome a lack of natural talent by sheer (not "mere") diligence? What if an immortal person, an average Joe, applies himself diligently and for enormous stretches of time to physics and ultimately discovers Einstein's theory of relativity (say that incidentally the only theory to which he had access was Newtonian), would this not be an incredible achievement? Certainly, such diligence should not be described as "mere" diligence because it is rather Herculean in scope.

One might wonder, however, is the thought that immortality would take away the possibility for distinguishing achievements a universally devastating thought or is it just devastating to a certain type of man? Borges appears to have had a horror that his own achievements, his writings, could have been written by someone else, or perhaps every man, even an everyman at some point given enough time. He thinks that he only has a reason to produce them if he knows that only he can. Borges's elitism was notorious. His comment about the beautiful game so deeply loved by Argentinians says it all: "Soccer is popular, because stupidity is popular." But what if we give up on this narcissism and settle for common accomplishments, those that the large majority of people in real life do settle for and are, in fact, highly motivated by? We could turn away from the enterprise of seeking to make ourselves special and take joy and pride in the great accomplishments of our fellow humans. If, for the sake of the argument, we all became one in the sense described by Borges, it would be an apotheosis for many mystics, something to celebrate rather than to fear.

7.7 Banging Our Heads against Epistemic Walls

Smuts argues that our individual and species relative limitations "will inevitably result in endless frustration, since the number of significant projects that one is capable of completing is finite, but the span of time is infinite."[17] Projects would fall into two categories: those that we can complete and those that we cannot complete. Frustration is the result of running out of the first kind and being forever thwarted by the second kind. With calculus as an example, Smuts argues that at a certain point we will have done everything we will ever do in mathematics, and what remains is unsolvable. Hence, we will be endlessly frustrated.

Here is why we must disagree with Smuts. The number of significant projects we can take on is infinite, and the projects themselves, like our quest for knowledge or moral perfection, are often open ended. There will always be more things to learn in an infinite evolving universe. We will never reach the last frontier. And since open-ended projects are never complete, it is not a problem that they are finite in number. Smuts's calculus case represents a particular type of knowledge, the timeless absolute Platonic kind of a priori knowledge, but knowledge can take many other forms. Often it consists in the capacity for synthesizing a multitude of facts into coherent narratives, and there can be a plurality of equally valuable ways of doing this. Other knowledge is emotional, such as the ability of a connoisseur of music to distinguish between the truly original and sublime and imitations thereof, or such as the intelligence needed to read and anticipate other persons' states of mind. This knowledge also appears to lack a precise endpoint. Other important open-ended projects are social and moral. The quest for moral perfection and the struggle to maintain a free and just society are never complete. Unresolvable tensions between values, such as that between freedom and equality, or that between order and chaos, will keep us permanently busy, adjusting society one way and then compensating the other way. The same is true for the tension between the individual and the collective. For the many who are hedonists, the most important project we can undertake is that of being happy and, for those who are utilitarian, the task is to try to ensure happiness and the absence of suffering for all sentient beings; both are clearly open-ended projects. Philosophers such as Plato and Aristotle believe that the most important project to undertake is to "contemplate the heavens." Part of this involved scientific understanding, part of it included a more passive appreciation and reverence for the universe. Perhaps watching snowflakes drift would be a significant project from this point of view.

What about the frustration regarding the existence of impossible projects? Well, first of all, how would we ever know that they are impossible? Even if we cannot solve certain problems, as long as we do not know that they are impossible to solve, we would not necessarily be discouraged. Many would no doubt believe themselves to know the answers to certain riddles, hence they would not suffer from this unknowability. Second, with so much else to occupy ourselves, we would probably be fine with it. To say that frustration is "inevitable" is far too deterministic, as if we did not have a choice in how to respond to the situation. We could, for example, tell ourselves that we are grateful for the mysteries or invent some other way to cope with the existence of impossible-for-us projects. We can just decide not to let unsolvable mysteries frustrate us. In fact, we can already guess that we will never wrap our minds around the concept of infinity, or the gulf between the world as it appears and the world in itself, but these Kantian antinomies are not keeping people awake now; they are not aware of them and, if they are, they do not care, and they probably would not be bothered by them even if they lived a very long time.

Borges's story has an interesting ending. In 1921, off the coast of Eritrea, the hero finds the mortality he seeks. Before this "happy" resolution, he delivers a brief summary of how he has spent his time:

> I travelled over new kingdoms, new empires. In the fall of 1066, I fought at Stamford Bridge, I do not recall whether in the forces of Harold, who was not long in finding his destiny, or in those of the hapless Haralda Hardrada, who conquered six

feet of English soil, or a bit more. In the seventh century of the Hegira, in the sub-urb of Bulaq, I transcribed with measured calligraphy, in a language I have forgot-ten, in an alphabet I do not know, the seven adventures of Sinbad and the history of the City of Bronze. In the courtyard of a jail in Samarkand I played a great deal of chess. In Bikaner I professed the science of astrology and also in Bohemia. In 1683 I was at Kolozsvar and later in Leipzig. In Aberdeen, in 1714 I subscribed to the six volumes of Pope's Iliad; I know that I frequented the pages with delight.[18]

Does this sound so bad? Does this not sound like an amazing life? If he had just hung on for another couple of centuries, he could have experienced the modern acceleration of history. He would have seen the first man on the moon. Today he could sit in front of his computer and blog about his storied past; it was a poor decision to end his life before the internet.[19]

7.8   The Threat of a Deadline

No little part of the torment of existence lies in this, that Time is continually pressing upon us, never letting us take a breath, but always coming after us, like a taskmaster with a whip.[20]
—Schopenhauer

It's like a hammer banging at the door, eventually you feel like it's going to break through. . . . You have to hold back the door and just not let that come to you.[21]
—Roger Federer

Herbert Spencer, who coined the phrase "survival of the fittest," nearly gave up on his aspirations because he thought he would fail to meet the final deadline:

When, in 1858, he was revising his essays for collective publication, he was struck by the unity and sequence of the ideas he had expressed; and the notion came to him, like sunlight through opened doors, that the theory of evolution might be applied in every science as well as in biology; that it could explain not only species and genera but planets and strata, social and political history, moral and esthetic conceptions. He was fired with the thought of a series of works in which he would show the evolution of matter and mind from nebula to man, and from savage to Shakespeare. But he nearly despaired when he thought of his nearly forty years. How could one man, so old . . . traverse all the sphere of human knowledge before his death?[22]

By a great amount of luck—he achieved twice the life expectancy of his age—Spencer was able to complete 10 volumes of his grand evolutionary

theory and thereby lay the foundation for the wide application of evolutionary thinking, including the kind that informed our discussion of the
existential arguments against prolonging life. His *Principles of Psychology*
introduced the notion of applying a biological perspective to our study of
the mind. If he had lived another 100 years, he would have seen the discovery of the double helix, the decoding of the human genome, and an
empirical turn in philosophy, realizing his dream of a greater cooperation
among the disciplines. He could have read E. O. Wilson's *Consilience* and
felt vindicated. More than that, he would have been able to participate
in, collaborate upon, invent, and teach new ideas, bringing to the table a
unique and irreplaceable historical point of view. He could have shown up
at TED talks and entertained us with stories about the science and politics
of the Victorian age. Spencer was fortunate that, despite his fragile consti-
tution, nature permitted him to live long enough to complete his grand
project. Other creative minds were less lucky. It is more common that they
leave unfinished symphonies, heaps of drafts, and lists of future undertakings. How would the world be different if Leonardo da Vinci had been given
enough time to invent and realize all of which he was capable? What we
have is but a sliver of his full potential.

We have moved away from the time where the ordinary human being
would have had her course staked out for her since birth, a time when if
one's father was a farmer then one, too, would be a farmer, as would one's
son, and so on. We now enjoy much more freedom to shape our lives.
Young people today foresee undertaking a string of different projects and
positions throughout the course of their lives. They may work in finance
and then become a farmer and then own a store, and so on. It looks like
we, sensibly, adjust our level of aspiration to the time available. With more
time, we would not only be able to complete grander projects, but we could
undertake a greater number. This is not only true for creative geniuses, but
for all of us. I once had a student in my class who, in his mid-thirties, was
hesitating to take the long educational road required to become a physician. For many, the ultimate deadline prevents them from changing careers
to something closer to their heart, perhaps. People settle into mediocrity
because they feel that there is not enough time to change track; the time
constraint tempts us to walk down a path that is not our true destiny.
Their awareness, on some level, of their mortality makes them aspire to
less, not more. Indeed, is it not one of the most unpleasant things about

being alive today the many worthwhile paths we would take if we only had more time? A person may be faced with the choice of becoming a musician or a lawyer or a mother. She picks one and feels something missing; she tries to pick everything, and she is running around playing catch-up. Despite having added 30 years to our life expectancy over the last century, we still feel short of time. One might argue that we should just focus and manage our time better. Seneca, for example, famously claimed that, "It is not that we have so little time but that we lose so much. . . . The life we receive is not short but we make it so; we are not ill provided but use what we have wastefully."[23] It is less often noticed that Seneca also thought that almost everything that we generally like to do is wasteful. We should, ideally, spend most of our time alone with our thoughts and if that is what we want to do, we will find that there is plenty of time. Since few but the wise philosophers would agree with this prioritization, time remains in short supply. The time-management literature is a manifestation of this dearth. Anyone who is not a type-A personality will not be able to optimize their time. Besides, would it not be nice to procrastinate a bit more? We like to procrastinate because when we do, we often do things we enjoy doing more than the important task at hand. Procrastination can be fun. It can also be useful because we may need the time for thoughts to settle.

We hear about these great achievers, perhaps we want to be them. But do we really? How often did they play with their children? Did they keep in touch with family? Were they attentive to their partners? Which parts of themselves did they fail to cultivate? Those illustrious names we venerate often neglected their health, their family and friends, and so much else in order to achieve greatness. Many are special talent monomaniacs on a spectrum of Asperger's and autism. As argued above, the value of an activity is not constituted by the sacrifices made on its behalf and the time constraint we are under forces us to make tragic decisions. As an illustration of this point, consider the popular debate about whether women "can have it all." This usually refers to the challenge of taking on a high-pressure job as well as the role of being a mother at the same time. This situation has created an industry of books about how to manage these different roles: strategies, tactics, shortcuts, lean-in-and go-for-it-sister -isms. There are political calls for supporting dad-at-home policies and more access to daycare. There are, though, no easy answers here. A work-life balance proves elusive. In 2012, Anne-Marie Slaughter, former director of planning for the US State

Department, offered a reality check in a widely noted *Atlantic Monthly* article titled, "Why Women Still Can't Have It All." Here is an excerpt:

> On a Wednesday evening, President and Mrs. Obama hosted a glamorous reception at the American Museum of Natural History. I sipped champagne, greeted foreign dignitaries, and mingled. But I could not stop thinking about my 14-year-old son, who had started eighth grade three weeks earlier and was already resuming what had become his pattern of skipping homework, disrupting classes, failing math, and tuning out any adult who tried to reach him. Over the summer, we had barely spoken to each other—or, more accurately, he had barely spoken to me. And the previous spring I had received several urgent phone calls—invariably on the day of an important meeting—that required me to take the first train from Washington, D.C., where I worked, back to Princeton, New Jersey, where he lived. My husband, who has always done everything possible to support my career, took care of him and his 12-year-old brother during the week; outside of those mid-week emergencies, I came home only on weekends.[24]

This is what life can be like for a woman who has made it. And this is someone successful, whom young women want to emulate. From the outside her life looks glorious; from the inside it is a different story. Slaughter continues:

> I was increasingly aware that the feminist beliefs on which I had built my entire career were shifting under my feet. I had always assumed that if I could get a foreign-policy job in the State Department or the White House while my party was in power, I would stay the course as long as I had the opportunity to do work I loved. But in January 2011, when my two-year public-service leave from Princeton University was up, I hurried home as fast as I could. . . . I'd been the woman congratulating herself on her unswerving commitment to the feminist cause, chatting smugly with her dwindling number of college or law-school friends who had reached and maintained their place on the highest rungs of their profession. I'd been the one telling young women at my lectures that you can have it all and do it all, regardless of what field you are in. Which means I'd been part, albeit unwittingly, of making millions of women feel that they are to blame if they cannot manage to rise up the ladder as fast as men and also have a family and an active home life (and be thin and beautiful to boot).

One moral might be that we should make it easier for women to be both mothers and successful professionals. The other moral is that life is too short. Think about the philosophers' claim that our projects derive their value from their opportunity cost and how wrongheaded this idea is when applied to the choice between one's career and family. Slaughter's career did not become more valuable because she could not be with her sons; rather, it was compromised by it. Both roles turned into sources of guilt and feelings of insufficiency. The problem was not that she wanted a career and that she wanted children. The problem was that it had to happen within an all-too-short time span as she is racing against entropy. More time would not remove all painful trade-offs, but it would remove many of the more inhuman ones. It is, of course, not just women who are under an inhuman time pressure; any ambitious person is. In a 2015 piece, Slaughter expands her considerations to encompass not just women but everyone.[25] A memorable passage describes how, at the funeral of the late top diplomat Richard Holbrooke, his son admits to not having known or seen his father much. These are the forced sacrifices of brutal time pressure.

We do not see it because it is part of the framing condition of our lives, but the time constraint of mortality is often our chief problem. Nothing more than another twenty years in our prime would allow us to undo many poor choices and compensate for the effect of an unfortunate beginning. It is said that youth is wasted on the young, but we cannot blame the young. The tragedy is that we do not learn how to live until most of life has already passed and many doors have already been closed to us. We either have too little experience behind us, or too little time ahead of us. With more time we could have both children and a career, the poor could become rich, the ignorant could become knowledgeable, the knowledgeable could become wise, and everyone could try on more roles to find out what they are really good at. Under the current time pressures most of us have to make a tragic choice between being narrow and specialized or broad and unsuccessful.

7.9   Life Is Short So . . . What?

> Then I commended mirth, because a man hath no better thing under the sun, than to eat, and to drink, and to be merry.
> —*Ecclesiastes*

There is an abundance of bon mots of the form: life is short so . . . They most often implore us to "to make the most of our life" and be appreciative of each day. We should love more, be more aware of consequences, be less worried about what people think of us, dream bigger, take action today, risk mistakes but not repeat them, live each day as if this is our last, and so on. We have only one shot at life, and we therefore need to be mindful that we leave behind a life testifying to the best of which we were capable, a life of moral conscientiousness and accomplishments. It is as if we are writing a book and the first draft must be of publishable quality. This is what the apologist writers we have just discussed have in mind.

Others may interpret "live each day as if it were your last" in a different way. They might see it as a reason to take life less seriously. "To eat, drink, and be merry" or as Kesha, a half-forgotten pop princess, sings,

> This is all we got and then it's gone
> You call us the crazy ones
> But we gon' keep on dancin' 'til the dawn.
>   . . . [26]

If all lives are rapidly vanishing into an abyss, then why not abandon oneself to the moment rather than build a legacy, since it is soon to be forgotten. Or is this her way of taking life seriously? Are the "crazy ones" those serious people she walks past in the morning as she stumbles home from her dance party? Certainly, Kesha would not be alone in drawing this lesson from the fact that life is short. People with entirely different personalities and proclivities from hers can sometimes feel that the ephemeral nature of life undermines the value of their efforts. Imagine a scholar who wonders why she should keep cramming knowledge into her brain when it is destined to be consumed by worms long before her intellectual work is done. What is the point, she asks herself, of reading all those books when the internal world she is painfully constructing is scheduled for demolition tomorrow? What about the French she learned? What was the point, when the opportunities she dreamt of to practice it are vanishing? She could read Proust's *À La Recherche Du Temps Perdu* and perhaps it would give her epiphanies about how to live, but what is the use when many of her life choices have already closed most doors to her and there is so little time left to live? What is the point in achieving something and aspiring to do so if everything turns to nothing, not even a memory, just silence?

Our possible responses are underdetermined. Sometimes we think the fact that we are soon dead puts pressure on us to achieve something sooner rather than later; at other times the thought that it is all over soon is seen as a reminder not to take life too seriously. We vacillate between two contrary attitudes, and there is therefore no good reason for thinking that a belief that one will soon die is necessary to avoid procrastination or for finding life valuable and meaningful.

8 Mortality, Character, Virtue, and Moral Excellence

8.1 Immortals Cannot Be Noble

It is common to think that living longer is selfish and immoral: that it is taking more than one's fair share, and it contributes to overpopulation and various social ills. Philosophers have also argued that our moral virtues depend on our mortality. Kass writes,

> [T]here is the peculiarly human beauty of character, virtue and moral excellence. To be mortal means that it is possible to give one's life, not only in one moment, say, on the field of battle, but also in the many other ways in which we are able in action to rise above attachment to survival. Through moral courage, endurance, greatness of soul, generosity, devotion to justice—in acts great and small—we rise above our mere creatureliness, spending the precious coinage of the time of our lives for the sake of the noble and the good and the holy. We free ourselves from fear, from bodily pleasures, or from attachments to wealth—all largely connected with survival—and in doing virtuous deeds overcome the weight of our neediness; yet for this nobility, vulnerability and mortality are the necessary conditions. The immortals cannot be noble.[1]

True to his style, Kass reaches back to Homer to exemplify the connection between virtue and mortality. In the Odyssey, Odysseus is offered immortality by the beautiful nymph Calypso. However, Odysseus rejects the offer:

> Goddess and Queen, do not be angry with me. I myself know that all you say is true and that circumspect Penelope can never match the impression you make for beauty and stature. She is mortal after all, and you are immortal and ageless. But even so, what I want and all my days I pine for is to go back to my house and see that day of my homecoming. And if some god batters me far out on the wine-blue water, I will endure it, keeping a stubborn spirit inside me, for already I have suffered much and done much hard work on the waves and in the fighting.[2]

Kass believes that, like Odysseus, we face the choice of virtue and moral excellence on one side and the siren song of ageless immortality on the other. According to Kass we cannot have both, since without death there can be no courage, no endurance, no greatness of soul, no devotion to justice, and no rising above our creatureliness.

8.2   Immortals Can Be Noble

Our question is: Is moral excellence possible for an immortal? Let us begin by considering Kass's key example, courage. Courage is usually defined as the ability to do something that frightens one and having strength in the face of adversity. Since many things besides death frighten us and adversity need not be deadly, courage is obviously possible for immortals. The everlasting punishments of Sisyphus (pushing up a rock), Tithonus (senility), Tantalus (frustration), and Prometheus (an eagle pecking at his liver) show that the risks and, correspondingly, the possible sacrifice can be higher under a condition of immortality. The stakes are higher when you risk eternal punishment rather than simply death. Kass's reference to the choice of Homer's Odysseus—love or immortality—also misses the target, since our choice would not be between life and love but rather between life and love, on the one hand, and aging and death, on the other; between immortality where we can be forever with those we love and mortality where we will rapidly lose everyone we love, and they us.

Another proposed connection between death and virtue suggests that without the threat of death we would all be liars. American philosopher William R. Clark writes, "In a world where no one would be required to keep their word [by threat of death], no words are more than wind."[3] Clark implicitly references Thomas Hobbes's claim that in a state of nature, defined as a time where there is no power that we all fear, our promises to each other are empty because we have nothing more to fear from breaking them than each other's imperfect power to punish such a breach. Fear of death in this picture is the beginning of morality because it forces us to make a compact of peace. Clark suggests that without fear of death, we would have no reason to make the compact, and hence we would have no reason not to lie (and rob and steal and so on by extension). Again, this seems like an unwarranted worry. The Hobbesian state of nature with its poverty and continual threat of violence would be worth bargaining our way out of even if we were immortal. If we want more than to merely survive and to get what we want, we need to collaborate and follow certain rules. Once we are a part of a society, we must be careful not to be known as a liar because it would exclude us from the benefits of cooperation. Sellers on eBay are honest not because they fear that they will be killed if they misrepresent their products, but because they fear that bad reviews will kill their business. In most cases, lying is simply not worth it to us. The Hobbesian self-interested reasons for being honest are one path to honesty and other virtues, are generally favored by contract theorists, and they expand to cover all virtues. Vicious and otherwise immoral actions make enemies rather than friends and, therefore, prevent us from reaping the benefits of cooperation. If we wish to live and prosper, we should wish to remain morally decent. Moral philosophers have proposed several other avenues to virtue and right action. Plato, Kant, and other moral rationalists hold that reason can tell us to respect others, just as reason can tell us that a straight line is the shortest distance between two points. Plato believes that we can grasp the form of the Good with our minds, and Kant believes that acting immorally embodies a contradiction: If we act in a way that violates what we would want to be the law governing all rational beings, then we are in conflict with ourselves. And if we treat people as if they have no other value than as an instrument for our desires, then we are confusing people with inanimate objects. In either case, we are irrational. A third answer places virtue in our emotions. This is the favored view of more empirically minded philosophers such as David Hume and contemporary moral psychologist Jonathan Haidt.[4] They argue that we have a natural compassion that in the right circumstances will lead us to be morally good. This compassion is a consequence of having to take care of our very vulnerable offspring. We may also, according to Haidt, have an innate natural capacity for making judgments concerning what is just and fair, what loyalty to our community demands, whom to submit to, and what to regard as sacred. These judgments are given shape by experience, similar to how we are all equipped with the capacity to speak a language, but what particular language we speak depends on where we grow up. Finally, a Christian perspective would say that the moral law is written in our hearts, and that we are equipped with a moral conscience. None of these four accounts gives us any reason to predict that moral virtue would be impossible if we were immortal.

Further support for the view that we would be moral even under some form of longevity or even immortality can be garnered from the psychology of the self and personal identity. The previous chapter detailed how Kagan did not want to live on if living on meant becoming Jo-Jo, who did not care about the downtrodden. Kagan is not alone in this sentiment. Studies have shown that people are more disposed to think they could survive a complete amnesia about who they are than they are to think that they could survive a complete reversal of their moral values.[5] Our moral values are an important part of who we understand ourselves to be. Once we become socialized in a certain world of values, we seek to associate with those who share them and distance ourselves from those who do not. We avoid close interactions with people who have differing values, not only because we disagree with them, but because they threaten our identities. This means that the desire to protect the integrity of our self (understanding) and the role a moral community plays in this gives us an additional reason to suppose that moral virtue does not generally depend on the threat of death or the possibility of dying.

It also does not appear that the thought that life is short has any generally morally edifying import. There is an online dating website called "Ashley Madison" whose niche is facilitating married people having affairs with each other. Its slogan is, "Life is short; have an affair." The people behind this site consider the brevity of life as a reason to be less morally serious. Who will care a hundred years from now? This once more takes us back to the point about underdetermination. People will draw different practical conclusions from whether life is short or in fact far longer. Far more important are the thoughts about punishments and rewards in an afterlife.

8.3   Is Wanting to Live a Character Flaw?

One of the most common attacks on the prolongevists' character is that we are suffering from excessive self-love and greed for life. Are we? Only if it is excessive to love oneself enough to want to continue living, and it is not. If, as Kant taught, we are irreplaceable as individuals and possess an intrinsic value, then self-preservation is the morally correct attitude. (Kant was strongly against suicide.) Existence is a miracle and not something to throw away after a couple of decades. Moreover, it is not as if prolongevists are only concerned with their own existence. As this book attests, they are keen to persuade others that they too would benefit from living longer. We want our families, our friends, and people in general to live longer and healthier lives. The accusation of selfishness is therefore baseless.[6] The allegation that we are greedy simply begs the question. If wanting more life is an appropriate attitude given the value of life, then it cannot be greedy to want it. We do not want too much life. Rather, we simply want the right amount of it, which happens to be much, much more than what we have. If life is good, then there is nothing shameful about wanting to preserve it. We do not have to excuse ourselves for choosing life over death. If we wanted, we could easily turn the tables on the apologists. We could, for example, accuse them of not fully appreciating the great gift of life, of being dull since they claim that they would quickly be bored if they lived longer, of being cruel because they want us to suffer all the pain and humiliation of aging, of being intellectually dishonest because they whitewash all the harm for which aging and death is responsible, of failing to respect the worth of the individual by their trivializing of death, of being cowards for not daring to admit that death is both inevitable and terrible, or of thoughtlessly and irresponsibly standing in the way of saving billions of lives and preventing enormous amounts of suffering. Nevertheless, apologists are not bad people. They are decent people who cannot stomach the truth that unless heaven awaits, they are heading toward a grim end.

The Wise View presents itself as morally and intellectually superior. These sophisticates have made peace with aging and death and are therefore wiser and nobler than the great unwashed. This pretense is ever present in the ancient philosophers, who see themselves as approaching godliness while the commoners' lives are barely worth living. Kass follows in this tradition: "The virtues of finitude—if there are any—may never be widely appreciated in any age or culture," Kass writes, "if appreciation depends on a certain wisdom, if wisdom requires a certain detachment from the love of oneself and one's own, and if the possibility of such detachment is given only to the few."[7] But this perception is false. As I noted before, if you ask someone if they think that death is bad, they will most likely say no, it would be boring to live longer, and it's natural to die, they just want to see their grandkids grow up, and not have a painful death, and so on. Philosophers, sages, and religious figures of every age and culture have taught that death is nothing to fear, and people have listened and accepted this ideology at least on some level (even if, as I have argued, a fair amount of self-delusion is a part of the acceptance). To say that one accepts death is a quick and easy way to be admired as a virtuous and wise person. It is the position that everyone is comfortable with. The rebel's naïve insistence that youth and life is much better is an unwelcome threat to the anxiety-reducing truce that has been made with death.

9 Death Is the Mother of Beauty

9.1 Love and Beauty Depend on Death

There is a popular website called *Quora*, where users type in questions—any question at all—and then other users answer it, and also vote for the best answer. Someone asked: "Is death beautiful?"[1] A top answer was: "Dying is the purest form of Beauty." Someone else asked: "What makes death beautiful?" The most popular answers included: "death can be beautiful if a person dies in a good or meaningful way"; "Death is lovely since it speaks to change . . . dying is the most flawless type of Beauty" and "Love makes death beautiful." Another user asked: What is more beautiful, life or death? The most popular answer was: "Both are equally beautiful from their respective perspective. However, dying . . . is perhaps the most beautiful of all." Judging by the answers on *Quora*, it is normal to find death beautiful. Kass goes even further and speculates that death may also be both an ultimate cause and a necessary condition for beauty as such.

> Death, says Wallace Stevens, is the mother of beauty. . . . Perhaps he means that only a mortal being, aware of his mortality and the transience and vulnerability of all natural things, is moved to make beautiful artifacts, objects that will last, objects whose order will be immune to decay as their maker is not . . . Perhaps the poet means to speak of natural beauty as well, which beauty—unlike that of objects of art—depends on its impermanence. Could the beauty of flowers depend on the fact that they will soon wither? Does the beauty of spring warblers depend upon the fall drabness that precedes and follows? What about the fading, late afternoon winter light or the spreading sunset? Is the beautiful necessarily fleeting, a peak that cannot be sustained? Or does the poet mean not that the beautiful is beautiful because mortal, but that our appreciation of its beauty depends on our appreciation of mortality—in us and in the beautiful? Does not

love swell before the beautiful precisely on recognizing that it (and we) will not always be? . . . How deeply could one deathless "human" being love another?[2]

We can abstract four distinct propositions from Kass's cloud of rhetorical questions:

a. we make beautiful things because we are aware of our mortality;
b. the beauty of natural things depends on their impermanence;
c. the appreciation of beauty, both natural and artificial, is connected to our awareness of its and our own decay; and
d. we can only love each other because we are aware of our mortality.

We will begin by investigating the first three propositions (a–c) regarding aesthetics and then turn to proposition (d) regarding love. Since this is the last of the spiritual arguments in favor of death, the chapter ends with a reflection on the common fallacies of apologist arguments.

9.2   Does Beauty Depend on Death?

What is beauty? The ancients believed that we respond to harmonious proportions whether in the human form or in art and architecture. The Parthenon and the Discobolus of Myron are reminders of this ideal. Plato philosophized that each beautiful thing is a realization of an eternal abstract idea of the beautiful, perfect beauty. What we admire in these things is that they remind us of this idea. Empiricist philosophers of the Enlightenment agreed with the ancient Greeks that we are naturally disposed to approve of certain forms as pleasing and find them beautiful. In "On the Standards of Taste," written in 1757, David Hume explains that the reason why we admire the art of the ancients is that "general principles of taste are uniform in human nature," and he suggests that aesthetic value can be defined as those forms that survive "the test of time."[3] Today, evolutionary aesthetics, a branch of evolutionary psychology, explains our sense of beauty as an adaptation. Studies reveal that we prefer facial symmetry and pronounced sex-typical traits:

> An attractive man, in the eyes of female experimental participants, is generally one with relatively prominent cheekbones and eyebrow ridges and a relatively long lower face. Likewise, prominent cheekbones, large eyes, a small nose, a taller forehead, smooth skin, and an overall young or even childlike appearance add to women's allure in the eyes of male raters.[4]

What these features have in common is that they are indicators of good genes. People with these visual traits really are better to mate with. Choosing them means picking offspring who will be most successful in perpetuating your DNA.[5] Recently, it has been suggested that our preference for certain kinds of representations of landscapes may also have an evolutionary origin:

> When young children from different nations are asked to select which landscape they prefer, from a selection of standardized landscape photographs, there is a strong preference for savannas with trees. The East African savanna is the ancestral environment in which much of human evolution is argued to have taken place. There is also a preference for landscapes with water, with both open and wooded areas, with trees with branches at a suitable height for climbing and taking foods, with features encouraging exploration such as a path or river curving out of view, with seen or implied game animals, and with some clouds. These are all features that are often featured in calendar art and in the design of public parks.[6]

All universally loved landscapes have this in common: they would be good habitats. We think certain landscapes are appealing because such a preference helped our Pleistocene ancestors survive. Wallace Stevens may ponder that "death is the mother of beauty," but the truth is precisely the opposite.[7] Our sense of beauty reliably tracks that which gives and preserves life. Whether we believe that beauty is a platonic form, or an innate sentiment shaped by culture, beauty is found in form rather than in temporality and we can therefore answer Kass as follows,

1. The impermanence of objects is not generally part of their beauty. The spring warblers excite us when they show up after a "drab fall," to advertise the advent of a milder season, but it would be a mistake to say their beauty is best explained by the fact that their appearance is of limited duration. After all, the same could be said about mosquitos. Rather, their beauty is better explained by their cute round shape and their luminous yellow and blue plumage. If, as a thought experiment, some of the warblers were eternal and some remained during fall, they would both presumably be equally beautiful if they looked the same. It would be odd to say that some of these warblers—although indistinguishable from the others—are not beautiful, because they are imperishable.

2. Planets and stars, oceans and mountains, diamonds and gold are no less beautiful because they are lasting. The beautiful is therefore manifestly

not, as Kass claims, "necessarily fleeting, a peak that cannot be sustained."[8] The beautiful can be lasting. It is our attention to the beautiful that is fleeting and hard to sustain.

3. It is not essential to think about our own mortality when appreciating beauty. Responses to, say, a beautiful face, are instinctive and would not invariably trigger thoughts of one's own mortality. As for beautiful artifacts, our mortality also does not seem to play a necessary role. If you want to persuade someone that a certain thing is beautiful (e.g., a painting), you will point to pleasing aspects of it; you will not remind them of their death or tell them how the object will outlive them.

In sum, the major theories of beauty all imply that permanence/impermanence play no essential part in our appreciation of beauty. Rather they suggest in different ways that there are certain properties or universals, like symmetry, or the golden mean, or certain colors, that please us. This is not to say that death never plays a role in the experience of beauty. Death is a major theme in art and is the central experience in genres such as dark romanticism, gothics, and death metal. Death and decay certainly endow beauty with a certain anxious and melancholic bitterness, such as how, when in the moment of the greatest joy, we suddenly feel the pain of realizing that it is soon passing, and we cannot hold on to it no matter how hard we try. As the poet John Hall Wheelock observes in his "Song of Reaching Seventy,"

Oh, now
Before the coming of a greater night
How bitterly sweet and dear all things have grown! How shall we bear the brunt,
The fury and joy of every sound and sight,
Now almost cruelly fierce with all delight
. . . .[9]

Such feelings of bitter sweetness and the pain of a foreknowledge that all loves are vanishing into the black waters of darkness will no doubt impose themselves less in a world without death, but they would not necessarily entirely cease. Death and decay are not the only ways to experience loss, and all those other ways would remain. It may also be a relief to appreciate beauty without bitter sweetness. Kass worries that we would not relate to art created in reaction to mortality, but this is underrating our imagination. An immortal could understand the tragedy of Romeo and Juliet even if they themselves cannot die, in the same way that an enslaved person can know what it means to be free, or a poor person can imagine what it would be like to be rich. Death therefore does not have to continue to be a threat in order for us to appreciate art that was created in response to this threat. And even if the real threat of death is necessary for certain aesthetic experiences, it is, as we have seen, not necessary for the experience of beauty as such.

9.3   Mortality and the Motivation to Make Beautiful Objects

Kass thinks that we create art to preserve beauty and symbolically immortalize ourselves. This resonates as true. Wanting to capture beauty and create a legacy, something that remains after we are no longer in this world, is a common human motivation. However, it is not the only reason why we create art. Temporary objects of beauty such as table arrangements, ice art, fireworks, and so on, cannot be explained in terms of wanting to create something that outlasts us. Hence, there must be other reasons to create beauty. Three reasons come to mind: First, beauty pleases us. This may even be a necessary truth since it is only because some things please us aesthetically that we have a concept of beauty. Second, making beautiful things can bring us money, glory, and the attention of a potential mate.[10] The esteem of other people is one of the major motives for any action. Third, making beautiful things is fun and self-realizing. A world of immortals would likely be a world where the creation of beauty would be even more important than it is for mortals. Beauty, alongside the pursuit of knowledge, would serve as a worthy, open-ended activity added to the enjoyment of living for those with so much time on their hands. We could ask our own rhetorical questions back at Kass: Could it be that death is not the mother of beauty but its destroyer? Could it be that beauty is lost because of the grinding entropy of aging and death? Have you seen Bridget Bardot lately? A few years ago, I went to a Steely Dan concert at the Radio City Music Hall. It was wonderful. Soon thereafter Walter Becker died. Why do poets not write about how death destroys beauty and those who create it? Why this need to always excuse death?

9.4   Can an Immortal Love an Immortal?

Kass asks, "How deeply could one deathless 'human' being love another?" We could approach this question from an evolutionary point of view with the predictable conclusion that love is deeply embedded in our nature, motivating us to form bonds of trust for raising children and collaborate in other ways. Therefore, love is not likely to vanish over time or in the presence of a belief that we are immortal. But what else could we say? If Kass speaks of natural, erotic love then why think that two healthy immortals could not have this? Of course, this kind of love rarely lasts more than a couple of years, so immortality would leave things as they are. In any case, Kass more likely speaks of a spiritual connection, a deep form of loving friendship. This kind of love, he has already admitted, is capable of unlimited evolution; so he has, in effect, already answered his own question: immortals could love each other. But how long can love last? It is impossible to know. We would have to adapt to more time, and it is hard to predict how we would structure and manage loving relationships. Perhaps we would have to take breaks from each other, or perhaps we would spiritually merge so deeply over time that we would be inseparable. There would probably be a great deal of individual variation here. Let us leave it as an open question whether love can last forever. What is clear is that we have no persuasive grounds for doubting that immortals could love each other.

Once more we can ask our own rhetorical questions: Is not death the enemy of love just as it is the enemy of beauty? Why would our love for someone depend on their decay and death? Is this not rather bittersweet and does it not have a cloud hanging over it? Is not to love someone to say that it is good that they exist? It is, for instance, almost unthinkable to us that our parents will die, yet this horror awaits with merciless certainty. The pain of losing a loved one is unbearable to some. Remember how the Stoics advised detachment and recognition that like ceramic cups, your wife and children will break, so do not be "in the least disturbed" when they do.[11] Such a wise superhuman detachment would probably shield a person and make them emotionally bulletproof, but does it not also make love impossible? Is it not like saying, *do not love, because what you love will die?* Death has the potential to destroy love, not only by destroying a loved one, but by justifying the defense mechanism of a radical Stoic detachment. Immortals, then, might love each other better for the absence of this fear of loss. In any case there is no realistic obstacle to such love. This is where I leave Kass and the discussion of the most important spiritual arguments in favor of death based on alleged death-dependent values and our presumed inability to handle a longer life. Before continuing to a different class of arguments—appeals to the negative social consequences of prolonging life—I will derive some general lessons.

9.5   Eight Common Fallacies of Spiritual Arguments in Favor of Death and Decay

We have responded to four categories of arguments in favor of death that speculate about the various adverse psychological effects of longevity and immortality, which I have called spiritual arguments. We took as our starting point Kass's formulation of these arguments, but they are not his original arguments. Rather they are perennial aspects of the Wise View. A common weakness—a fallacy—of these arguments is that while being psychological hypotheses, they do not consider what we know about the human mind. There is nothing wrong with being inspired by poems and old apologist myths but claims about how we are likely to react to an absence caused by death and about the role death plays in our minds should consider what our best scientific understanding tells us.

There are several other recurring fallacies of apologist arguments:

The second is the failure of relevance. By speaking of absolute immortality when what is at issue is life extension and, at its limit, contingent immortality, the apologists' arguments fail to be relevant to the issue of life extension. Conclusions about what would be the case if we were unable to die do not necessarily extend to more realistic cases. We can, for example, agree that an immortal could not demonstrate courage by sacrificing his life (obviously), but this has nothing to do with courage in any realistic condition of longevity, or even under the condition of contingent immortality. Another example of the failure of relevance is when the immortal is assumed to be unique, as was the case in the story about Elina. This introduces problems that are not necessarily a part of immortality as such, and hence prevents us from generalizing from these cases.

The third is the problem of overgeneralization. As we have seen, apologists are quick to extrapolate from isolated cases. To stay with our example of courage, the impossibility for an immortal to sacrifice their life is used to support the much broader claim that courage as such would be impossible, as well as the even wider claim that all moral excellence depends on death. Another example is their tendency to think that everyone would react the same way to their imagined scenarios: for example, that we would all be alienated and suffer from ennui if we lived a couple of hundred years, rather than admitting that it is possible that some of us would and others would not.

Special pleading is the fourth fallacy. Often only cases supporting their argument are mentioned and counterinstances are ignored. For instance, Kass mentions sunsets and spring warbles to support the view that impermanence makes something beautiful, but he fails to mention the many near-permanent features of nature we find beautiful, such as stars and diamonds.

False dilemma is the fifth fallacy. Their arguments often give us a choice between either losing something of value (for example, interest, virtue, beauty, and love) or accepting that we die within our natural limit. However, this ignores that a better alternative could be to decide for ourselves when to die. For example, we can agree with Kass that we will one day get bored, but we need one more argument to show us that we should not ourselves decide when to die.

The sixth misstep is vagueness. It is often left unclear whether the apologists mean to say that it is the presence of a belief in our death or whether it is the absence of a belief in our immortality that is supposed to be a blessing. For example, is it the belief that we are going to die that makes us enjoy being with our friends and family, playing tennis, or listening to music, or is it the fact that we do not believe we are immortal that supposedly makes us enjoy these activities? Do we have to be aware of our mortality, or is it enough that we are not aware of our immortality? Furthermore, is the negative effect of thinking that we will not die or live much longer supposed immediately to make us bored, disinterested, loveless, lawless, and be liars? This would be the case if an awareness of death is "the condition for treasuring and appreciating all that life brings us."[12] Once we no longer have that condition in place, we would not be able to treasure and appreciate life. Or is the claim rather that over time life would lose its value? This sounds more plausible. But the question now is *when*? If the apologists' arguments are to have any bearing on current debates about life extension, then we need to know if the effects can be expected to happen after 100 years, 200 years, 10,000 years, or later. Sometimes we are given numbers, a 25 percent longer tennis career, 15 more years climbing ladders, a 300-year potion, and so on, but there is no systematic commitment to a timeframe here. Unless we are given some approximate timeframe, we can agree that someday in some very distant future, our lives are likely not to be worth living, but we insist that until then death is not a blessing.

Seventh, predictions of what belief that we are immortal/absence of a belief that we are mortal would do to our psyche has the systematic weakness that such beliefs would be unjustified. Barring supernatural intervention, we could never know that we cannot die. We can only know that we have been alive so far. This is an application of the problem of induction: it cannot give us necessary truths. The problem for their argument is this: If we cannot know that we are immortal, and if it makes us miserable to think that we are immortal, then we would probably stop believing that we are immortal, and therefore it would not be able to maintain its alleged corrosive power over us. (Besides, in a realistic scenario we would have nothing more than an indefinitely long life span, and hence whatever beneficial effects mortality is thought to have would remain.)

Eighth fallacy. Apologists often ignore an essential trait of humans: our ingenuity. Speculations about the psychological effects of altering our beliefs about death and longevity must consider that we are not passive bystanders of these effects. Why think that it would be harder for us to accommodate to contingent immortality than it has been to adapt to our current state of imminent mortality?

9.6   Speaking Nonsense to Desires

Imagine slipping a pill of contingent immortality into the coffee of a true believer of the Wise View, such as Kass. Upon realizing that he is now contingently immortal and can live for as long as he wants or as long as he is accident-free, his first reaction might be one of bewilderment: What now prevents me from postponing every undertaking? How will I now be able to enjoy spring warblers and sunsets? How can I love my family and friends? What reason do I have for not being a liar and a murderer? My life is meaningless! At first he would be confused, but is it not reasonable to suppose that given time, he would adapt and find a way to make the best of his new freedom? In any realistic scenario he would not be the sole immortal but belong to a community sharing this new human condition. Together with other longer living people he would develop intelligent ways to cope with more time. Perhaps one strategy would be denial. They would not think or talk too much about how long their lives have the potential to be but focus

on living day to day, year to year. Mindfulness practitioners would not let
the big perspective detract from the moment. Perhaps they would exaggerate the likelihood that they would be killed in an accident and low-ball
their life expectancy. "Don't worry, you will probably be hit by a bus before
your 500th birthday. In fact, you might die today, or tomorrow!" If, despite
adapting a new ethos that fits with his contingent immortality, Kass still
cannot find spring warblers and sunsets beautiful in the absence of a looming death, perhaps some form of cognitive therapy, meditation, or drugs
would restore this ability.

To be honest, I do not think that an erudite, productive, and successful
man such as Kass would have any problems adapting to having his youthful vigor restored. I am sure he has a long reading list, projects to do, and
people to see. Consider how he starts off his argument: "Against my own
strong love of life, and against my even stronger wish that no more of my
loved ones should die, I aspire to speak truth to my desires by showing
that the finitude of human life is a blessing for every human individual,
whether he knows it or not."[13] I propose that the truth is that there is nothing wrong with his "strong love of life" and his "even stronger wish that
no more of [his] loved ones should die." These are natural, healthy, honest,
and reasonable attitudes. The "truth" that he wishes to speak against them
and in favor of death and decay is the untruth. Death is not, unless heaven
awaits, bliss. Kass, like all proponents of the Wise View, desperately wants
a nontragic ending, when the truth is that, if death is final, then we are all
heading toward a personal disaster.

10 Death Saves Us from Overpopulation

There must needs be substance that the generations to come may grow.
—Lucretius, *De Rerum Natura*

10.1 Prolonging Life Would Bring Horrible Social Consequences

Could it be that life extension, while good for the individual, would be terrible for the world if universally achieved? Is life extension an instance of the tragedy of the commons? In the next two chapters, I will discuss a variety of apologist arguments that suggest that postponing or abolishing death would have a range of bad societal consequences. The discussion will start by considering one of the most common observations with regard to life extension—that it would cause overpopulation. Overpopulation means that there are more people than resources, and it is the harbinger of famine and war. If this is what we get for extending our lives, then our case against death is significantly weakened. Death, it turns out, does not rob us of a valuable future because if we do not die, the future will not be valuable; it will be unlivable. The accusation that wishing to prolong life is greedy and selfish reappears here since it would be wrong to insist on living longer if the price is the destruction of the world.

The argument about overpopulation can be seen as giving two distinct reasons against life extension: the first is that life extension would cause overpopulation, and the other is the more generally pessimistic claim that, whether or not life extension causes overpopulation, the future will be so crowded that it would not be beneficial to be alive in it. In what follows, I will argue that overpopulation is not likely to happen to the degree that the earth would be unlivable. Population growth is primarily driven by how many children we have rather than how long we live, and we can decide to have fewer children, which is a choice already made by the majority of the world's countries. Countries where people do not limit their fertility are likely to be overpopulated, but these are the exceptions, not the rule.

10.2 The Overpopulation Threat

Two perfectly matching hockey stick graphs break upwards from the Age of Reason. One describes the increase in life expectancy and the other describes our increase in population. We have improved from having a life expectancy at birth below 30 for most of human history to over 80 years in some areas.[1] At the same time, we have increased from a population of 10 million at 10,000 BC to 100 million at AD 1, to one billion at 1800, to seven billion now. Population growth has accelerated over time. It took all of history for us to reach the year 1800's population of one billion people. By 1900 there were two billion people and, by 2020, the population were nearly 8 billion.. Almost two billion people have been added since Lady Gaga's "Poker Face" was topping the charts in 2008. This looks like we will have exponential growth toward a disaster.

The specter of overpopulation has haunted many thinkers over the ages, most notoriously demographer and economist Thomas Malthus (1766–1834) who wrote that, "Population, when unchecked, increases in a geometrical ratio. Subsistence on the other hand increases only in an arithmetical ratio."[2] Therefore, "it has appeared that from the inevitable laws of our nature, some human beings must suffer from want."[3] Malthus, a pious man, offered the apology that the discrepancy between population and resources and the ensuing want and suffering is God's way of purifying our race and ensuring that we were spurred to develop our cultures. The fear of overpopulation once more gripped the population at the end of 1960s, in some measure due to Paul Ehrlich's 1968 tone-setting bestseller *The Population Bomb*, which added to Cold War–era anxiety and a general feeling of impending doom.[4] Like Malthus before him, Ehrlich predicted that the "population will inevitably and completely outstrip whatever small increases in food supplies we make. The death rate will increase until at least 100–200 million people per year will be starving to death during the next ten years."[5] The tone of *The Population Bomb* is one of despair:

"The battle to feed humanity is already lost, in the sense that we will not be able to prevent large scale famines in the next decades or so."[6] Ehrlich advocates that the US government launch a population policy with the aim of establishing an "optimal population size" and that it put pressure on other countries to do the same. He speculates about the possible means of implementation: "Many of my colleagues feel that some sort of compulsory birth regulation would be necessary to achieve such control. One plan often mentioned involves the addition of temporary sterilants to water supplies or staple food."[7] In a 2018 interview in *The Guardian*, 50 years after the publication of *The Population Bomb*, Ehrlich had not backed down but had simply deferred the "shattering of civilization": "It is a near certainty in the next few decades, and the risk is increasing continually as long as perpetual growth of the human enterprise remains the goal of economic and political systems," he says. "As I've said many times, 'perpetual growth is the creed of the cancer cell.'"[8]

While worries about overpopulation have recently been overshadowed by worries about global warming and more pressing concerns such as international terrorism, and global pandemics, they are still very much alive. Articles such as the one in *The Guardian* appear regularly. Physicist Steven Hawking in 2017 said that unless something is done, "By the year 2600, the world's population would be standing shoulder to shoulder, and the electricity consumption would make the Earth glow red-hot."[9] This pessimism seeps down to ordinary people and can have a serious impact on their lives. A particularly striking example is viewable on YouTube.[10] Actor-activist Alexandra Paul tells us how as a child she was taught to sing a song with the verse "three billion people in the world" and how one day the teacher told them to revise it to "four billion people in the world." Paul continues, "And I was shocked, I couldn't believe that the population was so big, and I was even more shocked by the fact that no one in the class was at all disturbed by this fact. A couple of days later I told my friend Suzie Hollander that since there seemed to be too many people in the world for it to handle, that I wasn't going to have any kids." Paul goes on to explain how we have increased the earth's population sevenfold in only 200 years, which is true, and warns that "there will be no more oil, and food and water," and we can expect "famine, disease, and war over resources," along with environmental disasters. "It will be our downfall!" she exclaims. Today she is 40-plus years old and childless.

10.3   Why Global Overpopulation Is Unlikely

Despite its impressive provenance and famous proponents, the worry about overpopulation is not well founded. We are not overpopulated, and we are not heading toward overpopulation. The United Nations' Population Division median prediction says that there will be 10.9 billion people in 2100.[11] This is, of course, a great increase (roughly three billion more than today) but from then on, the population is expected to shrink and stabilize at around nine billion over the next century afterward.[12] This is a consequence of a steadily declining growth rate, which was at an all-time high of 2.1 percent per year in the early 1960s. Now, it is roughly 1 percent, and it is projected to be 0.1 percent by 2100. The cause for the slowing growth is that women are having fewer children. In 1970, the global average number of children per woman was 4.3. Today, it is down to roughly 2.5. If it were to dip to 2.1, we will have zero population growth, as predicted by the United Nations for the next century.

Consider this: close to half of the earth's population already lives in countries with below-replacement levels of fertility. In 2018 the rates were distributed as follows: North America has a fertility rate of 1.7 children per woman; Europe and Central Asia have a rate of 1.7 and the EU countries have a rate of only 1.5; Russia has a rate of 1.6; East Asia and the Pacific has a rate of 1.8; Latin America and the Caribbean has a rate of 2.0. Rather than suffering from excessive population growth, many countries are facing a rapid population decline. By 2100, Bosnia, Lithuania, Ukraine, Poland, Italy, Greece, Serbia, Germany, the Czech Republic, Austria, Bulgaria, Croatia, Estonia, Belarus, and Spain stand to lose between 20 percent and 30 percent of their populations. Russia, the largest country by area in the world, expects to lose 22 percent of its population already by 2050. The very survival of some cultures is at stake and the threat to these cultures is underpopulation, not overpopulation. Africa is the only large region experiencing a significant population growth, where primarily Nigeria (200 million) and Ethiopia (100 million) are driving it. Outside of Africa, only Afghanistan, Iraq, and Yemen are rapidly increasing their populations.

The UN forecast factors in an increase of our life expectancy from a current age of 72.6 years to 82.6 years in 2100 and to 90 years in 2200. This means that a significant increase in life expectancy is compatible with a decrease in population size. Far from driving population growth, increased longevity is concomitant with population stagnation and even shrinkage. Japan, Switzerland, Singapore, Australia, Spain, Iceland, Italy, Israel, Sweden, and France have the highest life expectancies and also either modest growth, no growth, or negative growth in population size. Take Japan as a test case. Japan has an average life expectancy at birth of 83.1 years, the highest of any major country, yet the country has negative population growth. The average Japanese woman has only 1.4 children. Japan is expected to lose between one third and two thirds of its population by 2100. This means that Japan could soon return to its 1950s levels of population at the same time that it continues to lead the world in average life expectancy with 93.7 years.

The longer we can be expected to live, the fewer children we have. The United Nations' median prediction assumes that this pattern will continue into the future. However, what reasons do we have for thinking that this pattern will? Perhaps people in developed countries will revert to having large families and perhaps developing countries like Nigeria will keep having large families. The United Nations has a high variant prediction of nearly 16 billion people in the world by 2100. What reasons do we have for relying on the medium prediction rather than the high variant prediction? The answer is that there are certain conditions explaining the negative correlation between longevity and fertility. All have to do with modernity. First, improvements in prenatal and postnatal nutrition, sanitation, medicine, and access to basic goods have brought down infant and child mortality. The global average child mortality rate in 1800 was 43.3 percent, which is nearly half of all children who died before their fifth birthday. Today only three in 100 do not see their fifth birthday. When you can expect your children to survive, there is less pressure to have as many children as possible. Second, contraceptives are more efficient and more readily available today. Third, the weakening of religion means that there is less of a stigma surrounding contraceptives, and there is less of an inclination to respect the command to "multiply and fill up the earth." Fourth, industrialization has meant that children are not needed to perform labor-intensive farming. Children used to be considered an asset from around the age of eight when they could help around the house. Now they are often a liability until they are in their thirties. Fifth, the highly specialized nature of a modern society demands a higher level of education, which means both that women put off having children and that each child needs more time and resources to succeed. A professional can make 10 times as much as a laborer. It is, therefore, rational to invest more resources in fewer children than in having many children. Sixth, insurance schemes and the welfare state mean that children are not needed as an insurance against the infirmities of old age. Seventh, industrialization meant that women became wage earners, and a pregnancy was considered as lost income. Eighth, increased equality for women has meant that many women pursue careers and other ways of defining themselves as something besides being mothers and homemakers. This tendency is further spurred on by a general ideology of individualism and the celebration of self-realization: many women live for themselves, not just for their children. Ninth, the opportunity of having a career means that women do not face the same pressure to marry early and many wait too long before their first child to be able to birth many children. Tenth, industrialization means urbanization. The increased cost of space prevents having large families.

These are 10 of the most important reasons for why modernity brings us a longer life and also creates a world where women have fewer children. On the assumption that countries like Nigeria, Ethiopia, and Egypt become more modernized, we can expect that their life expectancy will continue to rise while their fertility rates and, therefore, their population growth will decrease. Of course, they may not, but this only means that a few exceptional countries will grow rapidly while most countries will remain at a stable level or shrink. Population growth, if any, will be local and not global. And it will not be primarily caused by an increase in life expectancy.

What if the UN is wrong, not about the global fertility rate but about global life expectancy? What if there is a gain not just of 10 or 20 years in the average life expectancy over the next few centuries, but of 40 or 50? Futurist author Ramez Naam has calculated that if we achieved an average life expectancy of around 120 in the developed world and around 113 in the developing world by 2050, this would add only 6 percent to the projected population size.[13] This is an increase that would be offset by a minor 5 percent decrease in fertility. So, while an increase in life expectancy could add to the population—in particular initially, before the first generation with access to life-extending medicine start to die—in the end, it depends on how many children these longer-living people decide to have.

But what if we conquered aging altogether? If almost no one goes away and we keep adding people, surely our planet would quickly fill up?

Renowned gerontologists Dr. Leonid Gavrilov and Dr. Natalia Gavrilova asked themselves this question. Working with Sweden as a model country, they summarized their findings as follows:

> A general conclusion of this study is that population changes are surprisingly slow in their response to a dramatic life extension. For example, we applied the cohort-component method of population projections to 2005 Swedish population for several scenarios of life extension and a fertility schedule observed in 2005. Even for very long 100-year projection horizon, with the most radical life extension scenario (assuming no aging at all after age 60), the total population increases by 22% only (from 9.1 to 11.0 million). Moreover, if some members of society reject to use new anti-aging technologies for some religious or any other reasons (inconvenience, non-compliance, fear of side effects, costs, etc.), then the total population size may even decrease over time. Thus, even in the case of the most radical life extension scenario, population growth could be relatively slow and may not necessarily lead to overpopulation.[14]

The Gavrilov study illustrates the relatively small effect on population growth that even radical life extension (their scenario of no aging after 60) would have. Here some might say that 22 percent growth, while manageable over this century, could become an enormous growth if it continued year after year, century after century. I did the calculation and at that rate Sweden would be as densely populated as France by the year 3000. This would, however, be to misunderstand the logic of population growth. If Sweden maintained its current fertility rate of 1.8 children per woman, its population would start decreasing again after the uptick brought on by the antiaging intervention. The increase is fast in the beginning because the first who benefit from the treatment will not die off, while new people keep being added. But once they start to die, the population can stabilize at a new point or, as in the case of Sweden if we assume a fertility rate of 1.8, go back to shrinking. Philosopher John K. Davies calls this, very descriptively, the lingering guest phenomenon: if every guest at a party stays for, say, six hours, then for the first six hours there will be more and more people and the party will grow.[15] But after six hours have passed, people will start leaving and the party will cease to grow, or even shrink. This means that the greatest challenge with regard to antiaging treatments and population growth will be in the early stage. Remember, even biological immortals will die at some point from nonaging-related causes. If this sounds strange, keep in mind that we have more than doubled the average life expectancy since 1900, yet the populations of most countries are stable or even shrinking.

It does not matter how long our life spans are, as long as we only have no more than two children per couple the population would ultimately stabilize and not grow. The most challenging scenario is one where (a) the treatment completely cures aging, (b) works on everyone, (c) everyone wants the treatment, (d) everyone has access to it, (e) fertility rates are high and there is little time between pregnancies. Then the earth's population may double or triple over only a century, all things equal. However, this is obviously an unlikely scenario. If we imagine instead that the treatments will only partly cure aging, that they work better on some than on others, that many are not interested in it, that for various reasons not all have access to it, and that fertility rates are low, then the challenges will be significantly less acute.

But what if couples want more than 2.1 children? Scenarios of overcoming aging may involve the expansion of the window of female fertility, and hence introduce the possibility of having hundreds of children per woman. Some philosophers have concluded that in order to prevent it from leading to overpopulation, we would either have to limit people's length of life or limit reproductive rights.[16] They see these measures as terrible and as reasons for rejecting immortality, but this seems like a hasty conclusion. First, the biological possibility of having untold number of children does not imply that it would be a popular choice among women to have as many children as possible. The advancement in fertility treatment has so far not been used by women to maximize the number of children they have, but to give them the opportunity to have children later in life. Second, there are several morally acceptable solutions to the possible problem. Davies has recently suggested what he calls a "forced choice" whereby the decision to have child beyond the sustainable average would enter the couple in a lottery with a chance of limiting access to antiaging medicine. So, a couple can still have as many children as they want, but they must also accept the risk of not having their life extended. Davies points out that the "forced choice" cannot be compared to morally problematic restrictions on reproduction such as China's one-child policy, since it is not forced on all, but rather a risk assumed voluntarily. This proposal makes sense: if you want to live like before life extension was a reality, you still can. Accepting a restraint on how many children we have in exchange for a longer, healthier life is not an unacceptable solution, since anyone who thinks that is free to abstain from life extension. Davis's proposal is but one example of how we can manage population growth. If we bear in mind the gruesomeness of the status quo, there are many acceptable solutions to avoiding overpopulation even in a world of biological immortals. Moreover, since we are here dealing with predictions over hundreds and thousands of years, we cannot—as do the smoothly flowing graphs of the UN's demographic projections—discount the possibility that natural and manmade disasters would occasionally decimate us as they have always done in the past. Nor can we dismiss the possibility that we have colonized other planets or built new artificial space colonies.

Ecological pessimists such as Paul Ehrlich compare humans to cancer cells, bacteria, and some noxious pests determined to kill Mother Earth. This is an awful philosophy. We are neither a cancer nor some virus destined to multiply until we kill our host planet. We are rational agents and can therefore adapt to changing demographics. Our reason and adaptability are among the few known variables in this equation. We are also universes in ourselves and irreplaceable as individuals, as Kant reminds us. Given that our life expectancy is not the prime driver of population growth, it is irrational and immoral to advocate death as the solution to (a merely possible) threat of overpopulation. The fact that Ehrlich is still predicting the end of civilization within decades despite the fact that half of the world's population live in nations with sub-replacement fertility rates, that is, despite being manifestly wrong, suggests that there may be an element of unreasoned misanthropic pessimism motivating his research.

10.4   Are We Running Out of Resources?

The first part of the overpopulation argument assumes that if we live longer, we will also increase in number. We have seen that this is not necessarily the case because birth rates are more important than death rates for population growth. Overpopulation, of course, is defined as a shortage of resources relative to population, and the second part of the argument concerns these. Will the earth's resources suffice for billions more people? Will there be enough water, food, and energy? And what about the toll on the environment? If the near future of humanity is one of extreme scarcity and severe environmental degradation, then this clearly takes away from the attraction of prolonging our lives (irrespective of the fact that longevity does not primarily drive population growth).

10.4.1   Water

The United Nations expects half of the earth's population will experience some level of water shortages over the next several decades. The United States is not the most fortunate country in this respect. California has already experienced droughts and 40 of 50 states are projected to have water shortages at some point over the next 10 years. Some of this is due to the natural fluctuations in precipitation, rising sea levels contaminating fresh water with saltwater and (to a small degree) pollution from fracking in some localities, all in combination with less-than-optimal water management. This sounds alarming, but as the UN study goes on to explain, most of these shortages are not expected to be calamitous. Rather, they are local, temporary shortages. Moreover, the concept of "water shortage" is not defined relative to what humans need to survive but rather to expectations—such as, for example, Southern Californians' desire to keep lush green lawns.[17]

Water is not like coal or some other finite resource; we are never going to use up water. The shortages arise because water is not always distributed and managed in such a way that it supplies an adequate or expected amount to all places at all times. During the last century, we did progress tremendously with regard to engineering and water management standards. In 1900 only about a third of US households had running water and only 15 percent had flush toilets. Today, these amenities are taken for granted. Water is also far cleaner today, a trend continuing since 1908 when cities (Jersey City in New Jersey was the first) began to disinfect their drinking water. Most countries have experienced the same progress. The World Health Organization estimates that over 90 percent of today's world population has access to an improved water source (a technical term for safe, treated water), a fine improvement over 1990 when 76 percent did.[18] There is no reason to suppose that countries today with successful water management would regress. On the contrary, we can expect a gradual improvement as technologies make agriculture less water demanding, desalination becomes more cost effective, and transport and distribution become more efficient. There will remain places on the earth that will have periodic water shortages due to their arid location (Texas, California, parts of the Middle East, parts of North Africa, and parts of China), poor management, natural disasters or war, or a combination thereof. It is, however, not too optimistic to predict that access to water will improve and that there will never be a global or a widespread water shortage.[19]

10.4.2 Food

Famines were common before the last century. The Great Famine (1315–1317) killed millions, and later the great famine in Ireland (1845–1849) killed one million Irish and forced another million to emigrate. Despite unforgettable calamities such as in the Darfur region, famines were rare during the last century. The catastrophes that did occur were primarily caused by war, oppression, and mismanagement. From 10 to 30 million people died as a result of Mao's Great Leap Forward (1958–1962); nine million people died in the Soviet Union due to Lenin's collectivization (1921–1922); three million, perhaps more, died in the Ukrainian Holodomor due to Stalin's industrialization and forced starvation policies (1932–1934); three million starved to death in Kim Il Jung's North Korea (1995–1999); two million died in Cambodia under the Khmer Rouge (1979); in Ethiopia, 400,000 starved under the Marxist militants; and several other African countries went down the same route of corruption, land redistribution, mismanagement, and starvation including Zimbabwe, Mozambique, and Somalia. There is a rumor that Venezuela is on the brink of a famine, proving that not even oil wealth guarantees that a country can survive poor governance.

Thankfully, the number of famine-related deaths has been steadily declining both in relative and absolute terms over decades even as the global population has increased. The proportion of deaths due to starvation was 194.6 per 100.000 over the first decade of the last century. This was down to 3.3 per 100.000 over the first decade of this century.[20] The world average was 2,196 kcal/person/day in 1961 and now it is just above 3,000 kcal/person/day. The improvement has been proportionally greater in the poorer regions of Asia and Africa. The average for Africa was 1,993 kcal/person/day in 1961; now it is 2,624 kcal/person/day. This is astounding. One of humanity's most persistent scourges has been reduced by 98.3 percent over just a couple of generations. And this has been done while doomsayers like Ehrlich predicted there would be mass starvation and deaths in the tens of millions. Ehrlich's *Population Bomb* was published in 1968. During that decade, the 1960s, there were 16.6 million deaths from starvation. During the next decade, there were 3.4 million deaths from starvation. During the decade of the 2010s, there have been less than 300,000 deaths. Contrary to Ehrlich's predictions, population growth has coincided with an increase in access to food, drastic reduction in death from starvation and, to repeat, every single instance of food shortages has been an effect of war or poor governance, not population size alone.[21]

The reason for this tremendous progress is, in a word, efficiency. Globally, land use efficiency has increased 68 percent since 1961. The amount of land needed to feed the world is, therefore, not much more than it was 50 years ago.[22] In the United States, agricultural land use has even decreased since the 1950s, despite a doubling of the population. There are still great gains to be had. It has been argued that farmers could triple yields without increasing land use if best farming practices and technologies were universally applied. As it is, we already produce more than enough food in the world to feed 11 billion people, but much is wasted. One estimate has it that only 40 percent of all produce reaches the table. Some waste is due to inefficient distribution and some of it is due to picky consumers who discard all but the freshest and best-looking produce. Another form of waste is in the choice of what we eat. Our taste for meat may be responsible for inefficient land use and there are many nutrient-dense foods that we are not used to, such as quinoa, algae, and insects. Yet even at current levels of wastefulness, there is no reason to think that we will run out of food.

A further ground for optimism is the technological progress we can expect over the next centuries. There are whole new approaches being explored, such as hydroponic vertical farming, where skyscraper farms service cities with locally grown produce. Greenhouses now enable us to grow produce in even the most arid areas. Genetic modification makes plants more nutritious and pest resistant. The number of new concepts for farming currently being developed inspires confidence in the future. We should expect that gains in efficiency in food production, food quality, and food distribution can keep pace with even a significant population growth.

10.4.3 Energy

What about crude oil? Many experts in the 1970s, including the US Department of Energy, predicted that by now we would have run out of oil and gas long ago. This prediction, as we can see, turned out to be entirely wrong. In 2000, the world crude oil production was 75 million barrels per day, 15 million more than in 1970. Today it is roughly 80 million barrels per day.

And yet, there is plenty of oil left. How much no one knows, but the well-respected Cambridge Energy Research Associates (CERA) has predicted that there are 3.74 trillion barrels of oil remaining in earth. This is certainly enough to take us through this century. Natural gas is expected to last at least another 90 years, not counting the discoveries of new reserves or any new advances in extraction methods. There is also a significant amount of coal left. A recent study by the US government concludes that coal reserves will last about 348 years, also not taking into account improvement in our ability to extract it over that time.

Pessimists also underestimated the emergence of alternatives to fossil fuels. Even if one day there will be no more crude oil, gas, or coal worth the effort to extract, this does not mean that we will be without energy. Since the 1980s, France receives 75 percent of their energy from nuclear plants. This keeps France clean and provides it with a large revenue stream as it exports its surplus energy. And it has almost zero CO_2 emissions. Nuclear energy is thus an already existing, superior alternative to fossil fuels. Promising—although so far inconclusive—research is being done on fusion reactors, which would be safer and cheaper than fission reactors and capable of solving all human energy needs forever. Solar energy is another promising alternative. In 2010, the United States produced 1,212 MVh per year from solar sources. In 2020, the number had increased sixty-five fold to 78,986 MWh per year. In the same time the share of solar energy of the total energy consumption increased from 0.03 percent, to 2.35 percent. In addition to solar and nuclear power, there are many other potentially revolutionary sources of energy currently being researched. For instance, at Argonne National Laboratory under the US Department of Energy's Office of Science, scientists are exploring ways to provide a near boundless supply of fuel by using tungsten diselenide to transform carbon dioxide to carbon monoxide, which in turn can be transformed into reactive substances like methanol that can be used to fuel our cars. Given the speed at which science is currently advancing, what we have now in terms of energy technology will most likely look as outdated as the Wright brothers' biplane by 2300. In any case, it is not too optimistic to predict that we will continue to have our energy needs met in the future.

The partial transition to solar and other alternative energy sources brings to mind another important dimension of population growth: its effect on the environment.

10.4.4 The Environment

Los Angeles obscured by thick smog is one of the iconic images of the doom and gloom of the 1970s. At the time it seemed inevitable that things would get progressively worse for the environment. Now, of course, we know that everything has been rapidly improving. The smog has lifted from LA and the air is much cleaner. And the same is true of other American cities. The EPA reports that there has been an almost 70 percent reduction in the six most common air pollutants. One of the greatest worries of the 1970s was the amount of lead in the air but removing lead from gasoline has reduced airborne lead by 98 percent; meanwhile carbon monoxide has decreased by 85 percent; and sulfur dioxide by 80 percent. Acid rain is another worry that entered into our public consciousness in the 1970s. Lately, though, we have not heard much of it because the risk of acid rain's distributing sulfur dioxide and polluting lakes and streams has been largely avoided by reducing power plant emissions. While we still hear of isolated cases of water contamination—like those in Flint, Michigan—overall, our water keeps getting cleaner. At the beginning of the last century, roughly one in four deaths was due to contaminated drinking water. Today only a handful of people, fewer than 10 per year, are documented to have died from water contamination.[23]

A similar trend has been visible in many other parts of the world. For instance, the former communist countries in the Eastern Bloc have made enormous progress. In 1990, after the fall of the Berlin Wall, it was revealed that East Germany was toxic: Only one third of all industrial sewage and only half of all domestic sewage received treatment. Almost half of its lakes were dead and unable to sustain fish. Nearly half its forests were damaged by acid rain.[24] Facts such as these help explain and excuse the excessive ecological pessimism of the times. Today a unified Germany has cleaned up its act. The German Environment Agency reports that 98 percent of bath water is in compliance with the European Union's Bathing Water Directive and drinking water "is very good virtually everywhere."[25] Acid rain has stopped falling and Germany today ranks among the most densely wooded countries in Europe. Wildlife such as wolves and elk are making a strong return. As in the United States, an awareness and willingness to prioritize the environment is high and the future looks clean and bright. The trend toward a better environment is global. NASA reports that the earth is greener than it was 20 years ago, partly due to efforts by, among others, developing nations like China and India, and oil spills in the ocean are down approximately 95 percent since the 1970s.[26]

The worst environments today are found either in underdeveloped areas or in places undergoing rapid economic growth like China, where it is experiencing its own version of the smoggy 1970s. China also contributes most of the plastic pollution of the oceans, mainly through the Yangtze River. Plastic pollution is one environmental problem that is getting worse. However, unless the Chinese are very different from us, they will begin to take steps toward redressing their environmental problem, if for no other reasons than having to keep foreign investors happy and skilled workers from fleeing to less polluted countries. There are early signs that the Chinese government is getting serious about the environment. They have invested in research on clean energy and, in October 2017, they shut down tens of thousands of factories in a pollution crackdown. Since 2014, air pollution is down more than 32 percent on average.[27] Every country that has gone through a successful industrial revolution has also gradually managed to improve its environment. Once basic needs are met, people want a safe and clean environment.

All that is fine, some will say, but what about global warming? The average global surface temperature has increased by 0.8 degrees Celsius since 1880. The United Nations International Panel on Climate Change (IPCC) projects a further increase between 0.3 and 4.8 degrees Celsius this century. By 2400, they are projecting either no further increase (best-case scenario), or an increase of eight degrees Celsius from today's average. Another couple of degrees may not sound so bad, but they can have calamitous effects. A 2018 IPCC report states that if the world gets two degrees warmer, 37 percent of the earth's population would be exposed to severe heat once every five years and once every 10 years the arctic sea would be free from ice. Sea levels would rise 0.46 meters (1.5 ft), 8 percent of vertebrates would lose at least half of their range of habitat, 16 percent of plants would lose half of their range of habitat, 18 percent of insects would lose half of their range of habitat, 4.1 million square miles of permafrost would melt, maize harvest yields would drop by 7 percent, 99 percent of coral reefs would be threatened, and marine fisheries would catch three million tons less fish. All this at a mere two-degree increase. Imagine what an eight-degree increase in global temperature would do. Would such an inferno be worth living in?

The observed and projected warming trend is in part the effect of an increase in so-called atmospheric greenhouse gases, primarily H_2O (water vapor and clouds) and CO_2 (carbon dioxide), preventing heat from escaping earth. Some of the atmospheric carbon dioxide is attributable to human sources, such as the burning of petroleum, coal, and natural gas. This human contribution is thought to be partly responsible for the one-degree Celsius increase in average temperature over the last 150 years. This is a cause for optimism since it implies that we have the power to stop the warming, or at least slow it down, until the next glacial period due within 50,000 years asserts itself. (On a geological scale we are now in an interglacial stage of an ice age.) Here is a second reason for optimism. As much as we may despair about the unwillingness of many to be serious about curbing emissions, there is a very strong reason to be certain that emissions will be drastically reduced: Alternative energy sources will hit a price point that makes burning coal and oil in particular, if hard to extract, uncompetitive. A third cause for optimism is that the IPCC appears to underestimate the rate of technological progress that we have ahead of ourselves. This means that the transition to sustainable energy may be ahead of schedule, but it also means that we will have more tools to deal with climate change. Consider the following. The number of reported natural disasters has increased over the last 100 years, but the rate of people dying in these has gone down from 27 per 100,000 in the 1920s to one per 100,000 in the 2010s.[28] Deaths due to extreme weather (mainly droughts, floods, and storms) have declined in absolute numbers by more than 90 percent since the 1920s, despite a fourfold increase in the population.[29] From the point of view of lives lost, extreme weather is less of a problem today than ever before. Global warming since the 1850s has been compatible with unprecedented advances in health, longevity, access to food, environment, and safety from natural disasters. Technology makes us resilient to environmental changes. Perhaps we need a climate shock. Humankind is one of those antifragile things that Nassem Nicholas Taleb talks about, namely things that get stronger when exposed to damage that would shatter more fragile things.[30]

The struggle against global warming has expanded our understanding of climate, accelerated the advancement of sustainable energy, and inspired the creation of global networks of collaboration. Thanks to this, we will be better prepared to deal with not only future climate challenges but also other kinds of risks requiring international collaboration. In fact, rising to meet the challenge of global warming may turn out to be the key to our survival as a species. If we are to survive, we need to colonize other planets.

This, in all likelihood, would require making these planets inhabitable by creating a suitable atmosphere. Drawing on our increased understanding of the causes of climate, scientists speculate that we may be able to ter-raform Mars and other planets by releasing greenhouse gases. The insight that we have an impact on the climate is empowering. We should feel a sense of excitement about finding out how we will meet the challenges of global warming and potential resource shortages rather than despair that the future looks too bleak to want to live in. In fact, challenges like these—there will always be looming catastrophes of one sort or another—give meaning to our existence and are one reason for why it would not be boring to live on.

10.5   Alexandra Paul's Tragic Mistake

In light of these facts about population, resources, and the environment, I found it a sad experience to re-watch Alexandra Paul's TEDx talk. Here we have a beautiful, intelligent, and caring woman who has made a momen-tous life choice not to have children based on utter confusion, in particular since she seems to want to have children. "[My] kids might be wonderful, but they would also be wasteful," she says. In order to save the planet from imagined shortages of food, water, and oil, she will not have "wasteful" children. She and her husband are ending their bloodline in a misguided hyperaltruistic gesture. It is "hyperaltruistic" because altruism begins with a desire to protect our offspring and in Paul's case this tendency is being used to prevent her from having any. It is a "gesture" because a few more kids in a world of billions would make no measurable difference. Her sacrifice, so momentous in her own life, is inconsequential in the larger picture. It is a sacrifice lacking any realistic connection with its desired result, and it is hard to imagine that she would want to universalize it. Surely, she does not mean that all women should abstain from procreation. So why does she think that other women have the right to have children, but she does not? This question is relevant here, since the same worries about overpopulation that lead Paul to abstain from having children, have been used to argue against prolonging our lives. What explains her terrible reasoning is that she thinks that there are too many Americans and other First World people on earth: "We should be having the babies, we are smart and we are edu-cated . . . we can afford kids, heck, our offspring might save the world . . .

but someone from North America uses 32 times the resources of someone from a developing country."[31] Paul's thought must be that, somehow, by not having a child she allows 32 children in, say, Nigeria to live. Perhaps she believes that if she has a child, it would somehow take away food, water, and other resources from 32 Nigerian children? Perhaps she pictures the resources of the world as a big pie, and if her child greedily takes 32 times as many slices, as say, a Nigerian child, then she is taking the food out of the mouths of other children. By not having one child, she can enable Nigerian women to have many children (provided they do not increase their level of consumption).

Paul's way of thinking of the global economy of resources as a big pie, a zero-sum game where each benefit to one is a cost to another, is common, perhaps even natural, but it is also deeply and dangerously flawed. It may sound counterintuitive, but American consumption levels of water, food, and energy have no important negative impact on the resources available to people in developing countries. Consider the scenario where Paul has a child, Lisa. Paul lives in New York, meaning that Lisa is drinking, showering, and cooking in water delivered by the force of gravity through pipelines from the Catskills and Delaware. Her water consumption has zero impact on the water supply in, say, Bangladesh, Afghanistan, or Nigeria. As to the food Lisa consumes, 81 percent of it is produced domestically. Only 19 percent is imported from other countries—for example, coffee, chocolate, tropical fruits, wine, and cheese. These food items are not taken from starving children. Rather, they create an income for the countries that produce them. The more we consume, the higher the demand for their produce, and the richer these countries get. Would Brazilians be better off if they drank all their coffee themselves? Would Panamanians be better off if they ate all their bananas themselves? Of course not. Trade is what makes these countries advance economically. Remember, the rate of death from starvation has been reduced 98.35 percent over the last 100 years and even the poorest part of the world has all but eradicated starvation.

As for the energy Lisa consumes, the majority is domestically produced (since 2019 the U.S. has been a net exporter of energy); besides, nothing provides the developing world with more resources than the fact that our industries need their oil. There was always oil in Saudi Arabia, but it only became worth something when the combustion engine was invented. We get oil and the developing world gets oil kleptocrats but also modern medicine, tractors, and smartphones. Trade explains why as rich countries have been getting richer, poor countries have been getting richer at an even faster rate. World GDP per capita has increased threefold since 1960. Countries such as South Korea have gone from rags to riches in a generation. The growth rate of the poorest area in the world, sub-Saharan Africa, was 3.07 percent in 2019. A drop in US demand for their products would be terrible for the developing world and would make the pie smaller. Consumers like Lisa are increasing the wealth of the world. The pessimism that Paul has absorbed from our culture concerning overpopulation is based on flawed economics..

Moreover, Paul is right. Her children might invent something that might "save the world." No recent groundbreaking, lifesaving, or life-enhancing invention has been invented in poor countries. It is the invention and dissemination of inventions made by people in the developed world—electricity, vaccines, tractors, and cellphones—that explains why poorer parts of the world have more than doubled their life expectancy over the last 100 years, which is the most tangible evidence for improved conditions. Paul should stop worrying about a nonexistent problem and feel free to have as many children as she wants since she can afford to raise them and lives in a country with below replacement level fertility. Those who argue on similar premises as Paul that we cannot prolong our own lives because we are so wasteful, should also stop worrying. No one needs to be prevented from living longer in order to save water, energy, and food or to save the environment.

10.6 Conclusions

The position "death is good because it prevents overpopulation" might be considered immoral since it holds that we should not seek to slow down aging, despite the immense pain, suffering—strokes, heart attacks, cancers, Alzheimer's disease, and so on—and the deaths of 100,000 irreplaceable human beings per day caused by it. It is appalling how quick people are to suggest—as a first answer—that we should die to save water, food, oil, or to make the world less hot or less polluted. Mom sorry, you have to die because our crude oil reserves are (perhaps) running out (someday) and you are contributing (imperceptibly) to population growth and the average temperature of the planet. And I am not giving you a grandchild for the same reasons. Would it not be better to think of less painful and nonlethal ways of achieving sustainability? Also disturbing is the tendency among some prophets of overpopulation to liken humans to cancers and other parasitic life forms. It reminds us of the holist view and its disregard for individual persons.

Think of Ehrlich—still a professor at Stanford—who speculated about the government putting sterilizers in the drinking water. One wonders how he and people like him in power would react if someone discovered a simple cure, a pill, say, that could double our life span. Would they recommend that individuals abstain from taking it by their own choice? Or would they, in an authoritarian way, recommend that the pill be illegal? Would they force us to get sick and die even if we no longer must? Francis Fukuyama has said that he thinks the government should be able to prevent people from living too long, so apparently this option is not unthinkable for some bioconservatives. It is bad enough as it is, given that government inaction potentially delays the development of antiaging science and thereby condemns millions or billions of people to needless aging, illness, and suffering. Much speculation with regard to overpopulation is carried on from an authoritarian, imperial world-controller perspective, where the multiplicity of individuals, cultures, and countries are reduced down to one world for which "we"—meaning the speculator and those who agree with him or her—must lay down law. This perspective hides the obvious fact that some countries can be underpopulated, and others overpopulated and so on. It would be absurd for a Japanese, a Lithuanian, or a Russian to let concerns of overpopulation limit their healthy life span. Overpopulation is an equation of people relative to resources, and population itself is the scarcest resource of these rapidly shrinking countries. Their cultures are threatening to disappear because of depopulation. There is nothing "we" must do, and the implied authoritarianism and collectivism of such an imperial point of view is simultaneously unrealistic, illiberal, and unsavory.

Pessimism regarding resources and the environment constitutes its own Wise View. To say that starvation is down 98.3 percent since 1900 sounds callous because there are still people starving. Likewise, to say that the air is much cleaner and that the water is infinitely safer to drink sounds as if one does not care about the environment. On the other hand, to express grave concerns about the future and to speak of the problems of the world rather than its improvements sounds caring and wise. Public intellectual Alain de Botton embodies this attitude when advocating for a "pessimistic realism" that he describes as "the root of wisdom" and as an antidote to "boosterish optimism," which is "dangerous and cruel."[32] Up to a point, such pessimism may be pragmatically justified if it spurs progressive action, as it no doubt once did in the case of the environmental movement. It is also generally a good idea to accept that things (and people) will never be perfect. Notwithstanding, projections about the future must be based on large-scale trends, numbers, facts, and statistics, and these do not back pessimism about overpopulation even given significant life extension.

In sum, apologists who argue that aging and death are good means for keeping the population down fail to see what comparatively little effect mortality rates have on population growth. They fail to notice that, so far, an increase in longevity has been correlated with a decrease in population growth; the countries with the highest life expectancy have a shrinking population. Moreover, they underestimate gains in productivity, misunderstand the fundamental non-zero-sum nature of the global economy, and think of resources as more limited than they are. Importantly, they ignore the continued progress of science and technology and, generally, humankind's ability to adapt to changing circumstances. Overpopulation is unlikely and it is not primarily caused by life extension. This is an important conclusion. It means that one of the most prevalent arguments in favor of the status quo of aging and death is nearly certainly unsound. However, our conclusion raises another worry, that of the greying of the world and having so many old people and so few who are young.

11 Death Saves Us from Social Consequences Worse Than Death

For the old ever gives place thrust out by new things, and one thing must be restored at the expense of others.

—Lucretius, *De Rerum Natura*

Worst of all they [the old] just refuse to get out of the way, not just of their children, but their grandchildren and great grandchildren.

—Francis Fukuyama, *Our Posthuman Future: Consequences of the Biotechnology Revolution*

11.1 The Graying of the World

Overpopulation is not the great threat that it is made out to be. An increase in longevity has come about with a decrease in fertility in much of the world, a trend we have reason to believe will continue. We may, however, be in a bind here. An increase in longevity plus a decrease in fertility equals upside down population pyramids with few young people at the base and many old people at the top. Today, 13 percent of the world's population is over 60. The United Nations anticipates that 22 percent of the global population will be over 60 by 2050, compared to 8 percent in 1950.[1] In the United States and Europe, roughly 25 percent of the population is currently 60 or older and this figure is expected to reach 35 percent by 2050. The number of octogenarians in the world is set to triple by 2050 and the number of centenarians is set to grow eightfold. In the face of so much aging, pessimists paint a picture of a stagnant society devoid of fresh minds and controlled by a perennial old guard, burdened by health-care costs and unable to defend itself. Would a society of the superannuated be a society in which we would want to live? Or would enhanced longevity, while a boon to the individual, have such bad effects when collectively realized that it is, in the end, in no one's interest? If so, then perhaps it is better to die within a natural life span after all.[2]

In this chapter, I will consider the effects of an increased median age on the economy, on our social hierarchies, and on progress. I will also address the fear that only the very rich will be able to afford life extension. The scenarios to be considered range from an average life expectancy, as projected by the United Nations, of 83 in 2100, 95 in 2200, and 100 in 2300, to the possible doubling of our life expectancy to roughly 150, which could result from a breakthrough in antiaging science. Beyond that point there are too many unknown variables. Will there still be countries hundreds of years from now? Or will the imperial perspective be realized in some form of a world government?[3] Will the capacities for complete surveillance be used for total control? How benevolent would the controllers be? Will democracy and liberal rights continue to be respected, or will societies go back to basics? We ourselves are also unknown variables in a new way. I have argued that we have a human nature and can therefore be expected to find a longer life valuable. As long as we are who we are, many things will stay the same, similar to the way in which much has changed since the year 1900 but most things have remained the same. This is why we still wrestle with ideas first formulated by the ancient world millennia ago. But will we remain who we are given a couple of hundred years more of science? Or will there be transhuman tweaks to our personalities? That in my view is the most dangerous aspect of emerging science and technology and it is an unknown unknown. It is not life extension that is a threat to humanity; rather, it is the dream of emotional and cognitive enhancement. I am not going to make any farseeing predictions here. It would be exciting to paint a picture of the year 2300 or 3000, but it would be pure speculation that science fiction writers and filmmakers do just as well. Instead, I will limit the discussion to those challenges that people today think are reasons not to radically extend our lives.

11.2   The Economy: The Main Challenges

[G]lobal aging . . . threatens to bankrupt the great powers. As the population of the world's leading economies age and shrink, we will face unprecedented political, economic, and moral challenges. But we are woefully unprepared.
—Former Secretary of Commerce Peter Petersen, *Gray Dawn: How the Coming Age Wave Will Transform America and the World*

In the 1950s, the global median age was 23 and there were, on average, 12 persons aged 15 to 64 for every person 65 and older. Economists call this the potential support ratio or PSR. It assumes that the working population is 15 to 64 and that the retired, "supported" population is 65 and above. Today the global average PSR has declined to eight and it is projected to decline to four by 2050.[4] Japan can give us a glimpse of this future. It has the world's second highest life expectancy after the outlier Monaco (89.52), its median age is 46.1, nearly a quarter of its population is above 65, and the country has already reached a remarkably low PSR of two.[5] This is due in equal measure to the increase in longevity of its retirees and the low fertility of its overall population. Japanese women have, on average, 1.43 children, which is far from the population replacement rate of 2.1. Consequently, Japan is projected to shrink from 127 million to 100 million inhabitants by 2050, a loss of nearly a fifth of its population. By 2050, the country is expected to have a PSR of 1.5.

This "graying" appears to hurt the economy. Since being heralded as a booming economic miracle in the 1970s and 1980s, Japan has long been experiencing slow economic growth. It is standard to describe the 1990s and the 2000s as Japan's "lost decades." Economists are worried and the headlines are outright despairing: "Japan's Sexual Apathy is Endangering the Global Economy," "Forget Greece, Japan is the World's Real Economic Time Bomb," "The Demographic Time Bomb Crippling Japan's Economy," and so on.[6] These worries are Malthusian in spirit but with a twist. This time the concern is not with general growth in population—there is no growth—but rather with the growth in the segment of the old and unproductive relative to the segment of those who are young and productive. As in the original Malthusian argument, the conclusion is that society will eventually run low on resources relative to population. Are the pessimists right this time? I will consider Japan in some detail since it is considered the canary in the coal mine.

11.3   The Economy: Troubles Are Overstated

Those who have had the opportunity to compare arriving at Haneda airport in Tokyo and taking the clean and efficient Tokyo Metro directly to the city with arriving at JFK airport and then making three changes on a leaky, rat-infested MTA subway to get to New York may find it ironic that American economists are talking about Japan as having lost several decades. The Japanese not only live longer but they are better educated, have newer electronics, have faster internet service, build more skyscrapers, and enjoy safer, cleaner cities than Americans. True, the growth of the economy in terms of the value of goods and services (GDP) has been slow since the 1990s, but developed economies always grow at a slower rate, and Japan is still the world's third largest economy. Furthermore, it is important to recognize that a country's GDP is not a reliable indicator of how its citizens are doing financially or otherwise. Measured by GDP alone, we would consider Nigeria rich and Monaco poor. What matters more is GDP per capita. When adjusted for purchasing power parity, Japan, as recently as 2017, noted its highest ever, twice that of the booming 1980s.[7] Japan then, despite the common wisdom, is not doing badly at all.

This requires an explanation. How can Japan continue to be one of the world's top three economies with an increasing GDP per capita while having a fifth as many workers per retiree as they did in the 1950s?[8] An increase in productivity is the answer. Productivity is growing at approximately 2 percent per year, which means that if it continues at the present rate, by 2050 each worker will produce about twice as much per hour as today. Despite the Cassandras of the economic press, the declining PSR has not been and will not be economically devastating because Japan does not need as many workers as the country previously needed in order to continue to prosper. In fact, a high PSR is usually indicative of a primitive economy. Afghanistan, for instance, has a PSR of 21. Wealth today is not created by having a large labor force but by having a highly productive labor force. This condition is reflected in the choices made by Japanese families: They have fewer children, but each child receives more education. Japanese students are consistently among the best performing in the world according to the OECD's PISA test.

A low potential support ratio is not terrible for an economy, but it is also not optimal to have a large part of the population outside of the productive economy. Japan is therefore seeking ways to add to its workforce. It can be instructive to consider some of these. Perhaps the most obvious way to increase the labor pool is for Japanese women to have more babies. That we are speaking of a need to encourage baby making in a society where the average life expectancy is the highest in the world reminds us of how weak the overpopulation argument (considered in the previous chapter) against life extension is. In real life, increases in life expectancy have come with decreases in fertility. The Japanese government is addressing the plummeting fertility of its population with incentives for couples to get married and have children, such as having increased access to childcare, family benefits, longer maternity leave, laws against pregnancy discrimination, and even a state-sponsored dating service.

Besides encouraging fertility, Japan has taken several steps to include more of its population in the work force. Companies in Japan have long had a policy of mandating retirement at 55. This was raised to 60 in 1998. The new retirement age is set to be 65 by 2025 and proposals to set it at 70 are being discussed.[9] In case someone would say that this is cruel to the aged, it is worth noting that the idea of working later in life is by no means unpopular in Japan. A government study has shown that seven in 10 workers over 60 want to continue to work. The encouragement of older workers to stay active has already made a significant impact on the PSR. The latest numbers from the OECD show that Japan now has the seventh highest labor force participation rate of those 65 and older (22.1 percent), and there is still room for significant growth. In Iceland, which tops the list, nearly 40 percent of those 65 and older still work. Raising the retirement age is a surprisingly powerful tool. Economists have calculated that if the global average retirement age were raised from 65 to 70, this would increase the current global PSR from eight to 13.[10] That current global PSR level of eight can be maintained to 2100 by raising the retirement age to 73. Given that the projected average life expectancy will be around 80 by 2100, this means that we would still gain in the time we can enjoy retirement. Since we can expect an increase in productivity over the next eight decades, a PSR of eight is likely to be twice as large as it needs to be, at the very least, to sustain a decent living standard for most. It could be that some decades from now the worry about support ratios will seem antiquated as there are fewer jobs for humans in a highly automized economy.

Perhaps what we see in Japan is less a "demographic bomb" and more a fortuitous convergence. Automation is replacing labor but since the labor pool is smaller there is work for everyone.[11] The unemployment rate in Japan is marvelously low at 2.8 percent and, since labor demand is high, so are wages. Nine out of 10 Japanese consider themselves middle class, and Japan ranks among the most economically equal countries in the world. Japan has thereby escaped one of the antinomies of capitalism described by Karl Marx in *Das Kapital*. Marx predicted that increased efficiency inevitably results "in the creation of that monstrosity, an industrial reserve army, kept in misery in order to be always at the disposal of capital."[12] But if there are fewer active workers, who produce more, the status and the value of the worker can be maintained and even enhanced.

The positive message is that it is possible to have a world-leading economy and a rising-per-capita GDP even as the proportion of the elderly increases. We can avoid some of Japan's initial mistakes by proactively adapting to the demographic transformation: reform benefits, raise the retirement age, and in other ways encourage people to remain professionally active; promote female participation in the workplace; allow for regulated immigration; and create incentives to have larger families. These are a few measures that can be considered. We can also try to balance the budget and encourage retirement savings. If we are to live significantly longer—whether this means to 100 or 130 or 150 or more—and avoid overpopulation, then a lower fertility rate combined with a more generationally inclusive labor market of highly skilled workers and higher productivity is ideal.

Finally, the challenges and opportunities of Japan represent an extreme case of graying. There is no reason why, as is the case in many countries, a higher life expectancy cannot combine with a stable or slightly growing or slightly shrinking population, in which case the adjustment necessary would not have to be as drastic as in the case of Japan. Remember, the United Nations predicts that we will arrive and stabilize at an average birthrate of two children per woman over the next several decades. The point is that even in the most extreme case of a graying population represented by Japan, it is not necessarily—all things considered—a terrible situation. And this is before any antiaging technologies have changed the equation, enabling societies to grow older without graying.

11.4   (Missed) Economic Opportunities of Longevity

I'm old enough to know you can't close your mind to new ideas. You have to test out every possibility if you want something new.
—Dr. John Goodenough, physicist and inventor, at age 94

One reason why we do not see the increased longevity of a population as a benefit is our prejudices about old people. They are seen as slow, tired, frail, forgetful, and so on; we know the stereotype. Few of these prejudices hold up to scrutiny, and they obscure the ways in which an older employee more than makes up for them. Recent studies consistently show that older employees (60 and over) are dedicated, punctual, honest, detail-oriented, focused and attentive, good listeners, take pride in a job well done, have better organizational skills, and are more loyal to their company. Peter Cappelli, a management professor at the Wharton School at the University of Pennsylvania, has found that "every aspect of job performance gets better as we age. . . . I thought that the picture might be more mixed, but it isn't. The juxtaposition between the superior performance of older workers and the discrimination against them in the workplace just really makes no sense."[13] In other words, insofar as there is any mental deterioration, it does not, all things considered, make older employees overall less well performing than their younger colleagues.

Physics is a field that is often mentioned as a young man's intellectual game, but this is a myth. A recent story from the *New York Times* tells us about physicist and inventor Dr. John Goodenough, born in 1922, who in 1946 was told that he was too old to study physics. He was 23 at the time and he did not listen. At 94, Dr. Goodenough filed a patent application for a new kind of battery that "would be so cheap, lightweight, and safe that it would revolutionize electric cars and kill off petroleum-fueled vehicles."[14] In 2019, he was awarded the Nobel Prize in chemistry. Dr. Goodenough is not an isolated case of late-onset creativity. Since the 1980s, the average age at which a Nobel Prize winner in physics made his landmark discovery is 50.[15] The *New York Times* story goes on to tell us that, contrary to the received wisdom connecting youth and creativity, most patents are received by those aged 46 to 60. Even more surprisingly, those aged 76 to 80 received as many patents as those aged 26 to 30. Clearly, our social stereotypes of

what it means to be old are unfair, outdated, economically counterproduc-
tive, and need to go the way of racial and sexual prejudices. Rather than
advocating for getting rid of the old, as many of our foremost bioethicists
do, we should help each other to achieve our potential regardless of age.

Now, let us consider the scenario where the average life expectation
increases, not because we become grayer, but because we stay younger. Public health professor Jay Olshansky of the University of Illinois at Chicago
argues that slowing aging just three to seven years would "simultaneously
postpone all fatal and nonfatal disabling diseases; produce gains in health
and longevity equivalent to cures for major diseases; and create scientific,
medical, and economic windfalls for future generations that would be
roughly equivalent in impact to the discovery of antibiotics in the 20th
century."[16] We hear less about the longevity dividend than we hear about
ticking population time bombs and fertility busts, perhaps because it is
good news. Still, the notion of a longevity dividend is in no way surprising.
Thus far in human history, wealth and longevity have been positively correlated: the longer and healthier our lives are, the more time we can be productive; the more time we can be productive, the more value our education
has, meaning that more people will have higher qualifications and create
more value. In her splendid *New York Times* best-selling book titled *100+*,[17]
Sonia Arrison cites a study by the University of Chicago economists Kevin
M. Murphy and Robert H. Topel who have calculated that for Americans
"gains in life expectancy over the century were worth over $1.2 million per
person to the current population" and that "from 1970 to 2000, gains in life
expectancy added about $3.2 trillion per year to national wealth."[18] There
is a two-way relationship between increased life expectancy and wealth; it
is one of those positive spirals that Japan and similar countries have been
in and that developing countries hope to enter. If a couple of additional
healthy years can yield an "economic windfall," then imagine what adding half a century to a person's productive life would do. Consider, for
instance, how much more one could save and invest if one had 60 more
years to do so.

Pessimists warn that this outlook is far too rosy. They think that what we
should expect is not a windfall from people living longer and more productive lives but rather a growing mass of resource-devouring elderly for whom
life has little meaning. Fukuyama, for instance, predicts that many developed countries will find themselves in a "national nursing home scenario,

in which people routinely live to be 150 but spend their last 50 years in a state of childlike dependency on caretakers."[19] If we cannot delay Parkinson's, Alzheimer's disease, and other forms of dementia, then longevity is clearly robbed of its charm. Why, though, should we be this pessimistic? We have already achieved a doubling of the health span with compressed morbidity of laboratory animals, so why guess that it would be different for humans?[20] In the caloric restriction experiments, for instance, animals showed all the signs of being younger including as it related to their mental abilities. That is, caloric restriction slowed the atrophy of brain cells. Also encouraging are a couple of very recent experiments in which stem cell therapy was shown to rejuvenate the brains of mice.[21] Perhaps these results will not translate to humans, but these experiments do support a cautious optimism.[22]

So far, we have considered the effects of longevity on the economy, but that is of course only one of many effects. Fukuyama identifies other potentially dangerous implications of life extension. He speculates that among other things it will lead to social and scientific stagnation, hierarchies dominated by old and incompetent leaders, and long-lived tyrants. I will consider these worries in the order mentioned.

11.5   Calcified Hierarchies and Stagnation

Fukuyama recognizes that we are status-conscious by nature and spontaneously arrange ourselves in pyramids of submission and dominance. He also predicts that increasing our life span will "wreak havoc" on these structures: "With people routinely living and working into their 60s, 70s, 80s and even 90s, however, these pyramids will increasingly resemble squat trapezoids or even rectangles. The natural tendency of one generation to get out of the way of the up-and-coming will be replaced by the simultaneous existence of three, four, even five generations."[23] This could mean that younger people would be dominated, frustrated, and kept down by their seniors far into their adulthood. It could also mean, worries Fukuyama, that there would be more incompetence at the top:

> Age-graded hierarchies make functional sense insofar as age is correlated in many societies with physical prowess, learning, experience, judgment, achievement and the like. But past a certain age, the correlation between age and ability begins to go in the opposite direction.[24]

If Fukuyama is correct, then we are purchasing longevity at the high price of progress. But there are plenty of reasons for doubting that there must be this trade-off. We have already seen that older workers generally outperform younger ones and that their social skills are superior. But does this mean that there will be no way forward for young people to advance in their careers? Fukuyama's dystopia of inflexible age-graded, progress-preventing hierarchies occupied by older incompetent leaders seems to rely on an out-dated model of a career life as a slow and deliberate climb up the corpo-rate ladder. Few people these days expect to stay within a firm until they become senior management. This is no longer the dream. Even most CEOs are often replaced after four to five years. Much work is organized as net-works of independent contractors in which age-graded hierarchies have no relevance. People shift employers when they feel that they have no more to learn from them or when they get a better offer from another employer. They start and join projects for as long as they make sense to them, then they move on. In the new economy, leadership can be held by people of all ages. There is room for old stalwarts like Warren Buffet and upstarts like Mark Zuckerberg. The free market is not respectful of age-graded hierarchies or sentimental toward old leaders. If they cease to perform well, they are fired or their company founders against its competition.

Academia is mostly outside of market forces, so it presents a case where one would think that age-graded hierarchies and the failure of old profes-sors to retire risk that old ways of thinking about the world would stay beyond their usefulness. Fukuyama, taking aim at the discipline of econom-ics, writes,

> There is a saying that the discipline of economics makes progress one funeral at a time, which is unfortunately truer than most people are willing to admit. The survival of a basic "paradigm" (for example Keynesianism or Miltonianism) that shapes the way most scientists and intellectuals think about things at a particular time depends on the physical survival of the people who created that paradigm. As long as they sit on top of age-graded hierarchies like peer review boards, tenure committees, and the foundation boards of trustees, the basic paradigm will often remain virtually unshakable. It stands to reason, then, that political, social, and intellectual change will occur much more slowly in societies with substantially longer life spans.[25]

The adage that "economics advances one funeral at the time" is mordant, but how accurate is it?[26] As Fukuyama's own examples show, paradigms can survive the demise of their founder: Keynesianism survived John Maynard Keynes's death and so-called Miltonianism survived Milton Friedman's, just like Marxism survived Marx. In fact, both Keynes and Friedman wrote within schools of economic thought that antedated them: Friedman wrote in the tradition of classical liberal free-market economics, counting Adam Smith's *Wealth of Nations* (1776) as his starting point and continuing through David Ricardo and the Austrian neoclassical school of Ludwig von Mises and Frederick Hayek and then over the Atlantic to the University of Chicago where Friedman worked. Keynes's *The General Theory* (1936) was similarly an outgrowth of classical economics, adding a modest role for the government to stimulate the economy occasionally to bring down unemployment. Today, both schools are thriving: Keynesianism in the "saltwater school" located at Berkeley, Harvard, MIT, Princeton, and Yale; and Miltonianism in the "freshwater school" of the University of Chicago, Carnegie Mellon University, University of Rochester, and the University of Minnesota. Outside of academia their popularity waxes and wanes. Paradigms do not die with their creator and one paradigm does not have to die to create room for another since—as we have seen—several paradigms can exist in parallel.[27]

If generational hegemony at the top turns out to be a serious concern, we could insist on a policy of generational diversity, similar to how male hegemony has been counteracted by policies of sexual diversity in many institutions. And if academics should—against what we have reason to suppose—become resistant to new and better ways, the private sector will be more welcoming. Intellectual progress can therefore not be prevented even if academia were to become stagnant. This may be true in particular of the hard sciences because in the private sector the theoretical rubber must constantly hit the road. As for the humanities, the idea of progress is difficult, perhaps even impossible to measure. Was, for instance, poststructuralism an advance over structuralism in literature studies? Was postmodernism an advance over modernism? Is new historicism better than either? Or was all this change, as many argue in conservative media, generally for the worse compared with more traditional approaches to literature? Or are these just different possible lenses that can be used depending on the reader's various goals and is the notion of "progress" therefore inapplicable?

Fukuyama's prediction that "intellectual change" (does he mean "progress"?) will occur more slowly in societies with substantially increased life spans also seems to be contradicted by our experience. The aging of a society has so far not hampered intellectual vigor and progress. Every single game-changing intellectual and technical advance in recent history has come from the countries with high life expectancy. A high median age is correlated with relatively higher intellectual output. Take as an imperfect measure the number of science publications in important peer-reviewed journals. In absolute numbers, the top five countries in the number of articles published are the United States, China, Japan, Germany, and the United Kingdom. Once more we see old, shrinking Japan doing very well. In terms of papers relative to population (papers per person), the top five countries are Switzerland, Denmark, Norway, Sweden, and the Netherlands. Denmark produces more science papers even in absolute measures than Nigeria, which is 70 times as large and where the median age is only 18. Old Denmark is known for its sleek designs and progressive values; youthful Nigeria is still burning witches, showing us that progress is not predicated on having a young population. Instead, it is predicated on having a functioning society and a commitment to freedom of inquiry and the scientific method. Add once more the possibility of having an old but youthful population because of antiaging technology, and the intellectual production could simply explode, as experience combines with youthful energy, together with the realistic prospect of carrying out ambitious long-term projects even when at an advanced age (relative to current measures).

But what about political progress? Fukuyama writes,

> Many observers have noted that political change often occurs at generational intervals—from the progressive era to the New Deal, from the Kennedy years to Reaganism. There is no mystery as to why this is so: people born in the same age cohort experience major life events—the Great Depression, World War II, or the sexual revolution—together. Once people's life views and preferences have been formed by these experiences, they may adapt to new circumstances in small ways, but it is very difficult to get them to change broad outlooks.[28]

Fukuyama thinks this means that as the proportion of old people "fixed in their views" grows, society will change more slowly. While initially plausible sounding, Fukuyama's conjecture is contradicted by the fact that there has never been a greater proportion of old people, yet society has never changed as fast, not only technologically but also value-wise. For instance, in 2001, Americans opposed same-sex marriage by a margin of 57 percent to 35 percent. Merely 16 years later in 2017, 62 percent support it while only 32 percent oppose it.[29] During the same time the median age increased from 35.5 to 38. Apparently, views are not that fixed, even in a graying society. In fact, we have grown older and more progressive over the last century, not just in the United States but all over the world. And we have grown more progressive in the grayer part of the world. When we think of a politically progressive society, we think of, say, Denmark or Sweden, not Nigeria. As already noted, the amount of progress one makes has less to do with a country's median age than it has to do with culture. This is empirical: countries with lower life expectancy typically value tradition and survival, not social progress. It is the commitment to certain ideas such as individual freedom and the rule of law that guarantees societal progress in the same way as it is the scientific method and the values of free and open inquiry that guarantees scientific progress. If these ideas are in place, then it is quite irrelevant whether we live to 80 or 120 or longer. It is, as said, manifest that countries with a higher median age are more progressive, so why are we so quick to think that a higher median age contradicts progress? Could ageism play a role here?

Speaking of politics, it is commonplace to remark that we become more conservative with age, and there is some data to back this up. Generally, people are more likely to vote more conservative (Republican in the United States) from the time they are in their 40s. There is also evidence that when someone comes of age—turns 18—the political climate of that time period impacts their voting. If, for example, they turned 18 under Reagan (Gen-X) or G. H. W. Bush, then they are more likely to vote Republican, and if they turned 18 under Clinton (Gen-Y), then they are more likely to vote Democratic.[30] Nevertheless, we might be tempted to think that if we lived longer, we would all be increasingly conservative, to the detriment of progress. But this would be too hasty. The picture is complicated. While we are more conservative after 40, the likelihood that we will be conservative does not increase significantly thereafter. In the 2016 US election, the 45–64 segment voted 53 percent for the Republican candidate, almost the same percentage as for those 65 and older. Moreover, age itself is a small factor among many others. Income, geography, marital status, religious affiliation, sex, and race are more significant predictors of voting patterns. Having studied voting patterns over time, Robert H. Binstock concludes, "Older people are as diverse in their voting as any other age group; their votes divide along the same partisan, economic, social, gender, racial and ethnic lines as those of the electorate at large."[31] If, for example, you are Latino, then you are significantly more likely to vote Democratic; if you are a Tennessean, you are more likely to vote Republican; and if you are a woman, you are more likely to vote Democratic regardless of how old you are or which administration was in place when you were 18. It should also be factored in that the older population is contingently different in other ways than simply being older and having grown up at an earlier time. It is, for example, also whiter, far less likely to be college educated, and more likely to be married. In other words, it is not mere age per se that explains current voting patterns. When the young today become the old tomorrow, they will be far less white, far more educated, and far less likely to be married. Thus, it is not a forgone conclusion that they will lean Republican.

To this complexity must be added that voters' values are often "lost in translation" from the voting box to Washington, DC. We have associated Republican with conservative and Democratic with liberal, but the two major parties are not pure and consistent in their ideologies and they are not particularly different in the wide view of things. They are both in favor of a liberal constitutional democracy and a welfare state with a limited free market; they are both for immigration; and they both borrow and wage wars. Neither is there any reliable correlation between their stated values and real-world effects. The "conservative" Republican Party under Bush added government spending, created a national debt of $10 trillion and took interventionist nation-building to new heights; the "progressive" Democrats under Obama further increased government spending, increased the gap between the top 1% and the rest, added another $10 trillion to the debt, continued Bush's wars, and started new ones. The Trump administration further increased government spending, further widened the gap between the top 1% and the rest, added to the debt at an even higher pace than the two previous administrations, but started no new wars. Perhaps more surprising was that immigration continued at a pace of just above a million immigrants per year, as it had under Bush and Obama. In fact, 2017 and 2018 legal immigration was higher than all but one year (2016) during the Obama administration. What we think we vote for and what we get are often very different.

We should also question Fukuyama's assumption that old people form a homogeneous class due to their common experiences. Not only is the range of 65 and over large, with some being born before the Second World War and others after it, even if people live through the same historical epochs, they experience them differently. To use Fukuyama's examples, the Second World War made some imperialists, some isolationists, and other pacifists. Most Americans were not at Woodstock or Haight/Ashbury or in Ken Kesey's LSD-powered bus tour; they were appalled by the sexual revolution and might remain so. The Kennedy years were a time when the working class started to migrate toward conservatism as the left embraced identity politics and became the party of immigrants and women. They were the most important years for the formation of the new conservatism. And the Reagan presidency, the apex of the New Right, was, depending on whom you ask, the best of times or the worst of times. History can be told from one end or the other. Consider the three most important presidential candidates of 2016—Hillary Clinton, 69, Bernie Sanders, 74, and Donald Trump, 70. They were the most distinctive political figures of the race: their membership in the same age bracket did not make them the same, despite having "experienced major life events . . . together." Old people are individuals. Fukuyama's images of the old as some sort of useless clogs in the societal machinery that need to "get out of the way" obscures this reality.

Not all new ideas are good and not all change is progress. What is crucial is the content of the views that the old "stick to." If among the views that the old are loath to give up are a commitment to individual rights and a limited government, then their "fixity" will enable an evolving society rather than prevent it. National Socialism and Stalinism were new ideas championed by the young. The young carried the medievalist mullahs to power in Iran, they were Mao's willing executioners during his Cultural Revolution, and they belonged to Pol Pot's Khmer Rouge in Cambodia where they killed anyone wearing spectacles or speaking a foreign language. Youth can be so dangerously self-righteous in their beliefs because they have no real-life experience to contradict them. With so little factual input, their ideas become everything and worth killing for. Is it not possible that we may gain in understanding as we age? Are not older voters more informed than young voters? Whom do you trust more to make political decisions, your current self or your younger self? When the arguments to invade Iraq were made in 2002, it was those 65 and over who were the least in favor of it.[32] Whether we agree with the war or not, something in the experiences of the older generation made them less enthused about it. Could it be that a more age-diverse society will be more prudent and less impressed by the crisis du jour?

As to the age of the political leaders, this should not be a major concern since either they are doing a good job, in which case their age should not matter, or they are not, in which case they will not be reelected. In addition, term limits also ensure a turn around. Such limits are now being proposed for the US Senate and Supreme Court.

11.6 Immortal Tyrants

Fukuyama recognizes that democracies have legal means to prevent people from staying in power for too long, but he worries about countries not equally blessed:

> We have already seen the deleterious consequences of prolonged generational succession in authoritarian regimes that have no constitutional requirements limiting tenure in office. As long as dictators like Francisco Franco, Kim Il Sung, and Fidel Castro survive, their societies have no way of replacing them, and all political and social change is effectively on hold until they die. In the future, with technologically enhanced life spans, such societies may find themselves locked in a ludicrous death watch not for years but for decades.[33]

This is a common worry, but it seems overly anxious and contrived. Of course, if everyone lives longer, then tyrants might also rule longer. But while this can be a tragedy for the people in the countries in which it happens, it is not a prevalent phenomenon. Looking at recent history, we see that an increase in longevity has correlated with an increase in democratization, and we find the world's best democracies in the longest-living parts of the world. Besides, it is not easy to tell whether the longevity of a bad ruler is the main obstacle to progress or not. There are often reasons, such as ethnic or religious diversity, that produce insecurity and a lack of trust for which despotism is the traditional answer. In such circumstances, the choice may be between suffering the instability of having a rapid succession of incompetent rulers or the stability of having a longer-ruling quasi-competent autocrat. Countries such as Liberia, Nigeria, and Sudan were ruled by a revolving door of crooks and maniacs, and they made little to no progress as a result. Libya, by comparison, was ruled by one eccentric leader, Muammar Gadhafi, and became Africa's most steadily advancing country. In 1970, life expectancy was roughly 50 in Libya and in Nigeria it was roughly 41. Forty years later, in 2010, the average life expectancy in Nigeria was 51, after a succession of 13 different leaders, compared to

70 in Libya after 42 years of Gadhafi, a gain of 20 years in life expectancy. Both literacy and per capita GDP advanced to become the highest on the continent. This progress itself lays the groundwork for an improvement in the political arrangements, since an educated middle class eventually will demand political influence commensurate with its economic and social status. The main point here is that, *pace* Fukuyama, replacing a ruler is not a guarantee of progress and in some cases prevents it. Without peace and order there can be no trust and no freedom, and without trust and freedom there will be little progress. The case of Gadhafi also illustrates that people do not need to wait for a leader to die to replace him. Whether Gadhafi would have lived another 20 or 50 years is moot since he was overthrown and killed. Other recent examples where strongmen have been deposed before their natural death include Saddam Hussein in Iraq, Pol Pot in Cambodia, Idi Amin in Uganda, Mobutu Sese Seko in Zaire, Nicolai Ceausescu in Romania, Jean-Claude Duvalier in Haiti, Ferdinand Marcos in the Philippines, Hosni Mubarak in Egypt, Fulgencio Batista in Cuba, Alfredo Stroessner in Paraguay, Ben Ali in Tunisia, Charles Taylor in Liberia, and Mohamed Morsi in Egypt. Correspondingly, it is also incorrect to assume that the natural death of a ruler marks the end of an oppressive regime. Fidel Castro is dead, but his brother Raoul Castro continued his legacy. The same holds for Fukuyama's other example, North Korea, where Kim Il Sung is dead, but Kim Jong Il and then Kim Jong Un have continued the oppression. The picture, then, is complicated: A high turnover of rulers appears to be neither necessary nor sufficient for progress, and we need not wait for a ruler to die a natural death to replace him or her. What is clear, though, is that the possibility of having longer-living bad rulers is not, in the grand scheme of things, particularly alarming.

11.7 Many Other Challenges

Fukuyama brings up a host of other possible consequences of having extended lives in combination with lower fertility: there will be an increase in the median age difference between the richer and poorer parts of the world; more women will be voting in our elections (since women live longer on average) with the result that foreign military interventions will be disfavored; there will be fewer young people to serve as soldiers; old people cannot appear attracted to each other and will dream of younger partners;

there will be more old people represented on the front pages in the magazine stands; our lives will feel empty and pointless given their added length in combination with an attenuation of relationships to family. Fukuyama is right to identify the challenge of finding a meaningful old age in a time when many have weaker ties to the family. The specter of lonely, isolated, and out of touch old people for whom life has little point is real enough. Thirty thousand elderly Japanese die alone each year. Often, they are discovered weeks after their death, as the smell of their rotting flesh alarms their neighbors. It is not hard to picture a future of physically healthy but socially deprived very old people lingering on, rather than living on. They would be sleeping, feeding, drinking, watching screens, and communicating with AI-nurses, on and on, alone and devoid of purpose. This may very well be what life extension would mean for many. However, extrapolating from the average life satisfaction of the very old today, many more can be expected to appreciate more time. It should also be noted that low fertility, loneliness, and isolation cannot be wholly blamed on longevity; rather these social anomies are the effect of factors associated with the same modernity that gives us longer lives. This is a new world, and it is not surprising that there are many aspects that we have not yet found a way to deal with as well as we would wish. Notwithstanding, the fact that some people will not know what to do with more life—just as some people cannot handle winning the lottery—is not a sound reason to prevent those who do from living longer.

We have done it before: in one century we have doubled life expectancy and transitioned from an existence where death was omnipresent and unpredictable, to one where death is seen as afflicting only the old. Despite the revolutionary transformation, we adapted quite well, and we now have a new normal, where the death of a child is seen as a singular tragedy, and we can expect to see 80. I take this as evidence that we could adapt to much longer health spans and regard our present situation as primitive and tragic. We have been able to tell and believe in stories that make sense of aging, decay, illness, and death before 100, and it is not hard to imagine that should we defeat aging we would be able to tell and believe in an alternative story that makes sense of our new condition of continued health. In such a future, it may be that a choice of taking the natural path of gradual enfeeblement and sickness is seen as immoral (what about your near and dear?) and irrational (you want to be less healthy rather than more?).

Most of the adverse social consequences brought up by Fukuyama would be greatly reduced if we assume that radical life extension is achieved by slowing, arresting, or even reversing biological aging. We should then imagine a population where experience is combined with youthfulness. Ask yourself, what would you want to do if you were given youthfulness and more than 100 years more to live. You swallow the pill and return to a state of prime physical functioning. What next? You take some time to just feel it. Likely, you will want to continue to pursue many of the things you are already pursuing, but now with more ambition. Then you might consider taking up some road never taken for one reason or another. Perhaps it is not too late to be a published author, or a 5.0 tennis player, or learn French. You can finally become an educated person. You will want to experience this respite with your favorite people and now you have time to open up for more new friends in your life. Imagine how interesting it would be if you could have met your great grandparents. The questions you would have and how much you could learn from each other. Now you have the chance of being a great grandparent and engaging with your great grandchildren. You could tell them about life before the internet, like your great grandparents could have told you about life before television, or perhaps before the car. Think what a support system and knowledge bank such an extended family or network of friends could constitute. It could provide the deeper roots—deeper than ever—that would work as a salutary antidote to the discomfort of the modern atomization of society.

None of the challenges posed by life extension discussed above are beyond our powers to solve and none of them are worse than the current state of aging and death. We lose each other so fast. If the choice is between death and the challenge of living well together, the latter is incomparably better. A society that values life and serves the interests of its members should regard life extension as one of its highest priorities.

This raises the worry that not all who want life-extending treatments can have them.

11.8   The Distribution of Life Extension

A frequent complaint—one of the first that comes to people's minds—is that only the very rich, or only some self-elected elite, or only certain countries will have access to radical life extension, further deepening the gulf between the haves and the have-nots. Will there be violent upheavals as people struggle to take a sip from the Fountain of Youth? Yoval Noah Harari imagines such a scenario in his recent book about transformative technologies:

> If you think that religious fanatics with burning eyes and flowing beards are ruthless, just wait and see what elderly retail moguls and ageing Hollywood starlets will do when they think the elixir of life is within their reach. . . . Once the scientific efforts are crowned with success, they will trigger bitter conflicts. All the wars and conflicts of history might turn out to be but pale prelude for the real struggle ahead of us: the struggle for eternal youth.[34]

As common as these worries are, they are not particularly well founded. If we assume, as a first scenario, that the treatment is very costly so that only billionaires can afford it, this would be unfortunate, but it would not necessarily create insurmountable problems for justice. Let the billionaires have it. It would in no way hurt us. We would not live a shorter time if Elon Musk, Bill Gates, Larry Ellison, Peter Thiel, and Warren Buffet lived longer. Good for them. It would be a distribution in accordance with the general principle that inequalities are acceptable if they make some people better off without making anyone else worse off in absolute terms. It is the same principle of distribution that, unfortunately, we must accept when it comes to other lifesaving treatments like heart transplants and expensive medicines such as Elaprase for sufferers of Hunter syndrome. It is better that some lives are saved than none. Inequality begins when not everyone has nothing.

But perhaps this kind of inequality *does* make someone worse off? If I see that Elon Musk in addition to all his wealth also does not age, and neither do his beautiful wife and children, whereas I and those around me fall apart and die, it may sadden me. In some way his longevity makes my own brevity worse. The levelling power of death is a perennial would-be solace. Philosopher John K. Davies calls all the negative emotions caused by the awareness that someone else has their life extended "distress."[35] There is no question that I would feel distress (mixed with being happy for Musk and his family) and it is reasonable to suppose that many people would feel distress. The question then is, is distress a good reason to deny Musk and other fortunate people a longer life? My gut reaction is: absolutely not. There is no way that I would consider my distress so important that Elon Musk and his family must be prevented from living substantially longer than me.

Generally, the distress of seeing someone else with something that I want is something to overcome and cannot by itself count as a moral reason for denying this person this something, *ceteris paribus*.

Since antiaging treatments may not come for another couple of generations it is possible that we are all in the position of the last person who cannot get on the lifeboat, and that makes our deaths feel even worse. Still, it would be terribly spiteful to want to deny these future generations life extension because we might miss out—analogous to not wanting to launch the lifeboats for fear that others may be saved but not oneself. Or to use a closer analogy, the fact that many in poor countries suffer and die from illnesses is made even worse when there are treatments for such illnesses available in rich countries. It adds to the tragedy. Still, the answer is not to deny everyone access to these treatments. The answer is to work toward providing it to everyone who needs it. And that is why, despite the distress felt by us who do not have access to antiaging medicine, Elon Musk and other fortunate few should not be denied life extension even if we cannot have it. Besides, Davies points out, preventing antiaging medicine from being developed would do little to alleviate the added tragedy, since it would remain true that in a close possible world it is developed and distributed to us. A world where we do not have access to a treatment because we are too poor, is still closer to a world where we have it, than a world where there is no treatment because we have abstained from finding one.

But is it not *unfair* that Elon Musk gets the antiaging treatment it rather than someone more deserving? No doubt a case could be made that someone as blessed with opportunities such as Musk is the last person who needs even more opportunities. Why not give it someone who through no fault of their own has lived a life bereft of valuable opportunities? It is a nice thought, but it would not be a rational choice in the world as it is. If companies developing antiaging treatments knew that they would be forced to give these astronomically expensive (we assume) treatments away as charity, they would not be able to justify developing them to their shareholders. And if it is suggested that we use public funds to purchase the treatment to give to a handful of unfortunates, it would be the most wasteful public program in history diverting funds from many other more essential services. If, on the other hand, Musk and other billionaires purchase the treatment for their own money, it would compensate the company for its research and development and make it an attractive investment with the possibility that they may continue to improve the quality and accessibility of the product. The ability to pay is therefore an acceptable principle of distribution as long as the treatment is affordable to billionaires only. The answer to one of the most common objections to life extension—"only the very rich will be able to afford it"—is surprisingly simple: let them have it.

Many would not stand for this answer. Radical egalitarians will want to deny the few a good if everyone cannot have it. Yet others will consider the thought of a longer life not just distressing but *intolerable* unless they themselves have a longer life. If there is life extension, they must have it. This is where Harari's violent dystopia takes off. A "war over eternal youth" is not unthinkable, but it is also far from obvious how it would play out. Are we to imagine that a retail mogul and an aging Hollywood starlet would join an armed militia with the purpose of taking over the factory of antiaging medicine or to sack the antiaging clinic and to kidnap the personnel and force them to perform the procedures? This seems far-fetched. There has long been inequality between those with access to life-extending technologies and procedures, such as antibiotics and clean hospitals, and those without, but this has never caused a significant violent conflict. Even with their lives at stake, no one has ever stormed plants or sacked clinics to get hold of the medicine Elaprase or to force a doctor and her team to perform a heart transplant. The grip of apologist attitudes is further reason for thinking that war is avoidable.[36]

There is a different answer to the worry that only the very rich will be able to afford life extension: antiaging medicine might not be enormously expensive. Usually, it is the research and development that makes treatments expensive, and the fewer potential users it has, the more expensive it will be. This is what explains the cost of Elaprase. Antiaging drugs, on the other hand, have billions of potential users and can therefore be expected to make a return even on an enormous investment almost immediately. Things would be more complicated and costly if life extension required some extensive and periodical treatment requiring the attention of medical professionals, but here there is reason to think that over time the process can become automated and streamlined. Robots might handle routine dips in the pool of life, or perhaps we would teach ourselves to perform it, or perhaps we would all be taught how to do so in school. In the larger picture, we have seen an exponential increase in the velocity with which new technologies proliferate. Electricity, the internet, and smartphones exemplify the trend. A highly relevant example may be the sequencing of the human genome. It took 13 years and cost roughly $2.7 billion to complete the first successful sequencing in 2003. Since then, the price has dropped to $1,000, it is publicly available, and the process only takes an hour. Perhaps life extension medicine will not be incredibly expensive but perhaps still relatively costly, like a new car or even a house. In this scenario, there are different reasonable ways a distribution could be realized. For those who cannot afford to pay for the cure up front, we can imagine payment plans akin to house mortgages and student loans. Those who want a longer life can use parts of that longer life to pay for it. Countries with a welfare state model, such as Japan, Canada, and the Nordic countries, could simply introduce a longevity tax under the assumption that their people prefer to stay young and healthy. Perhaps those who are not interested in life extension can be exempt, and those who are benefiting from the extension pay a higher rate. In fact, there is a straightforward theoretical argument in favor of a left-liberal society striving for an equal distribution of life extension.[37] Aging and ill health, and ultimately death, are encumbering the expression of the individual's chosen life plan, and just as liberalism wants to remove other obstacles to self-expression such as lack of access to education, or unemployment and poverty, or discrimination and prejudice, it should therefore seek to mitigate these as far as possible, consistent with other goals. Other kinds of societies may approach the distribution differently. Classical liberal and capitalist societies, for example, would simply trust that the market would efficiently cater to the interest in more life on the model, of smartphones, cars, and houses. The strongest reason for optimism that we will find reasonable principles of distribution is probably that there is a strong financial imperative from the point of view of the state to encourage its development and universal distribution. Better health, and added years of productivity, and even new peaks of intellectual creativity when experience is married with youthful energy in a novel way are all potentially enormous fiscal gains, making distribution more of a practical and less of an ideological issue.

In sum, the distribution problem is often brought up as if it proves that life extension is an impossibly unfair or morally compromised proposition but, as we have seen, in reality there is no reason to think that life extension must be very expensive, and there is a range of acceptable solutions for how to distribute it. The accidental virtue of this objection to life extension is that it treats life extension as a good thing. That is, although presented as a reason for why it is better to age and die the natural way, it also tacitly agrees with prolongevism in so far as it is concerned that not all who want it can have it. Perhaps the egalitarian making this objection is also opposed to life extension for other reasons, but it is hard to make sense of an insistence that everyone ought to have access to something that one also considers a bad thing for them.

11.9   A Question of Priorities

There is a different kind of justice-related argument, which says that as long as there are people who lack the bare necessities in life, like clean drinking water, we ought not to spend money on antiaging research. It is a question of priorities. Audrey R. Chapman makes this point:

> My position is that our first priority for health-related investments should be to provide basic medical services to everyone in our own country and to ameliorate health needs elsewhere in the world. Pursuing efforts to extend the human life span seems like a frivolous investment in comparison with these imperatives.[38]

This argument is most relevant as it relates to the use of tax dollars. Here is why I think it fails: The problem with health care is primarily that it is inefficient. Given what we spend on it, it should be able to provide basic medical services to every American. Other countries do a better job. Taking the money that goes to antiaging research to feed a malfunctioning system is therefore not the solution. That is, money may not be the solution, and certainly taking the money from antiaging research (a small amount in the context) rather than from somewhere else in the budget makes little sense. Why single out antiaging as the research to be put on hold, rather than, say cancer, diabetes, or Alzheimer's research? Chapman appears to suffer from the common misunderstanding that antiaging is divorced from the project of health, as if antiaging research aimed at making us live longer in some other way than making us less vulnerable to disease. Antiaging medicine is preventative medicine and therefore not only more humane in that it aims at giving people more healthy years free from suffering, but it is also potentially more economically sound. We have already discussed the incredible economic benefits of an increased health span, including the lower demand for medical services. This would in time enable us to spend more on basic medical care for all. Of course, Chapman is a supporter of the Wise View, and thus does not think it is very important whether we live to 80—as we now do—or to 90 or 100. But we care a great deal whether we, or perhaps our parents, or grandparents can count on living 10 more years or 20 more years at age 80, or whether they should expect their lives to end much sooner than that. It is hard to imagine a less frivolous way to spend health-related tax dollars than on research that promises to keep people healthy and alive.

As to the project of providing health care for citizens of other countries, this should be undertaken without putting research into cancer or aging on hold. Poor health care, when not the result of natural disasters and war, is usually the result of poor governance, and the solution is therefore not ultimately that American citizens provide it where needed (although in the short term this may be part of a solution). But is there not a risk that the poorer part of the world will be left out if we succeed in delaying or reversing aging? Yes, that is very likely to happen just as health inequality increased when doctors in the West began to wash their hands. We cannot deny ourselves progress on the grounds that it makes us better off than those who have not similarly progressed. Imagine if the roles were reversed (which could happen over time) and we no longer had the most advanced science and most prosperous economy. Clearly, we would not want to deny (begrudge) a more advanced country healthier longer lives for their populations as a result of their science, on the grounds that it would make them better off than us. And second, wherever the antiaging treatment is discovered and produced, over time the cure is likely to reach more parts of the world. The life extension revolution of the last century began in the developed world and then spread globally as habits and technologies were increasingly adopted. The greatest gains in life expectancy during the last 30 years have been in the developing world and the gap between the rich and the poor world is projected to continue to shrink. In 1950, the life expectancy at birth in the world was 48; and in the United States 65; today the average life expectancy at birth in the world is 72, and the average for the United States is 79. We should expect the same pattern to repeat itself if a cure for aging appeared. First the longevity gap will widen and then it will close as the rest of the world catches up. This time, though, it will probably close faster since we are more globally connected. In sum, we have good

reason to progress with life extension even before all other health-care needs
have been met for all. To deny this would amount to embracing a principle
that makes medical scientific progress impossible.

11.10   The Fog of Future Technology

A longer-living society is one for which we can rationally wish. Such a society would pose new kinds of challenges but none that are more serious than
our current problem with aging and death. It is not only ill informed, but
callous and lacking in imagination to suggest that the best solution for such
problems is that people get frail, become ill, and die. Wanting to extend
our lives now rests on the conviction that we will enjoy the future and
it will be worth living in. It is the same optimism directing us to want to
have children and we have seen that that is justified. I have sought to show
that provided the increase comes with health, most of the common worries
about the economy, progress, and so on, are misplaced.

The X factor here is the evolution of technology. Future technology
may present new possibilities bearing both on our access to resources and
our psychological capacity for longevity. We are at the very infancy of the
relevant sciences of genetics, nanotechnology, and robotics, which may
expand our mastery of nature, both outside and within us, in radical ways.
We can already, on a rudimentary level, manipulate individual atoms, edit
DNA, and control external objects with our thoughts. Who can tell with
any certainty what, say, 100 years' more research will deliver? This X factor
makes it impossible to say what kind of society we would have if we lived
to, say, 150 on average.

When we imagine not dying, we are naturally imagining our dear old
selves on a long, interesting, and open-ended journey, somewhat like the
hero in Borges's story "The Immortal." That is, we assume a fundamentally
unchanged human psychology, but this assumption may turn out to be
incorrect. Radical life extension will come, if it comes, in concert with a
cluster of new powers. Our intelligence may reach superhuman levels either
through gene editing or through merging our minds with computers. And
through gene editing or through psychotropic drugs or brain stimulation
or computer implants or some other way, we may design ourselves in accordance with our ideals. If this becomes a possibility, then it is no longer relevant if an unenhanced person would be bored, alienated, or incapable of

appreciating spring warblers and sunsets; she would just need a tweak and an upgrade and then eternity would be supremely enjoyable. This raises the disturbing question (touched upon in chapter 8) of whether we would then have survived or perhaps, as bioconservatives warn, in fact replaced ourselves? For these are the possibilities that feed nightmare scenarios of dystopic science fiction. As our myths tell us and our political history bears testimony to, our search for perfection can land us in a perfect hell; if it does this time, how will we ever know the way back? How do we un-bite the apple? Hence, yes, things may turn out to be disastrous, but we must keep in mind that whatever ills we can conjure as the effect of conquering aging and extending our lives must be compared to our horrific status quo.

Moreover, whether we like it or not, there are conditions in place that make it nearly impossible to prevent the development of these transformative technologies. In the same way that our thoughts about the next 100 years must be based on an allowable illusion that we have a grasp on the many variables creating it, discussions about the promises, perils, and relations to morality of transformative sciences and technologies involve the equally allowable illusion of agency: that we are able judiciously to give green lights and red lights to control what will happen. In reality, we are not in a significantly different position from the first hunter-gatherers who thought it a good idea to stay and cultivate a strain of wild wheat, not knowing that they took the first step toward modernity and their own lifestyle's obsolescence. The technologies that will transform the human condition are likely to be decentralized, the agendas multifarious, and the market forces powerful. We can perhaps, only perhaps, prevent certain specific unpopular applications such as human reproductive cloning.[39] However, as Leon Kass himself noted, "the train has already left the station" and there is no emergency brake to stop it. If we find a way to stave off death, we will take it, whether it is a road to salvation or a road to perdition.

12 The State of the Debate and a Concluding Dialogue Concerning the Badness of Human Mortality

12.1 The State of the Debate

Will the public change its view of aging and death and life extension technologies? I think so. I believe that much of the resistance stems from the feeling that aging is impossible to cure, or at least not in our lifetime. More youth and life are sour grapes. The sense that life extension is a hopeless pursuit is understandable given the terrible track record of false claims about the fountain of youth. The fear is that if we reach for more life, what we end up with will be something similar to existing resource-demanding life extension technologies used to treat the terminally ill to marginal benefit. There is a sentiment that there is a tragic and inescapable trade-off between quantity and quality of life. Some of this resistance will weaken as the public becomes more aware of the many promising avenues pursued by antiaging science, and as it learns that its goal is really to prevent us from getting sick. If successful, we can expect something very different from existing technologies: something that increases quantity of life by increasing quality of life.

Once the public is open to the possibility of addressing aging it opens itself up to the powerful rhetoric of health. The term "geroprotective"—medicine that affects the root cause of aging and aging related diseases—is not yet in common parlance but it encapsulates this strategy since it frames the issue as one over protecting from loss of health ("sensible"), rather than as extending life ("extreme"). Do we want a lower risk of cardiovascular disease, diabetes, heart disease, Alzheimer's disease, and cancer? What do we want for our children? The public will find it hard to keep up its resistance to life extension technologies whether they are conceptualized as such or not. It is hard to argue against health. Once a pill (or some other means) is available and proven to be a safe way to add healthy decades to our lives, I surmise that even long-standing moral and philosophical arguments will fade away and eventually be nearly incomprehensible to future generations. Did people in the 2020s really say that they were not interested in living longer, healthier lives by slowing aging?

In a world where autonomy is sacred and where even genders are seen as social constructs, it is strange that so many still think that nature must be obeyed if it tells us that we must make do with the time it gives us. Often, they combine their apologism with a strong personal interest in appearing young and healthy through (unnatural) cosmetic products: do they really want the appearance, but not the real thing? I have tried to explain this on the cultural level: we are in the grip of a perennial apologist ideology that provides us with a narrative that tames death and assuages our fear of it: the Wise View. The Wise View used to make sense, but its time has passed. Before modern science it was reasonable to accept whatever nature offered up, but these days such quietism is irrational and harmful and once we have geroprotectors that work, this will become even more obvious. We are always suspicious about new biotechnology, but antiaging medicine is likely to gradually assimilate with accepted life-extending technologies such as vaccinations, antibiotics, and preventive medicine in general. Many will cease to think of it as unnatural once it is normalized.

Prolongevity is consonant with liberal democracy because the foundation of the liberal conception of society is that it exists to further the ends of its members, first and foremost their self-preservation, rather than some transcendent aim of an imagined emergent whole. In other words, it is not so simple to contrast the personal good with the good of society. This is why some conservatives and what is sometimes called the regressive left meet in their rejection of both the liberal view and of radical life extension technology and converge on bioconservatism. Their view—thoughtlessly embraced by many—that the best solution to a possible shortage of resources, or an environmental emergency, or a stagnation of culture and science is that we die, even when we could have healthy years ahead of us, is profoundly illiberal and collectivist. I am not prepared to die for the GDP or ask of anyone else that they do so; that is not the kind of society I want to live in. The contract is that we hand over power to the government so that they can protect our rights, not so that they can prevent us from living in order to save resources or to promote some other larger goal; that is not what we signed up for. Resistance to life extension is reactionary and, assuming that society progresses, will eventually be regarded as fringe.

These are not merely hopeful speculations. There is already one country whose people break with the Wise View. A recent study of Canadians shows that 59 percent would want to live to 120 if science made it possible to do so in good health.[1] Forty-seven percent believed that it will be possible as soon as by 2050. Only 31 percent agreed that "living to 120 is unnatural." Those who believed that it will be possible by 2050 were also more inclined to disagree that it is unnatural. Notwithstanding the Canadian avant-garde, the Wise View is still the received opinion among thoughtful people. Like the great philosophers of the past, they claim to find little fault with death. Article after article scolds Silicon Valley's quest for immortality and makes the old ponderous apologist talking points about hubris, narcissism, boredom, overpopulation, inequality, and so on. Still, overall, the case against death is gaining ground. Important leaders like Peter Thiel, Larry Page, Larry Ellison, Sergei Brin, Mark Zuckerberg, and Elon Musk provide the necessary assurance of authority to timid believers to dare admit that if death is the end it is not such a great blessing after all. In so far as adherence to the Wise View is an instance of preference falsification, such modeling of death-resistance is more powerful than philosophical arguments. The 2016 presidential election included for the first time a candidate, Zoltan Istvan, running on a platform "to conquer death with science and technology," not to win the election of course, but to broadcast the idea to a wider public. Once the benefits of slowing aging with the hope of defeating death become part of common knowledge, there may come a time, perhaps even just a few elections down the road, when candidates are asked what they plan to do to prevent us from dying and when an antiaging stance is essential for any electable candidate. With increased political will and with more interest and research going toward science-based antiaging medicine, a breakthrough might be nearer than we think. Until then, stay alive.

12.2   A Dialogue Concerning the Badness of Human Mortality

While writing this book I have had many good conversations with friends and strangers. By way of recapitulation, here is a stylized composition of these conversations:

Death is a terrible thing. I do not wish to die, and I do not wish that my loved ones die.

But why fear death? Either you go to a better place or you are extinguished and therefore cannot suffer.

True, if death is a transition to a better state, then it would not be terrible to die. It would not really be death in the sense that bothers me. I hope to continue beyond the grave, but I'm not persuaded that I will. And the alternative, that death is the final end, is one of the worst things that I can imagine happening to me, to you, or to anyone who has a valuable life.

But, if death is the permanent end of you, it will be like a deep, dreamless sleep. What is so frightening about that?

Imagine that tonight when you close your eyes, you will never open them again. You will never see anything again. You will never sense anything again. There will be no waking up to see the room flooded in morning light, no hugging the person next to you, no smell of coffee, no shower, no planning of the day, no listening to your favorite music, no more skies and oceans, no more seeing your family and friends. All your most precious memories and feelings and unfulfilled dreams—that whole internal world you inhabit—will be erased. Soon thereafter no one will know you ever existed.

So what? I'm not existing, so I won't know what I'm missing.

You don't get it. Meditate on it some time when you are alone at 4 a.m. in the morning.

I think it's easy: either I'm alive or I'm dead. If I'm alive, fine, and if I'm dead, fine, because I will not be alive to regret not existing.

Of course, if death is the end, then you cannot regret not existing but nevertheless and equally true you will no longer enjoy being alive. You will, for example, never again see your loved ones. How can you not prefer to see them over being dead?

But perhaps I appreciate life and the things and the people in it precisely because time is limited?

I hear that a lot. We need a deadline to appreciate life. And to love someone, we need to know that we will not be around forever. I don't think that's true. If I learned that my mother would not die, I don't think I would stop loving her. I also don't think I would cease to enjoy playing tennis, or drinking gin and tonics, or listening to music, or watching snow drift, and so on. The "deadline hypothesis" is most likely false. Moreover, there is a logical error in the way that it's formulated.

What error would that be?

Even if I agreed that we need a deadline—and I don't—we need not agree that the deadline would not work just as well if it were around 200 years or even further out than that. Hence, the deadline argument fails to show that the natural life span is also the perfect deadline.

Two hundred years! You would be bored to death before that!

You can't be serious. When I imagine living to 200, I feel panic—I'm already a quarter of the way into it! There are books I want to read, trips I want to take, and people I want to meet, which would take me far longer than my natural life span. And the longer I live, the longer I expect the list will be. It's an insult to God to say, "Life in this world quickly gets so uninteresting and boring that I'd rather be dead." That is such a sad lack of understanding and curiosity. I wish people who did not appreciate life and found it boring could give their time to me and to others who feel that it is too short.

Ok, I admit, I could probably find something to do for a couple of centuries, but the idea of living forever frightens me.

What would it mean to live forever?

To never die. Is that not what you want?

I certainly don't want to be unable to die—what if I got buried under a house, or was at the bottom of the ocean, or was in immense pain for millions of years? Immortality is a strange concept. Even if we live "forever," we always find ourselves at some specific point in time. It's impossible to know if there would come a time when I'd want to end my life, and it's impossible to say when exactly that would be. I also don't like the terms "forever" or "immortal" because we will never be immortal in a physical world. It's not a realistic option. What I want is to go on living for as long as I want, and I see no reason that I would want to die just because I hit some arbitrary number of years, say 90 or 100.

But these numbers are not arbitrary! They set the limits that define a human life. We are given sufficient time to complete most important projects. Someone who has lived well will feel full of days and would leave this world in peace, and that person would not greedily clamor for more life. Was it not Seneca who said that "it is not that we have a short time to live . . .

. . . but that we waste a lot of it." Yes, it was. Then he goes on to explain that unless you are living alone and withdrawn from the world, you are wasting your time. Seneca was wasting his time on power struggles in Rome. I am wasting my time. You are wasting your time. We are all wasting our time, and therefore—on Seneca's understanding of what constitutes a waste of time— none of us have enough of it. And for those of us who are not attracted to a monastic life, we have plenty of interesting and open-ended projects that cannot be completed within a normal life span—or perhaps even ever. Projects such as becoming thoroughly educated or becoming fluent in the most important languages of the world, or figuring out how the mind works, or visiting other planets, or discovering the fate of humanity, are all open-ended. I'm more than halfway through life, and I have mastered nothing. I can't recite a complete poem beyond eight lines or play a single piece by Chopin on the piano. I study philosophy, but I don't even know how to read Greek and Latin. I haven't seen *Sleepless in Seattle*, although I have always intended to. I hear that it's groundbreaking. My death will be *in medias res*. Also, I don't like this emphasis on "projects" and "accomplishments."

Why?

Because it brings to mind a shopping list: Grow up, get educated, marry, have children, raise them, play golf, done: check out. As if we do things just to have them done. No one studies French just to have done it but as a preparation to practice it. No one makes friends just to have made friends and be done with it, and so on. Not only are many projects open ended, but much of the enjoyment in life is constituted, not by undertakings, but rather by small moments: a memory, a feeling, a touch, an observation, and so on. I enjoy watching snow drift on a winter's day. That's enough for me to hate death.

Look, it's not that I love death. Life is great, but even good things must have an end. Your favorite movie would not improve by never ending; it would become unendurable. Likewise, it's sad that life ends, but it must end at some point.

Calling death "sad" is like calling Hitler naughty. It's bearable that music, films, and books have endings because we can finish them, set them aside, and pursue some other interest. The movie does not have self-awareness and an inner world; putting it in the recycled box on your laptop's desktop isn't murder. Because the movie lacks subjectivity, it can easily be copied and played on millions of screens; you are unique and irreplaceable.

But I'm not! That's such a self-important, not to say self-indulgent, perspective. I'm here as the result of everyone who came before me, and when I'm done, someone else will take my place. I participate in eternity through procreation. Things live because things die.

The circle of life.

Yes.

I don't think that works as an argument. If I die, or my mother dies, or my father dies, or my brother dies, there is no one replacing any of us. One ant in an anthill may be as good as another, but the subjective worlds we are take us to a different category of existence. Granted, to look at humans as no more than ants in an anthill cycling through their stages may relieve our anxiety over death, but we have this anxiety precisely because we are not ants. Call me a ridiculous humanist, even call me a Kantian, but I'm not ready to take Nature's careless (and wholly imaginary) point of view on my existence.

But is it not a fact, according to evolutionary theory, that death is the means by which we have been created? Without the death of our ancestors, we would not be who we are. Why should we decide to transcend nature?

Most people do not accept evolution as the account of why we are here, but even if it's true, it would not justify death. First, because even if my death serves some evolutionary purpose, it would not mean that it would be good for me as an individual to die. Second, my death would in fact serve no evolutionary purpose whatsoever. The human race would not increase in intelligence or health by me dying. Third, even if my death would advance the human genome in some miniscule way, I'm not prepared to die for eugenic purposes and I'm not prepared to argue that others should either.

I didn't mean it that way. I meant that everyone who lived before us has died, why should we be different?

Our ancestors had a life expectancy in the thirties and half of their children died before reaching adulthood. Let's not live like them. Do you really think that just because something happens to everyone by nature, then it can't be bad? Here is a counterexample: Aging happens to everyone by nature, and no one should think that aging is good.

Forever young? What a nightmare. I would hate to be forever stuck at one age. Once more, this is a juvenile and self-centered daydream, a sign of our society's obsession with youth. You want to break out of the cycle of life that has always provided the parameters defining the human condition?

You have internalized the Wise View of aging and death perfectly. Congratulations! You are so wise and well-adapted. It will make aging and death appear acceptable to you.

So, you agree that my reasoning can ease your fears?

I'm not cowering in fear and trembling, although this would be an understandable response to a deeply felt horror at ceasing to exist. Life is too short to spend it in fear. But I will never accept death and never say that it is not fearsome.

You were going to persuade me that aging is bad.

Right. Do you like cancer? No, you don't. Aging is the greatest cause of cancer, so you don't like aging. End of argument.

Listen, not everyone who ages gets cancer.

We all get cancerous cells every day. Aging weakens our bodies' defenses against them. If we are not dead from something else before getting cancer, it will come. It's struggling to conquer us when we are weak. Like in a horror film, it stalks you because it is inside you. You cannot say that this is acceptable because it is a part of the circle of life.

I said I want to age, not that I want to get sick.

An illusory distinction. Aging is the accumulation of damage that makes you more likely to die. If you get no damage, then you are not aging. The thought that there is healthy aging is arguably the deadliest idea in the world since it guides the insane misallocation of resources, whereby we seek to address each age-related illness after it occurs, rather than fix the underlying cause. Now, whether you want to call aging a disease or not is a matter of semantics. The fact is that it is the main cause of illnesses that kill people.

Even if you could convince me that it is in my interest to stay forever young, I want to know how this benefits the world. If no one dies and people are still being born, we will be overpopulated.

Don't worry about it.

Don't worry? That's your response?

Yes. Life expectancy has been rising, but the rate of population growth has been decreasing the last 50 years. Population growth is almost entirely driven by how many children we have and not how long we live. The countries with the highest life expectancy are either stable or shrinking: United States, Russia, and many countries in Europe and Asia have less-than-replacement-level fertility rates. Even radical life extension would make little difference. So don't worry about it.

I don't know. I hear that Africa will triple in population size this century.

It's not because they live longer. It's because they have many children. Thus, it is not relevant. And in any case, it's not a global problem. Nigeria will probably be crowded, but Japan, the world's grayest country, will become less crowded.

But Japan is a warning sign. It is going to collapse economically, socially, and culturally under the weight of all their old people.

Japan is always presented to illustrate that life extension is a publicly unrealizable goal. But it's sloppy thinking. First, "retirement age" is a social construct, not a biological reality. If we stopped aging, there would be no compelling retirement age. We would be healthier and therefore an economic asset rather than a burden. We should also take into account the increased use of AI and robotics. Many jobs requiring youthful brawn will be eliminated. It will probably be more of a problem than a benefit to have a more traditional, broad-based population pyramid. Beyond these economic facts, there is a more fundamental moral reason for dismissing your argument.

I thought I was making the moral argument.

No. Condemning people to decay and death for bad economic reasons is not a morally sound position. I'm not prepared to die for the GDP, and I'm not prepared to ask others that they do. This is not excessive self-loving; it's just proper respect for human life, including my own.

Even if you win this argument, what is the point? You are going to age. You are going to die. Deal with it.

I don't want to think that death and decay are okay, even if it made me feel better. I don't like to have false beliefs. Besides, complacency prevents efforts to deal with these evils. The Wise View causes suffering and costs lives by retarding antiaging research.

. . . .

The End

Notes

Chapter 1

1. United Nations Department of Economic & Social Affairs, Population Division, World Population to 2300 (New York: United Nations, 2004), https://www.un.org/development/desa/pd/sites/www.un.org.development.desa.pd/files/files/documents/2020/Jan/un_2002_world_population_to_2300.pdf

2. United Nations Children's Fund, Levels and Trends in Child Mortality, Report 2017 (UN Inter-agency Group for Child Mortality Estimation, 2017), http://www.childmortality.org/2017/files_v21/download/IGME%20report%202017%20child%20mortality%20final.pdf.

3. Ricki J. Colman, T. Mark Beasley, Joseph W. Kemnitz, Sterling C. Johnson, Richard Weindruch and Rozalyn M. Anderson, "Caloric Restriction Reduces Age-related and All-cause Mortality in Rhesus Monkeys," *Nature Communications* 3557 (April 1, 2014), https://www.ncbi.nlm.nih.gov/pmc/articles/PMC3988801/.

4. Leanne M. Redman, Steven R. Smith, Jeffrey H. Burton, Corby K. Martin, Dora Il'yasova, and Eric Ravussin, "Metabolic Slowing and Reduced Oxidative Damage with Sustained Caloric Restriction Support the Rate of Living and Oxidative Damage Theories of Aging," *Cell Metabolism* 27, no. 4 (2018), 805–815.

5. Redman et al., "Metabolic Slowing," 806. An explanation for why caloric restriction slows aging is that the body assumes that it is in a time of famine, which would not be conducive to successful reproduction, so it tries to delay aging to prolong fertility.

6. Aubrey de Gray and Michael Rae, *Ending Aging: The Rejuvenation Breakthroughs That Could Reverse Aging in our Lifetime* (New York: St. Martin's Griffin, 1998).

7. Raymond Kurzweil, *The Age of Spiritual Machines* (New York: Viking Penguin, 1999).

8. David Ewing Duncan, *When I'm 164: The New Science of Radical Life Extension, and What Happens If It Succeeds* (TED Conferences, 2012).

9. Pew Research Center, "Survey of Aging and Longevity, Living to 120 and Beyond: Americans' Views on Aging, Medical Advances and Radical Life Extension," August 6, 2013, http://www.pewforum.org/dataset/survey-of-aging-and-longevity/.

10. I will refer to it as the Wise View, not just because wise philosophers have held it, but because the heart of wisdom is standardly thought to be the acceptance of that which we can do nothing about. The label is therefore not meant ironically or with scare quotes, at least not entirely so. Death will always be with us, barring supernatural intervention, so acceptance then would seem to be the wise attitude. The problem I have with the Wise View is not so much that is not wise—in the way just defined—but that it is false and stands in the way of efforts to prolong healthy life. Those may be reasons enough to think of the Wise View as unwise, if one prefers to, even if it is historically a part of what we call wisdom.

11. Lucretius, *On the Nature of Things*, trans. Cyril Bailey (Oxford: Oxford University Press, 1986), 133–138.

12. Thomas Cathcart and Daniel Klein, *Heidegger and a Hippo Walk Through Those Pearly Gates: Using Philosophy (and Jokes!) to Explore Life, Death, the Afterlife, and Everything in Between* (New York: Penguin, 2009), 89. This is an overstatement. Roger Bacon, Francis Bacon, Condorcet, Renée Descartes, and Benjamin Franklin had prolongevist ideas. Still, the main point stands: to be an apologist is the default view of philosophers.

13. Gerald J. Gruman, *A History of Ideas about the Prolongation of Life* (New York: Springer, 2003), 55.

14. These writers were in various ways envisioning a future in which we control our biology and thereby transcend naturally given limits, including the limits on our life spans. See Mark B. Adams, "The Quest for Immortality: Visions and Presentiments in Science and Literature," in *The Fountain of Youth: Cultural, Scientific, and Ethical Perspectives on a Biomedical Goal*, edited by Stephen G. Post and Robert H. Binstock (Oxford: Oxford University Press, 2004), 38–71.

15. Peter Jackson, *The Lord of the Rings: The Fellowship of the Ring*, special extended DVD edition (New Line Home Entertainment, 2001).

16. "Muggles' Guide to Harry Potter/Characters/Voldemort," Wikibooks, accessed January 31, 2019, https://en.wikibooks.org/wiki/Muggles%27_Guide_to_Harry_Potter/Characters/Lord_Voldemort.

17. Star Wars Episode III, Revenge of the Sith, dir. George Lucas (Los Angeles: Lucasfilm Ltd., 2005).

18. Leon Kass, *Life, Liberty and the Defense of Dignity: Challenges for Bioethics* (San Francisco: Encounter Books, 2004), 264.

19. Francis Fukuyama, *Our Posthuman Future: Consequences of the Biotechnology Revolution* (New York: Farrar, Straus and Giroux, 2002), 9.

20. Daniel Callahan, *Setting Limits: Medical Goals in an Aging Society* (New York: Simon & Schuster, 1987), 65.

21. This is my summary of the Wise View. Most adherents would accept some or all the claims made. In some cases, this view goes as far as celebrating death. Consider, for example, the following paean to death posted on the website Death Café by a user with the handle Abrasax:

> Everything must have its end, or there is no Beginning. Death is not the opposite of Life, but the counterpart to Birth. Death is beautiful because it represents change. I have no fear because I Trust Life. I Respect Death and only accept it's Calling when I know it's my Time. Dying is the most pure form of Beauty. We Return to our Innocence as a molecule of the body of the Creator, only to be Reborn in a higher form than before. I long for Death as I Return to its semblance each Night in my Dark Sleep. Death is Peace. Death is Joy. Death is Purity. Death is True Freedom.

Accessed December 15, 2018, https://deathcafe.com/.

22. A study from 2015 asked participants if they would avail themselves of radical life extension technology in their old age, with the result that 59 percent were neutral (did not know), 39 percent were negative, and only 5 percent were positive. Allen Alvarez, Lumberto Mendoza, and Peter Danielson, "Mixed Views About Radical Life Extension," *Etikk i praksis—Nordic Journal of Applied Ethics* 9, no. 1 (2015): 87–110. The public is also generally more prone toward recognizing the negatives rather than positives of radical life extension. In a 2009 study, 36 percent of participants saw no personal benefits to life extension, compared to 80 percent who saw personal negatives; 48 percent saw social benefits, compared to 78 percent who saw social negatives. B. Partridge, J. Lucke, H. Bartlett, and W. Hall, "Ethical, Social, and Personal Implications of Extended Human Lifespan Identified by Members of the Public," *Rejuvenation Research* 12, no. 5 (2009): 351–357. One exception to the trend is a study from Canada, where life extension up 120 years was supported by 59 percent of the participants. The study also finds that an individual's general orientation toward science and technology predicts support for radical life extension. N. Dragojlovic, "Canadians' Support for Radical Life Extension Resulting from Advances in Regenerative Medicine," *Journal of Aging Studies* 27, no. 2 (2015): 151–158.

23. Thomas Hobbes, *Leviathan*, Part 1: Of Man, Chapter XIII, ed. C. B. MacPherson, 4th ed. (New York: Penguin Classics, 1982).

24. Richard Momeyer, *Confronting Death* (Bloomington: Indiana University Press, 1988).

25. The New Atheists is a label for modern-era thinkers pursuing an aggressively atheist line. Daniel Dennet, Sam Harris, Richard Dawkins, and the late Christopher Hitchens count among its foremost exponents. Christopher Hitchens, *God Is Not Great: How Religion Poisons Everything* (New York: Hachette Book Group, 2007).

26. Philip Larkin, "Aubade," *Collected Poems* (New York: Farrar Straus and Giroux, 2001).

27. The concept of preference falsification was first introduced by social scientist Timur Kuran in his book *Private Truth, Public Lies* in 1997 and it is meant to capture the phenomenon that members of the public frequently communicate preferences that differ from their real preferences, in particular to pollsters and researchers. Individuals will tailor their expressed preferences to conform to what they think is the social norm, and thereby make surveys unreliable measures of public opinion. The psychological mechanism underlying the phenomenon is primarily the need for social approval, and the fear of standing out and attracting unpleasant or dangerous attention. Even when the polling is presumed to be preserving the anonymity of the respondents, these mechanisms apparently cause the individual respondent to self-censor. The shy Tory phenomenon, whereby polled voters pretend not to favor the Conservative Party in the UK, is one example of falsified preferences. Preference falsification, Kuran argues, has the terrible effect of perpetuating bad systems—both political and ideological—since it produces the impression that these systems enjoy a wider support than they actually do. The inauthentic responses reinforce the mistaken belief that a system is socially acceptable, and thereby create continued incentives for individuals to pretend to accept the system. The Soviet Union, East Germany, and the Indian caste system are some of Kuran's examples. Kuran's theory explains why pollsters get a false impression of the public's preferences and also why seemingly popularly supported systems suddenly are overthrown: they were not that popular, and everyone was waiting for someone else to say so. I think this also applies to the case of attitudes to antiaging treatments. Once more people publicly say that it is alright to want to stay young, we might see that there is much more interest in availing themselves of such treatments, should they become a reality, than today's surveys would have us believe. Timur Kuran, *Private Truth, Public Lies* (Cambridge, MA: Harvard University Press, 1997).

28. Nick Bostrom suggests this explanation of people's contradictory responses to these kinds of questions. Nick Bostrom, "Why I Want to Be Posthuman When I Grow Up," in *Medical Enhancement and Posthumanity*, ed. Bert Gordijn and Ruth Chadwick (New York: Springer, 2008), 107–137.

29. Callahan, *Setting Limits*, 58.

30. Kass, *Life*, 263.

31. Michael J. Sandel, "The Case against Perfection," *The Atlantic*, April 2004, https://www.theatlantic.com/magazine/archive/2004/04/the-case-against-perfection/302927/.

32. This approach is known as naturalist moral realism. The basic idea is that humans, like other organisms, have certain needs given their nature and that these determine what tends to flourish and what does not. The reason that we know,

for example, that it is wrong to deprive a child of love, is because we think that there is human nature and not every child is, as they say, unique. It is not unlike flowers: the right amount of sun and water is determined on the species level. But who decides what is sane, normal, and so forth for a human? Is that not itself a normative claim? Yes, welcome to moral philosophy. It is a trade-off: either we have to give up on the idea that it can be true that smoking heavily is a bad choice for a pregnant woman, unless the woman thinks so, and unless she does not want to harm herself and her baby—in effect give up on making any prescriptive judgments about people's actions beyond "whatever"—or we can recognize that to be a human is to be a certain way and that this way sets certain (broad) parameters for the sane rational "real" human. The woman in the example transgresses these, and she contradicts her real interests as a human and as a mother. A full defense of this perspective would take volumes. Notice that my argument does not stand or fall with any particular meta-ethical position. A rationalist could say that it is obvious that one ought not to harm oneself and others, and therefore the mother is wrong, whatever she herself believes. This is what Platonists and Kantians would say. The most common form of realism is supranatural. On this view, the mother can be seen as violating an order established by God and is therefore in sin. As long as it is admitted that there can be moral and value truths that are different from opinion, my argument is possible. This, fortunately, is generally conceded in practice—even by those who in philosophy question the possibility of truth in matters of morals and values. Naturalist moral realism is historically associated with Aristotle and has recently been defended by David Brink. David Brink, *Moral Realism and the Foundations of Ethics* (Cambridge: Cambridge University Press, 1989).

33. Leon Kass, *Life, Liberty, and the Defense of Dignity: The Challenge for Bioethics* (San Francisco: Encounter Books, 2002), 264.

34. Or to be more precise: death is bad, assuming that death is the end; and more so, the better the life that is lost is.

35. Aubrey De Gray, "Strategies for Engineered Negligible Senescence: Why Genuine Control of Aging May Be Foreseeable," *Annals of the New York Academy of Sciences* (2004).

36. Robert Sinsheimer, "The Presumptions of Science," *Daedalus* 107, no. 2 (Spring 1978): 23–35.

37. Raymond Kurzweil, *The Age of Spiritual Machines* (London: Viking Press, 1999).

38. Swedish transhumanist philosopher Nick Bostrom imagines such an enhanced life:

> Let us suppose that you were to develop into a being that has posthuman healthspan and posthuman cognitive and emotional capacities. At the early steps of this process, you enjoy your enhanced capacities. You cherish your improved health: you feel stronger, more energetic, and more balanced. Your skin looks younger and is more elastic. A minor ailment in

your knee is cured. You also discover a greater clarity of mind. You can concentrate on difficult material more easily and it begins making sense to you. You start seeing connections that eluded you before. You are astounded to realize how many beliefs you had been holding without ever really thinking about them or considering whether the evidence supports them. You can follow lines of thinking and intricate argumentation farther without losing your foothold. Your mind is able to recall facts, names, and concepts just when you need them. You are able to sprinkle your conversation with witty remarks and poignant anecdotes. Your friends remark on how much more fun you are to be around. Your experiences seem more vivid. When you listen to music you perceive layers of structure and a kind of musical logic to which you were previously oblivious; this gives you great joy. You continue to find the gossip magazines you used to read amusing, albeit in a different way than before; but you discover that you can get more out of reading Proust and Nature. You begin to treasure almost every moment of life; you go about your business with zest; and you feel a deeper warmth and affection for those you love, but you can still be upset and even angry on occasions where upset or anger is truly justified and constructive. As you yourself are changing you may also begin to change the way you spend your time. Instead of spending four hours each day watching television, you may now prefer to play the saxophone in a jazz band and to have fun working on your first novel. Instead of spending the weekends hanging out in the pub with your old buddies talking about football, you acquire new friends with whom you can discuss things that now seem to you to be of greater significance than sport. Together with some of these new friends, you set up a local chapter of an international nonprofit to help draw attention to the plight of political prisoners. By any reasonable criteria, your life improves as you take these initial steps towards becoming posthuman. But thus far your capacities have improved only within the natural human range. You can still partake in human culture and find company to engage you in meaningful conversation. Consider now a more advanced stage in the transformation process . . . You have just celebrated your 170th birthday and you feel stronger than ever. Each day is a joy. You have invented entirely new art forms, which exploit the new kinds of cognitive capacities and sensibilities you have developed. . . .

And it goes on from there, ever upwards. Life extension is not enhancement in the same way, since it is compatible with remaining fundamentally the same limited creature, only longer living.

Nick Bostrom, "Why I Want to Be Posthuman," 112.

39. Some have argued that transhumanism is a religious view or an ersatz religion. Is transhumanism also a form of Wise View? No: It does not offer reasons for why it would be ok to die, but rather wishes for technological ways to avoid dying.

Chapter 2

1. Leonard Hayflick, *How and Why We Age* (New York: Ballantine Books, 1994), 341.

2. There is no generally accepted definition of aging, nor a universally accepted theory about the fundamental mechanism at work, but we can assess the value of aging even in the absence of such a theory. What matters to us is what aging does to us and how we experience it. For our purposes, the best way to understand aging is to list all that happens in our body that cause the recognized symptoms of aging. For instance, gray hair is a symptom of aging, hence aging includes the process that causes gray hair. To learn more about theories of aging consider reading Vern L.

Bengtson and Richard A. Settersten, eds., *Handbook to Theories of Aging*, 3rd ed. (New York: Springer, 2016).

3. Pew Research Center, "Living to 120 and Beyond: Americans' Views on Aging, Medical Advances and Radical Life Extension," August 6, 2013, https://www.pewforum.org /2013/08/06/living-to-120-and-beyond-americans-views-on-aging-medical-advances -and-radical-life-extension/.

4. S. J. Olshansky, L. Hayflick, and Bruce A. Carnes, "Position Statement on Aging," *Journal of Gerontology* 57, no. 8 (August 2002): 292–297.

5. David Gems, "Tragedy and Delight: The Ethics of Decelerated Ageing," *Philosophical Transactions of the Royal Society* B 366 (January 2011): 108–112.

6. The version I have in mind here is a lithograph by German Artist F. Lieber, *Das Stufenalter des Mannes*, published by Gustav May Söhne, Frankfurt, 1900.

7. Gilbert Meilaender, *Should We Live Forever: The Ethical Ambiguities of Aging* (Grand Rapids, MI: Eerdmans, 2013), ix.

8. Plato, *The Republic*, Book I, trans. Benjamin Jowett (The Internet Classics Archive), http://classics.mit.edu/Plato/republic.2.i.html.

9. Plato, *The Republic*, Book I.

10. Plato, *The Republic,* Book I.

11. Natalie C. Ebner and Håkan Fischer, "Emotion and Aging: Evidence from Brain and Behavior," *Frontiers of Psychology*, September 9, 2014, https://doi.org/10.3389 /fpsyg.2014.00996.

12. *VANITY FAIR on Twitter*, June 4, 2014.

13. Jonathan Raush, *The Happiness Curve: Why Life Gets Better after Midlife* (London: Bloomsbury, 2018). However, other researchers question this result. See, for example, S. J. Laaksonen, "A Research Note: Happiness by Age Is More Complex Than U-Shaped," *Happiness Studies* 19 (2018), 471–482. https://doi.org/10.1007/s10902 -016-9830-1.

14. Mhaske, R. "Happiness and Aging." *Journal of Psychosocial Research* 12, no. 1 (2017): 71–79.

15. David Millwar, "Eric Clapton Struggling to Play Guitar Because of Damage to His Nervous System," *The Telegraph*, June 12, 2016.

16. Lesser-known poet Pat A. Fleming, "I Still Matter," September 2017, http://www .familyfriendpoems.com/poem/i-still-matter.

17. Rod Dreher, "Old Age Is A Humiliation," *The American Conservative*, November 30, 2014. Notice how Dreher says that he is not afraid of dying. This, in my

experience, is the normal view. Almost no one that I have talked to, or have read, say that they are afraid of dying.

18. Michel de Montaigne, "That to Philosophize Is to Learn to Die," in *The Complete Essays of Montaigne*, ed. Donald M. Frame (Stanford, CA: Stanford University Press, 1958), 63.

19. Leon Kass, *Life, Liberty and the Defense of Dignity* (San Francisco: Encounter Books, 2002), 264.

20. Meilaender, *Should We Live Forever*, 12.

21. Gems, *Tragedy and Delight*, 109.

22. Sven Bulterijs et al., "It Is Time to Classify Biological Aging as a Disease," *Frontiers in Genetics* 6, no. 205 (June 2015), https://doi.org/10.3389/fgene.2015.00205.

23. Adam Woodcox, "Aristotle's Theory of Aging," *Cahiers des Etudes Anciennes* 55 (2018): 65–78.

24. The Declaration of Geneva was adopted by the 2nd General Assembly of the World Medical Association, Geneva, Switzerland, on September 1948. It was a response to the fact that German doctors had to a large extent supported and participated in the holocaust and other Nazi atrocities. It contains The Physicians Pledge where respect for all human life is emphasized.

25. Categorizing aging as a disease would allow the FDA to certify antiaging drugs, allowing for a safety and efficacy standard, and the market for such a drug would be further stimulated since it could secure more money for research, just to mention some practical effects. It would also allow a mental shift in perspective from meek acceptance to rebellion against the imposition of aging.

Chapter 3

1. Atomism does, some think, allow for life after death if we imagine that the atoms dispersed are once more put together. Star Trek-style teleportation and Biblical resurrection suppose this possibility. But Epicureans like Lucretius did not believe that we would ever be reconstituted. For them, the dispersal was final and death was the end.

2. Epicurus, *Letter to Menoeceus*, trans. Robert Drew Hicks, *The Internet Classics Archive*, http://classics.mit.edu/Epicurus/menoec.html

3. Seneca, *Epistles, Volume I: Epistles 1–65*, trans. Richard M. Gummere, *Loeb Classical Library* 75. (Cambridge, MA: Harvard University Press, 1971), 17.

4. From a debate with Sam Harris, David Wolpe and Bradley Shavit Artson in Los Angeles, 2011. Hitchens continues by provocatively claiming that death is still preferable over having to party forever in heaven under godly supervision.

5. I owe this example to Swedish philosopher Eric Ohlsson from his "The Epicurean Death," *Journal of Ethics* 17, no. 1–2 (2013): 65–78.

6. Phillip Larkin, *The Broadview Anthology of British Literature*, vol. 6, eds. Joseph Black et al. (New York: Broadview Press, 2004), 704. Philip Larkin completed "Aubade" in November 1977 and the poem was first published in the Times Literary Supplement on 23 December the same year.

7. Fred Feldman, "Death", in *Routledge Encyclopedia of Philosophy* (London: Routledge, 1998).

8. It would be akin to an argument that a couple that does not have a child is harming this potential by not bringing it into being. Such reasoning is problematic, however, since we must recognize that there is no end to the number of potential people. What about all the potential children, and their potential grandchildren, and so on? Are we to countenance them as part of reality, and pity all of them? Perhaps we could stipulate that the potential person must have existed at some point. Still, a merely possible person is not a real person, and it is therefore hard to see her as the subject of a misfortune.

9. The eternalist block universe, in Albert Einstein's mind, supports the Epicurean conclusion that death means nothing. In a letter to the family of Michele Besso, his friend and collaborator, Einstein writes,

> Now he has departed from this strange world a little ahead of me. That means nothing. People like us, who believe in physics, know that the distinction between past, present and future is only a stubbornly persistent illusion.

This quote found its way into an article in *Forbes*, with the title, "Einstein Believed in a Theory of Space Time That Can Help People Cope with Loss," December 28, 2016, written by Paul Mainwood, https://www.forbes.com/sites/quora/2016/12/28/einstein-believed-in-a-theory-of-spacetime-that-can-help-people-cope-with-loss/#2c41aa5155d2. Perhaps it can help people cope, but Einstein's conclusion does not follow from eternalism. Clearly, Besso would no longer be showing up to work or to family dinners. Does that not mean something? If he loved his family and friends and they loved him, how can his absence be insignificant? Whatever it means to deny the distinction between past, present, and future, why would it not be better for Besso to continue his work and be with his friends and family, rather than die? It is interesting to see that even Einstein had a need to tame death.

10. Ben Bradley develops one such account in "When Is Death Bad for the One Who Dies?" *Noûs* 38, no. 1 (March 2004): 1–28.

11. Bradley, in correspondence.

12. Thomas Nagel, "Death," *Noûs* 4, no. 1 (February 1970): 73–80.

13. Nagel, "Death," 77.

14. Shelley Kagan, *Death* (New Haven, CT: Yale University Press, 2012), 214.

15. Epicurus, *Letter to Menoeceus*, trans. Robert Drew Hicks, The Internet Classics Archive, http://classics.mit.edu/Epicurus/menoec.html

16. Lucretius, *De Rerum Natura*, trans. Cyril Bailey (Oxford: Clarendon Press, 1910), 135–136. Over the course of two millennia, fires, bookworms, and religious purges destroyed 99 percent of all antique literature, and the Roman poet Lucretius's *De Rerum Natura* was destined to perish among other masterpieces had it not been for the Italian book collector Poggio Bracciolini, who in 1417 found a tattered, foxed, and disintegrating copy in the Benedictine library of the Fulda monastery. It became a central text for the early Renaissance, reviving atomic theory and inspiring a naturalist, scientific outlook. Dante, Machiavelli, and later Montaigne and Thomas Jefferson owned copies of it. Today it is read in many introductory philosophy courses. In the religious climate of the early Renaissance, knowledge of the poem could be dangerous, and copies of it were handed around with the greatest discretion and kept out of view. If naturalist philosophers had believed in ancient sacred texts, then *De Rerum Natura* would have been it.

17. Stephen Luper, "Annihilation," *Philosophical Quarterly* 37, no. 148 (1987): 233–252.

18. Lucretius, *De Rerum Natura*, trans. Cyril Bailey, 138.

19. Derek Parfit, *Reasons and Persons* (Oxford: Oxford University Press, 1986).

20. See Saul Kripke, *Naming and Necessity* (Cambridge, MA: Harvard University, 1980).

21. I think that when we picture ourselves as Romans, or Vikings, or pirates, we are not clearly imagining that we could have been born earlier. Rather we take ourselves, with part of our autobiography, including perhaps who our parents are as well as some of our values and beliefs, and then we simply drop down into an imagined historical theater. This leap in time borrows from our spatial imagination, where we imagine ourselves to be somewhere else. Such a spatial leap is possible, however, because it does not threaten our personal identity in the way that temporal transitions do.

22. Christine Overall, *Aging, Death and Human Longevity* (Berkeley: University of California Press, 2003), 25.

23. Titus Lucretius Carus, *On the Nature of Things: De Rerum Natura*, trans. Anthony M. Esolen, (San Francisco: Cengage Learning, 1995), 144.

24. Marcus Aurelius repeats this argument in his meditations, where he seeks consolation in the thought that life is ever vanishing and bookended by "void of infinite time on this side and that." Marcus Aurelius, *Meditations*, Book IV, trans. Georg Long, The Internet Classics Archive, http://classics.mit.edu/Antoninus/meditations.html

25. Epicurus Us. 221 = Porph. Ad Marc. 31, p. 209, 23 N. Quoted from Nussbaum, *Therapy*, page 5. This paragraph is attributed to Epicurus by classicist Herman Usener (1834–1905).

26. Martha C. Nussbaum, *The Therapy of Desire: Theory and Practice in Hellenistic Ethics*, reprint ed. (Princeton, NJ: Princeton University Press, 2018).

27. Lucretius, *De Rerum Natura*, trans. Bailey, 107.

28. Lucretius, *De Rerum Natura*, 136.

29. Lucretius, *De Rerum Natura*, 139.

Chapter 4

The epigraph from Silenus is thought to come from a lost work by Aristotle, *Eudemus*, or *Of the Soul*. Aristotle is recounting what Silenus tells King Midas.

1. Declinism has been shown to be predictive of less support for life extension technology. It is also correlated with a less favorable view on science, which is also predictive of less support for life extension technology. Enlightenment progressivism is—not surprisingly—predictive of support for life extension. N. Dragojlovic, "Canadians' Support for Radical Life Extension Resulting from Advances in Regenerative Medicine," *Journal of Aging Studies* 27, no. 2 (2013): 151–158.

2. Arthur Schopenhauer, *The World as Will and Idea*, trans. E. F. J. Payne (Mineola, NY: Dover Publications, 1966), 635.

3. David Benatar, *Better Never to Have Been: The Harm of Coming into Existence* (Oxford: Oxford University Press, 2008), 70.

4. Benatar, *Better*, 72.

5. Benatar, *Better*, 72.

6. Arthur Schopenhauer, *Studies in Pessimism*, trans. T. Bailey Saunders (London: Swan Sonnenschein & Co., 1891), 14.

7. Sophocles, *Oedipus at Colonus: The Tragedies of Sophocles*, trans. Sir Richard C. Jebbs (Cambridge: Cambridge University Press, 1904), lines 1211–1225.

8. Unknown writer. "Did You Consent to Being Born? Why One Man Is Suing His Parents for Giving Birth to Him," *The Guardian*, February 5, 2019, https://www.the guardian.com/lifeandstyle/shortcuts/2019/feb/05/consent-being-born-man-suing -parents-for-giving-birth-to-him.

9. H. Singh Gour, *The Spirit of Buddhism* (Whitefish, MT: Kessinger Publishing, 2005), 286–288.

10. According to findings of a Harris Poll survey of 2,345 US adults surveyed online between April 10 and 15, 2013, by Harris Interactive, a third of Americans (33 percent) are "very happy." See https://theharrispoll.com/new-york-n-y-may-30-2013 -has-the-pursuit-of-happiness-left-americans-unhappy-maybe-according-to-the-harris -polla-happiness-index-which-uses-a-series-of-questions-to-calculate-americans/.

11. My direct aim here is not to refute antinatalism, but to defend the view that life is good enough that we can rationally prefer to live on. I think that it follows that we have reason to want to create new people who will be in a similar position as us, and so on. Benatar will disagree because he thinks that the absence of the good things in life is only bad if there is someone there who experiences the absence. But the absence of bad things is good even if there is no one there to experience the absence. Hence it is better never to come into existence: you are not harmed by the bad things in life, since you are not, and that is good, and even if you are not benefited by the good things, that is not bad (it is neutral) since you do not exist. I reject this reasoning since I think that the situation is symmetrical: if you do not exist then it is not good for you that you are not in pain, just as it is not bad for you that you are not experiencing pleasure; or alternatively (my preferred alternative), if it is good for you that you are not in pain, then it is also bad for you if you are not experiencing pleasure. Intuitions clash here. It brings to mind the modal conundrums of the Epicurean arguments. For someone who does not have any firm intuitions regarding the asymmetry asserted by Benatar, it is probably better to focus on the question whether they themselves are happy to exist. Or they can picture the crystalline state and ask themselves if a view with such a horrendous implication is sound. I have argued that it is not.

12. Plato, *Phaedo* in *The Dialogues of Plato*, vol. 2, trans. Benjamin Jowett, 3rd ed. (Oxford University Press, 1892), 193.

13. Plato, *Phaedo* 191.

14. Plato, *Phaedo*, 191–192. Platonism influenced the development of Christendom and a similar denigration of earthly pleasures and projects can be seen in, for example, the writings of Calvin:

> Let believers, then, in forming an estimate of this mortal life, and perceiving that in itself it is nothing but misery, make it their aim to exert themselves with greater alacrity, and less hinderance, in aspiring to the future and eternal life. When we contrast the two, the former may not only be securely neglected, but, in comparison of the latter, be disdained and contemned. If heaven is our country, what can earth be but a place of exile? . . . [L]et us ardently long for death, and constantly meditate upon it, and, in comparison with future immortality, let us despise life.

John Calvin, *Institutes of the Christian Religion*, vol. 2, trans. Henry Beveridge (Edinburgh: T & T Clark, 1860), 29.

15. Lucretius, *De Rerum Natura*, Book III, lines 1069–1094, trans. Cyril Bailey (Oxford: Clarendon Press, 1910), 142.

16. Lucretius, *De Rerum Natura*, 141.

17. I recently had a conversation with a Buddhist philosopher who maintained that Buddhism does not have to deny the existence of God and does not have to deny the reality of the soul, or the self, and does not have to conceive of Nirvana as total annihilation. However, on this understanding, this life and this world are still not the best state of things. There is suffering, and it is important to have compassion for each other and other suffering creatures. Life is not just suffering, but also occasionally pleasurable. However, wanting to live on here, in this world, is as foolish as wanting to have lunch at the same lousy cafeteria day after day after day rather than wanting to visit a better restaurant. Buddhists, on his understanding, are not necessarily against living long, or even living longer, but it is not important to them.

18. Schopenhauer, *World*, 573.

19. Schopenhauer, *World*, 635.

20. Schopenhauer, *World*, 390.

21. Schopenhauer, *World*, 507–508.

22. Perhaps some of the rejection of desire should be understood in its historical context. At the time of Plato, Lucretius, and even Schopenhauer, most people could do nothing but scramble for safety and sustenance. Ninety percent of the world's population was living in poverty, 80 percent was living in extreme poverty. Today even the poorest among us in the West and in other level one and two countries (roughly 80 percent of the world) have access to water and food and can expect to live nearly three times as long as an average Bronze Age person. The hard toil and monotonous diet of most people in the past makes the wish to have no desires understandable.

23. Plato, *Phaedo*, 191.

24. Friedrich Nietzsche, *Twilight of the Idols*, Thought 14, Anti-Darwin (Indianapolis, IN: Hackett, 1989 [1889]), 59.

25. *The Bible*, New International Version, Eccles. 12:13–14.

26. Bertrand Russell, "A Free Man's Worship," in *Mysticism and Logic* (London: Routledge, 1976 [1903]).

Chapter 5

1. Empirical studies confirm that the unnaturalness of radical life extension technologies is the most prevalent moral reason given in several studies of public attitudes to such technologies. See, for example, Brad Partridge, Jayne Lucke, Helen Bartlett, and Wayne Hall, "Ethical, Social, and Personal Implications of Extended Human

Lifespan Identified by Members of the Public," *Rejuvenation Research* 12, no. 5 (2009): 351–357. A 2015 study also shows that people are wary of manmade means of life extension. Fourteen percent would take no means toward life extension, 24 percent would countenance both natural and artificial, and 62 percent would only consider natural means. This is startling. If offered a pill that would allow them the youthfulness to live to 120, 69 percent would turn it down because it is manmade. It is hard to believe that this could possibly be their considered view, but it is consistent with the generally negative views the public has toward living longer. Allan Alvarez, Lumberto Mendoza, and Peter Danielson, "Mixed Views about Radical Life Extension," *Etikk i praksis. Nordic Journal of Applied Ethics* 9, no. 1 (2015): 87–110. In another study a participant speculates, "It seems totally unnatural. It seems to be upsetting the natural sequence of things. That's a philosophical view on my part—it's probably a very old-fashioned view. But I think doubling life would be . . . I don't like it at all . . ." Brad Partridge, Jayne Lucke, Helen Bartlett, and Wayne Hall, "Ethical Concerns in the Community about Technologies to Extend Human Life Span," *American Journal of Bioethics* 9, no. 12 (2009): 68–76.

2. The Scottish Enlightenment philosopher David Hume famously observed that no natural fact, a fact about how things are, can by itself imply any fact about how things ought to be. This means that even if we could determine what is and what is not natural, this does not by itself settle any dispute over values. Hume's insight is important enough to be simply referred to as "Hume's Law." Later, the Bloomsbury Group's favorite philosopher, G. E. Moore, emphasized much the same point when he claimed that it is always an open question whether something that is natural is also good. It is, for instance, a fact that we pursue happiness, but it is an open question whether we ought to pursue happiness. Applied to our topic, the insight is that while it is a fact that we age and die, it is an open question whether it is a good thing to age and die.

3. Jean-Paul Sartre, *Existentialism Is a Humanism*, trans. Annie Cohen-Solal, reprint ed. (New Haven, CT: Yale University Press, 2007).

4. It is outside the scope of this book to argue for this thesis. The job has recently been done by Steven Pinker in *The Blank Slate: The Modern Denial of Human Nature* (New York: Viking Press, 2002).

5. Homer, *Iliad* (London: Penguin Classics, 1998), 6.146–150.

6. Lucretius, *De Rerum Natura*, trans. Cyril Bailey (Oxford: Clarendon Press, 1910), 137–138.

7. Marcus Aurelius, *The Meditations of Marcus Aurelius*, trans. George Long (New York: Digireads.com, 2015), 9.

8. Epictetus, *The Enchiridion*, trans. Elisabeth Carter, The Internet Classics Archive, http://classics.mit.edu/Epictetus/epicench.html.

9. John Hardwig, *Is There a Duty to Die and Other Essays in Medical Ethics* (New York: Routledge, 2000), 160.

10. Daniel Callahan, *False Hopes: Why America's Quest for Perfect Health is a Recipe for Failure* (New York: Simon & Schuster, 1988), 116.

11. Callahan, *False Hopes*, 116.

12. David Wendler, "Understanding the Conservative View of Abortion," *Bioethics* 13, no.1 (1999): 32–56.

13. J. Baird Callicot, *In Defense of Land Ethics* (Albany: State University of New York, 1989), 113.

14. Patrick Curry, *Ecological Ethics: An Introduction* (Polity Press, 2011).

15. Bill Devall and George Sessions, *Deep Ecology: Living as if Nature Mattered* (Salt Lake City. UT: Peregrine Smith Books, 1985), 66.

16. Walt Whitman, "Song of Myself," *Leaves of Grass* (Mineola, NY: Dover Publications, 2007).

17. Thomas Nagel, "Death," *Noûs* 4, no. 1 (1970): 80.

18. To clarify, the argument here is not over the relevance of appeals to nature. The argument is rather about how best to understand such appeals. Appeals to nature make sense when they refer to natural propensities in human beings, but not when they refer to nature as an external agent and source of value. Consider, as an illustration, the claim that women are mothers by nature and should therefore have children. This makes sense when suggesting that a woman may be better off having a child than not, because of her innate psychology. Not having a child would leave her less satisfied. But it does not make sense as some external command that— whether she wants to or not—nature wants her to have a child.

19. Freud thought that we have a death instinct, or death drive. If this is correct, then nature did equip us with an individual goal of going extinct. However, this part of Freudianism is generally considered to be incorrect even by practicing psychoanalysts. Besides, even if there was such a natural drive to self-destruction alongside our will to live, it would not mean that we would have to accept that it overrides our will to live, or that it must be allowed to assert itself more later in life.

20. This theory has been most notably advanced by T. B. L Kirkwood and colleagues. In a dangerous environment, most offspring come from young couples, hence no bad genetic disposition that expresses itself later in life prevents its bearer from successful replication. This means that there is no mechanism for filtering out bad genes that express themselves later in life, hence there is aging and death. For example, cancer that expresses itself later in life is not selected against by evolution, since its carrier would be dead before it expressed itself (due to starvation or predations, etc.)

and would already have reproduced this disposition to late-onset cancer in their offspring. T. Kirkwood, *Time of Our Lives* (Oxford: Oxford University Press, 1999).

21. Sherwin B. Nuland, *How We Die: Reflections on Life's Final Chapter* (New York: Knopf, 1995), 133–134.

22. H. G. Wells and Aldous Huxley, *The Science of Life* (New York: The Literary Guild, 1934), 1434–1435.

23. George Orwell, *1984* (New York: Signet Classic, 1961), 186.

24. Orwell, *1984*, 186.

25. Georg Lukács, *The Destruction of Reason* (London: Merlin, 1954).

26. Luc Ferry, *The New Ecological Order*, trans. Carol Volk (Chicago: University of Chicago Press, 1995), 10.

27. Anne Harrington, *Reenchanted Science: Holism in German Culture from Wilhelm II to Hitler* (Princeton, NJ: Princeton University Press, 1996), 175.

28. Adolf Hitler, *Mein Kampf*, vol. 1, trans. Ralph Manheim (London: Houghton Mifflin Company, 1998), 287. Hitler, inspired by Johan Gottlieb von Herder and Wilhelm Fredrick Herder, regarded Jewish life as unnatural. This is another example of how questionable the appeal to nature often, but not always, is.

29. Leon Kass, *Life, Liberty, and the Defense of Dignity: The Challenge for Bioethics* (San Francisco: Encounter Books, 2002), 266. Kass is referring to Thomas Hobbes here; namely, his idea that a fear of violent death motivated us to enter a contract to limit our freedom for our mutual benefit. For Hobbes, this was the beginning of civilization.

30. Phillipe Aries, *Western Attitudes Toward Death: From the Middle Ages to the Present* (Baltimore, MD: Johns Hopkins University Press, 1974), 28.

31. Aries, *Western Attitudes*, 88.

32. Daniel Callahan, *Setting Limits*, 57.

33. Daniel Callahan, *Setting Limits*, 57.

34. Giovanni Pico della Mirandola, *Oration on the Dignity of Man* (Chicago: Gateway Editions, 1956).

35. Francis Bacon, *Novum Organum*, in *The Philosophical Works of Francis Bacon*, trans. R. L. Ellis, ed. J. Spedding Robertson (London: Routledge, 1905), 24.

36. Francis Bacon, *Novum*, 25.

37. But did Thomas Hobbes not defend an absolute monarchy? Yes, he did, but on the grounds that it would serve the interests of the individual members of society. He was not a monarchist on principle, but a pragmatic monarchist. If a constitutional

republic with an elected president such as in the United States can guarantee peace, then he would not object to it. His worry about such an arrangement is that it could disintegrate to fierce partisanship of, as we would call it today, special interest groups, and civil war.

38. John Stuart Mill, *On Liberty* (Mineola, NY: Dover Publications Inc., 2002), 56.

39. Immanuel Kant, "An Answer to the Question: What is Enlightenment?" *Perpetual Peace and Other Essays*, trans. Ted Humphrey (Indianapolis, IN: Hackett, 1983).

40. John Rawls, *A Theory of Justice* (Cambridge, MA: Belknap Press, 1971).

41. Steven Pinker, *The Better Angels of Our Nature: Why Violence Has Been Declining* (New York: Viking Press, 2011).

Chapter 6

1. Mikel Burley, "'The End of Immortality!' Eternal Life and the Makropulos Debate," *The Journal of Ethics* 19, no. 3/4, Special Issue: Immortality (September 2015), 305–321.

2. Leon Kass, "L'Chaim and its Limits," *Life, Liberty, and the Defense of Dignity: The Challenge for Bioethics* (San Francisco: Encounter Books, 2002), 264.

3. Kass, *Life*, 266.

4. Lucretius, *On the Nature of Things*, trans. Cyril Baily (Oxford: Clarendon Press, 1910), 137.

5. They shook hands and embraced as gentlemen after the match.

6. Christine Overall, *Aging, Death and Human Longevity, A Philosophical Inquiry* (Berkeley: University of California Press, 2003), 45.

7. Daniel Callahan, *Setting Limits: Medical Goals in an Aging Society* (New York: Touchstone, Simon & Schuster, 1988), 67.

8. Physical health is an assumption here. The argument here is not that we would be so broken down and ill that it would have unbearable mental effects.

9. Celeste Kidd et al., "The Psychology and Neuroscience of Curiosity," *Neuron* 88, no. 3 (2015): 449–460.

10. D. E. Berlyne, "Curiosity and Exploration," *Science* 153 (1966): 25–33.

11. Bernard Williams, *Moral Problems: A Collection of Philosophical Essays*, 2nd ed., ed. James Rachels (New York: Harper & Row, 1979).

12. Bernard Williams, "The Makropulos Case: Reflections on the Tedium of Immortality," in *Moral Problems: A Collection of Philosophical Essays*, 2nd ed., ed. James Rachels (New York: Harper & Row, 1979).

13. Williams, *Moral Problems*, 416.

14. Karel Capek, *The Makropulos Case, in Four Plays*, trans. Peter Majer and Cathy Porter (London: Methuen, 1999), 165–259.

15. Williams, *Moral Problems*, 420.

16. Williams's argument appears to assume what philosophers refer to as the "personality view" of personal identity, which, in short, says that our memories, beliefs, preferences, and so forth, make us who we are as individuals. His worry is that if we were open to experience and change, then we would lose our original personality and literally become someone else, and therefore have no personal interest in surviving. However, this is to misunderstand the view. The personality view does not say that we must remain precisely the same psychologically in order to remain the same person. It is enough that there is a continuity and overlap; if the change is gradual then we remain who we are. The analogy here is that of a rope with overlapping threads, none of which stretches through the entire rope. Yet they are part of one and the same rope. Or like an Italian sourdough passed on for generation. Each time the part is used it is replaced with a new piece, but it is still regarded as the same dough over time. It is aptly called *anima de pane*, the soul of the bread. This is how we can remain the same person from five years of age to 20 years of age despite drastic differences. The personality view's two main competitors are the bodily view and soul view. Neither of these views would see Elina's transformation as a threat to her personal identity. According to the bodily view, it suffices that she remains the same living body or, in some versions, that she remains the same brain, to remain the same person, and she clearly does. (As in the personality view, change is allowed if it is gradual.) Thus, also on the bodily view is her personal identity preserved even if she lived for 300 years and beyond. According to the soul view, as long as she has the same soul, she remains the same person. There is no question here of Elina having her soul replaced, and there is no problem here of personal identity if we accept the soul view. There is no agreed-upon account of personal identity or identity of objects over time in general, but we can conclude that on none of the three main accounts—personality, body, soul—of personal identity would having an evolving psychology necessarily constitute a threat. There is one more theory of personal identity: identity is an illusion. Many philosophers and scientists would deny the idea that there is a fixed self. We are literally not the same person from one year to the next; we only make ourselves believe so. David Hume famously argued that we can never observe a self, but only experience a succession of variating impressions. The idea that there is a persisting personal identity, a persisting essential "I" surviving all change over time is but an illusion. Just as we tend to say that there is a thing, say an "oak tree," that remains the same from sapling to big oak, when in fact nothing really remains identical over time, we have a tendency to think that there is some essential self that remains the same over time despite all the changes that we observe. Our empirical

observations give us series of diverse impressions over time, and then our mind says they all belong to the "same" object; but this, as said, is not real, rather it is a product of our imagination. The Buddhist notion of Anatta is similarly the denial that there is a permanent, unchanging self, soul, or essence. It is one of the three "right understandings" alongside Dukkha (suffering) and Anicca (impermanence). Consistent with both Buddha and Hume is the theory present in Jung and many other psychologists that our self is part of a story that we tell to make sense of our actions and experiences. Often we work in genre or archetypes, where we appropriate various cultural, or perhaps even innate, models of self-construction. "I am a man/woman who" is not a discovery, or a report, but an act of creation. We are to some extent born self-authors and will therefore be able to weave together a narrative that makes sense of ourselves to ourselves when even given more material (more years that is) to work with. The constant self-creation is also a central idea of existentialism. For Sartre, the self is not given but created out of nothing in each moment. This is just to say that denying the existence of an essential self persisting over time is not a fringe idea, but part of various philosophical traditions. It is, of course, outside the scope of this book to inveigh against the validity of denying the self. The point here is that if there is no self to protect, then Williams's second lemma is moot.

17. Shelly Kagan, *Death* (New Haven, CT: Yale University Press, 2012), 166.

18. Kagan, *Death*, 167.

19. Of course, even if she had not been the only one with a 300-year extension of life, maintaining love and friendships over 300 years or more would be a challenge. But it would not necessarily be impossible. It could be that, as Kass wrote, our relationships would deepen as never before. Given that we would know more about each other simply by having a greater sample in terms of years, we would be more intimate and, perhaps, recognize the virtue of being more accepting since given more time there will be more to forgive and forget. While we would face challenges, we would also have time to deal with them.

Chapter 7

This epigraph is attributed to Samuel Johnson by his biographer, James Boswell, in the work *The Life of Samuel Johnson*.

1. Leon Kass, *Life, Liberty, and the Defense of Dignity: The Challenge for Bioethics* (San Francisco: Encounter Books, 2002), 266.

2. Victor Frankl, *The Doctor and the Soul* (New York: Alfred A. Knopf, 1957), 73.

3. Kass, *Life*, 266.

4. Willard van Orman Quine, *Word and Object* (Cambridge, MA: MIT Press, 2013).

5. Sigmund Freud, *Reflections on War and Death*, trans. A. A. Brill and Alfred B. Kuttner (New York: Yard & Co., 1918). Freud goes on to say that the belief in our immortality makes us less prone to risk our lives.

6. Thomas Nagel, "Death," *Noûs* 4, no. 1 (February 1970): 80.

7. Kass, *Life*, 265.

8. Introspectively, I find that the thought of death rarely enters as a spur. When I eat supper, I am spurred by my hunger and have no thoughts of death. When I play tennis, I am spurred by the joy of playing, and thoughts of death only enter as a reminder of the hopelessness of my desire to improve as a player. Here it acts as an antispur.

9. Martha C. Nussbaum, *The Therapy of Desire: Theory and Practice in Hellenistic Ethics* (Princeton, NJ: Princeton University Press, 1994), 229.

10. Jean Kazez, *The Weight of Things: Philosophy and the Good Life* (Hoboken, NJ: Wiley–Blackwell, 2007).

11. Hadrian Wise, "Death Is Good for You," *Fortnight*, no. 436 (June–August 2005): 30.

12. Ludwig Wittgenstein, *Tractatus Logico-Philosophicus*, trans. C. K. Ogden (Mineola, NY: Dover Publications, 1999), 75.

13. Aaron Smuts, "Immortality and Significance," *Philosophy and Literature* 35, no. 1 (2011): 134–149.

14. Jorge Louis Borges, "The Immortal," in *Labyrinths: Selected Stories and Other Writings*, ed. Donald A. Yates and James E. Irby (New York: New Directions, 2007).

15. Borges, *Immortal*, 114.

16. Smuts, *Immortality*, 146.

17. Smuts, *Immortality*, 114.

18. Borges, *Immortal*, 116.

19. One thing is missing from his life though: the companionship of other immortals. But this, as in the case of the story of Elina, is not intrinsic to being immortal—there is scant risk of this ever being the case since life extension requires a communal scientific effort—it is just a particularity of Borges's hero. There are other problems with Borges's story: the Immortals are not unable to die; for Borges' narrator, a member of the Roman military, recounts that, "The body for them was a submissive domestic animal and it sufficed to give it, every month, the pittance of a few hours of sleep, a bit of water and a scrap of meat." So they are contingently immortal. This unfortunately renders his story incoherent, for why would the hero have to go searching for a river of mortality when he could simply abstain from drinking water?

20. Arthur Schopenhauer, *The Essays of Arthur Schopenhauer; Studies in Pessimism*, trans. T. Bailey Saunders (New York: The Project Gutenberg eBook, 2004) 1.

21. Roger Federer, "Roger Federer Pays Emotional Tribute to Rafael Nadal at Laurus Awards," ESPN Online, February 28, 2018, https://www.espn.com/tennis/story /_/id/22598117/roger-federer-pays-emotional-tribute-rival-rafael-nadal-laureus -awards.

22. Will Durant, *The Story of Philosophy: The Lives and Opinions of the World's Greatest Philosophers from Plato to John Dewey* (New York: Simon & Schuster, 2006), 471.

23. Seneca, *On the Shortness of Life*, trans. Garreth D. Williams, https://archive.org /stream/SenecaOnTheShortnessOfLife/Seneca+on+the+Shortness+of+Life_djvu.txt.

24. Ann Marie Slaughter, "Why Women Still Can't Have It All," *Atlantic Monthly*, July/ August 2002, https://www.theatlantic.com/magazine/archive/2012/07/why-women -still-cant-have-it-all/309020/.

25. Ann Marie Slaughter, "The Failure of the Phrase 'Work-Life Balance,'" *The Atlantic*, December 16, 2015.

26. Kesha Rose Sebert, "Crazy Kids," recorded 2012, 5th track on *Warrior* (2012), RCA, CD and LP.

Chapter 8

1. Leon Kass, *Life, Liberty, and the Defense of Dignity: The Challenge for Bioethics* (San Francisco: Encounter Books, 2002), 267.

2. Kass, *Life*, 268.

3. William R. Clark, *Sex and the Origins of Death* (New York: Oxford University Press, 1996), 56.

4. Jonathan Haidt, *The Righteous Mind, Why Good People Are Divided by Politics and Religion* (New York: Vintage, 2013).

5. Larisa Heiphetz, "The Role of Moral Beliefs, Memories, and Preferences in Representation of Identity," *Cognitive Science* 40, no. 7 (2016): 744–767.

6. There is another way of making the accusation, namely by suggesting that by not dying we are harming others due to our consumption of resources. We will deal with this objection in chapters 9 and 10.

7. Kass, *Life*, 268.

Chapter 9

1. Quora, "Is Death Beautiful," https://www.quora.com/Is-death-beautiful.

2. Leon Kass, *Life, Liberty, and the Defense of Dignity: The Challenge for Bioethics* (San Francisco: Encounter Books, 2002), 267.

3. David Hume, "On the Standards of Taste," in *David Hume: Selected Essays* (Oxford: Oxford World's Classics, 2008), 133–158.

4. Eric Wargo, "Beauty is in the Mind of the Beholder," *Association of Psychological Science: Observer*, April 2011, https://www.psychologicalscience.org/observer/beauty -is-in-the-mind-of-the-beholder.

5. Some may object, but is not beauty to a large degree a social construct? Does not a survey of cultures reveal that what is beautiful in one place, is not so in another, and has not our ideal of beauty changed a great deal over time? Is it not all relative? Consider the obese Venus of Willendorf, the 20-inch waists of French courtesans, the enormously elongated necks of the giraffe women of Northern Burma, the mutilated feet of Chinese women, the blackened teeth and paste-white faces of Japanese geishas, or the anemic girls and the boy-men of the Paris runway—are these and many more examples not disproving the idea of universal beauty? Not quite. They remind us that culture has a great power to work on our perception of beauty, and that just as there will always be great deal of individual variety, there will also be social variety, but underneath it all remains an unchanging natural baseline that cultures will naturally gravitate back to. While some traits may be cultivated with a particular idiosyncratic fervor by a community, most others will typically be left untouched; the geishas may have black teeth, but otherwise they presented forms we would still appreciate. Also, the variation most often remains within the boundaries of health and symmetry. It is often complained that our culture has moved from celebrating Marilyn Monroe's curves to Calvin Klein's heroin chic, a change that may on the surface amount to a great shift in our ideal of beauty; but this ignores that both types of women are still young and display symmetrical faces. Moreover, the average person is not swayed by what the fashion world and the media present as ideal. Men, in general, will still always prefer Marilyn. In fact, confirming the idea of universal beauty, heroin chic was a temporary aberration and we have rebounded, via Kim Kardashian, to our natural baseline. Just like brutalist architects tried to persuade us to live in large concrete boxes with square windows, separated from the bustle of a living city, this was an ideal that violates what most of us find appealing. And, to return to the main point, even if the social constructivist view of beauty were correct, it does not support the view that death is its mother.

6. Denis Dutton, "Aesthetics and Evolutionary Psychology," in *The Oxford Handbook of Aesthetics*, ed. Jerrold Levinson (Oxford University Press, 2003), 698.

7. Kass, *Life*, 267.

8. Kass, *Life*, 267.

9. John Hall Wheelock, "Song on Reaching Seventy," *Songs of Experience: An Anthology of Literature on Growing Old*, ed. Margaret Fowler and Priscilla McCutcheon (New York: Ballantine Books, 1991), 20–21.

10. Some may object that we also have an innate awareness of our mortality, but I have not found any evidence for this. It appears that we learn that we are mortal and, for most people, as I have argued in previous chapters, this awareness is at best as a half-awareness for most parts of their lives.

11. As a reminder, Epictetus wrote, "With regards to whatever objects give you delight, are useful, or are deeply loved, remember to tell yourself of what general nature they are, beginning from the most insignificant things. If, for example, you are fond of a specific ceramic cup, remind yourself that it is only ceramic cups in general of which you are fond. Then, if it breaks, you will not be disturbed. If you kiss your child, or your wife, say that you only kiss things which are human, and thus you will not be disturbed if either of them dies." Epictetus, *The Enchiridion*, trans. Elisabeth Carter (Cambridge, MA: The Internet Classics Archive), http://classics.mit.edu/Epictetus/epicench.html.

12. Kass, *Life*, 268.

13. Kass, *Life*, 264.

Chapter 10

1. The concept of average life expectancy at birth is ambiguous. It can either mean the number of years a child can be expected to live if it is born today or it can mean the number of years a child born today can expect to live given current mortality patterns. The second interpretation implies that on the assumption of scientific and medical progress a child can be expected to live longer than its life expectancy at birth.

2. Thomas Robert Malthus, *An Essay on the Principle of Population* (New York: Electronic Scholarly Publishing Project, 1998), 6.

3. Malthus, *Essay*, 6.

4. Paul Ehrlich, *The Population Bomb* (New York: Ballantine Books, 1968).

5. Paul Ehrlich interviewed by Peter Collier, *Mademoiselle*, April 1970.

6. Ehrlich, *Population Bomb*, 36.

7. Ehrlich, *Population Bomb*, 135.

8. Paul Ehrlich interviewed by P. D. Carrington, "Paul Ehrlich: 'Collapse of Civilization Is a Near Certainty Within Decades,'" *The Guardian*, March 22, 2018.

9. Hawking speaking at the Tencent WE Summit in Beijing, 2017.

10. Alexandra Paul, "Overpopulation Facts—The Problem No One Will Discuss: Alexandra Paul at TEDx Topanga" (Topanga, CA: 2013 presentation), https://www.youtube.com/watch?v=fNxctzyNxC0.

11. United Nations, Department of Economic and Social Affairs/Population Division, "World Population Prospects, Key Findings and Advance Tables," 2019 Revision. https://population.un.org/wpp/Publications/Files/WPP2019_Highlights.pdf.

12. United Nations, Population Division, Department of Economic and Social Affairs, Population Newsletter, "World Population in 2300," December 2003, https://www.un.org/en/development/desa/population/publications/pdf/newsletter/News76.pdf

13. Ramez Naam, *More Than Human: Embracing the Promise of Biological Enhancement* (New York: Random House, 2005), 106.

14. Leonid A. Gavrilov and Natalia S. Gavrilova, "Demographic Consequences of Defeating Aging," *Rejuvenation Research* 13, no. 2–3 (April 2010): 329–334.

15. John K. Davies. *The New Methuselahs: The Ethics of Life Extension.* (Cambridge, MA: MIT Press, 2017).

16. For example, Christine Overall, *Aging, Death and Human Longevity* (Berkeley: University of California Press, 2005).

17. The average American consumes three times as much water as, for instance, a Japanese. "Need" is to a large extent governed by cultural expectations.

18. WHO/UNICEF Joint Monitoring Program (JMP) for Water Supply and Sanitation, https://www.unwater.org/publication_categories/whounicef-joint-monitoring-programme-for-water-supply-sanitation-hygiene jmp/#:~:text=JMP%20is%20the%20only%20drinking,SDG%20targets%206.1%20and%206.2).

19. There is no firm definition for when to count a problem as global. Technically, it should mean a problem that directly affects everyone on earth. A clear case would be a hole in the ozone layer with global effects in terms of radiation and climate change. In this usage few problems are global. A wider definition would count a problem as global if it affects a majority of people on the earth. It is this wider concept that is intended in this and the following chapter. Judging by how the term global is used in the common discourse, it is often even more loosely applied intending something that affects many, but this is an unfortunate corruption of its meaning. The reason for this corruption is that adding "global" to some favored cause makes it seem worthier of our attention.

20. Joe Hassell and Max Roser, "Famines," Our World in Data, December 7, 2017, https://ourworldindata.org/famines/.

21. Max Roser and Hannah Ritchie, "Food Per Person," Our World in Data, 2017, https://ourworldindata.org/food-per-person.
   Daily per capita food supply by world region, measured on the basis of average caloric supply (kilocalories per person per day). Note that this measures the food available for consumption at the household level but does not account for any food wasted or not eaten at the consumption level.

22. Max Roser, "Land Use in Agriculture," Our World in Data, September 2019, https://ourworldindata.org/land-use.

23. United States Environmental Protection Agency, "EPA's Report on the Environment," 2017, https://cfpub.epa.gov/roe/

24. Colin Grabow, "If You Think Communism Is Bad for People, Check Out What It Did to The Environment," *The Federalist*, 2018.

25. Umwält Bunesamt, "Data on the State of the Environment in Germany: A Mixed Picture," The German Environmental Protection Agency, December 18, 2017, https://www.umweltbundesamt.de/en/topics/data-on-the-state-of-the-environment-in-germany-a.

26. Abby Tabor, "Human Activity in China and India Dominates the Greening of Earth, NASA Study Shows", NASA, Feb 11, 2019, https://www.nasa.gov/feature/ames/human-activity-in-china-and-india-dominates-the-greening-of-earth-nasa-study-shows

27. Michael Greenstone, "Four Years After Declaring War on Pollution, China Is Winning," *New York Times*, March 12, 2018.

28. The OFDA/CRED International Disaster Database, 2011, Université Catholique de Louvain, Brussels, Belgium, http://www.em-dat.net.

29. I. M. Goklany, "Deaths and Death Rates from Extreme Weather Events: 1900–2008," *Journal of American Physicians and Surgeons* 14, no. 4 (2009): 102–109.

30. Nassem Nicholas Taleb, *Antifragile: Things That Gain from Disorder* (New York: Random House, 2012).

31. Alexandra Paul, "Overpopulation Facts—The Problem No One Will Discuss: Alexandra Paul at TEDx Topanga" (Topanga, CA: 2013 presentation), https://www.youtube.com/watch?v=fNxctzyNxC0.

32. Alain de Botton, *Munk Debates*, (Toronto, House of Anansi Press, November 6, 2015), https://munkdebates.com/debates/progress.

Chapter 11

1. United Nations, "United Nations Population Prospects, Key Findings & Advance Tables: 2017 Revision." All population data are from this publication unless otherwise stated.

2. The belief that radical life extension technology would create adverse social consequences is the second most prevalent moral reason (behind its perceived unnaturalness) given by the public for being against it according to a 2009 study. Brad Partridge, Jayne Lucke, Helen Bartlett, and Wayne Hall, "Ethical, Social, and

Personal Implications of Extended Human Lifespan Identified by Members of the Public," *Rejuvenation Research* 12, no. 5 (2009): 351–357.

3. Nick Bostrom lists authoritarian world government as the fifth most likely calamity after nuclear war, extreme climate change, and designed pandemic. "Existential Risk: Analyzing Human Extinction Scenarios and Related Scenarios," *Journal of Evolution and Technology* 9 (March 2002).

4. The United States currently has a support ratio of 4.5.

5. In 2017, Japan had a life expectancy of 83.7 years, with a life expectancy of 80.5 for males and 86.1 for females.

6. Max Fisher, *Washington Post*, October 22, 2014; Chris Matthews, *Fortune*, February 26, 2015; Milton Ezrati, *National Interest*, March 25, 2015.

7. Purchasing power parity is when, in this case, the yen is compared to the dollar in terms of what it can buy in terms of a basket of basic goods. This measure is seen by many to give a realistic assessment of the relative economic standard when countries are compared on a dollar currency scale.

8. Japan dropped from a PSR of 10 in 1950 to a ratio of two in 2017.

9. There is nothing morally problematic with this: the idea was never that retirement benefits would provide people with a "fourth age" of two decades of leisure during which to travel and develop their tennis game. When the retirement age was set at 60 or 65 in developed countries, most people were genuinely worn out. When the US Social Security program, for instance, was introduced in 1935, the retirement age was set at 65 because the average life expectancy was only 61 and only roughly 55 percent of the population survived from adulthood to 65. Those who did were expected to live 13 years more, compared to 20 more years today. US Social Security Administration, "History of Social Security, Life Expectancy for Social Security," September 2019, https://www.ssa.gov/history/lifeexpect.html.

10. Joseph Chamie, "The Number of Workers per Retiree Declines Worldwide," Yale Global Online, December 22, 2015, http://yaleglobal.yale.edu/content/number -workers-retiree-declines-worldwide

11. It is probably not a coincidence that Japan is a world leader in robotics, a technology that will continue to transform the workplace. Oxford University researchers recently published a study finding that 47 percent of jobs in the United States are at risk of being eliminated in the next 20 years. The following jobs have a 99 percent chance of being eliminated over the next couple of decades: data entry clerks, library technicians, new accounts clerks, photographic process workers and processing machine operators, tax preparers, cargo and freight agents, watch repairers, insurance underwriters, mathematical technicians, title examiners, abstractors, and telemarketers.

12. Karl Marx, *Capital: A Critique of Political Economy*, vol. 1, trans. Ernest Untermann from 4th German edition (New York: The Modern Library, 1906).

13. Peter Capelli, *Managing the Older Worker, How to Prepare for the New Organizational Order* (Cambridge, MA: Harvard Business Review Press, 2010).

14. Pagan Kennedy, "To Be a Genius, Think Like a 94-Year-Old," *The New York Times*, Sunday Review, April 7, 2017. The data about patents come from the Information and Innovation Foundation.

15. Zoe Corbyn, "Experience Counts for Nobel Laureates," *Nature*, November 7, 2011, https://www.nature.com/news/2011/111107/full/news.2011.632.html.

16. Jay Olshansky, "Adding Years to Life: Current Knowledge and Future Prospects," *Session 1*, Testimony to President's Council on Bioethics, December 12, 2002, https://bio ethicsarchive.georgetown.edu/pcbe/transcripts/dec02/session2.html.

17. Sonia Arrison, *100+* (New York: Basic Books, 2013).

18. Kevin M. Murphy and Robert H. Topel, "The Value of Health and Longevity," *Journal of Political Philosophy* 114 (2006): 872.

19. Fukuyama, *Our Posthuman Future*, 69.

20. Robert Arking, "Extending Human Longevity: A Biological Perspective," in *The Fountain of Youth, Cultural, Scientific and Ethical Perspectives on a Biomedical Goal*, ed. Stephen Post and Robert H Binstock (New York: Oxford University Press, 2004), 179.

21. Lida Katsimpari et al. "Vascular and Neurogenic Rejuvenation of the Aging Mouse Brain by Young Systemic Factors," *Science* 344, no. 6184 (May 2014): 630–634.

22. At this point we know very little about the brain but the more we learn the greater the likelihood that we will be able to figure out ways to keep it younger. The Harvard Aging Brain study is currently pursuing research to be completed in 2019 based on the discovery that abnormal levels of the naturally occurring protein amyloid beta are linked to Alzheimer's. By normalizing the level of this protein, researchers hope to halt or delay the onset of the disease. Perhaps they will fail, but it is merely one of many approaches and we are, of course, still at the utter infancy of brain science. It may be exceedingly pessimistic to believe that every effort to revitalize our brains will fail. Besides biomedical solutions, we can also count on a continued reliance on artificial intelligence to make up for our own deteriorated mental capacities. Philosophers Andy Clark and David Chalmers suggest that we should understand our minds to extend beyond our brains to include our tools, such as our cellphones, meaning that we can nearly count the knowledge and capacities of our cellphone as our own. Even if our synapses are firing more slowly and our memory for names and dates is unreliable, as long as we can look up the information we need, we can be said to possess it. Our AI gadgets pick up the slack. Moreover, it is

not impossible that over the next 100 years the capacities of our cellphones will be moved from our hands to our brains via implants that literally will be a part of our minds. As a sign of times to come, Elon Musk has recently invested in a company called Neuralink, which is developing brain implants—"neural laces"—to improve memory and allow for direct communication with computing devices and by way of these devices, the internet. It seems premature to pronounce on the possibility of maintaining our mental faculties as we increase our health spans. Granted, it is speculative, like Chalmers and Clark, to think that cyborg-esque interventions can one day make up for mental decay and even enhance our minds, but it is equally speculative to assume the status quo. At this point we do not know how long we can keep our minds healthy.

In another recent case for cautious optimism, a two-year study of healthy non-obese humans on voluntary caloric restriction concludes that caloric restriction may have a slightly positive effect on working memory. Emilie Leclerc et al., "The Effect of Caloric Restriction on Working Memory in Healthy Non-obese Adults," *CNS Spectrum* (April 2019): 1–7.

23. Fukuyama, *Our Posthuman Future*, 65.

24. Fukuyama, *Our Posthuman Future*, 65.

25. Fukuyama, *Our Posthuman Future*, 67.

26. Fukuyama is here paraphrasing and adapting Max Planck's more general claim that a scientific truth does not triumph because it convinces its opponents but because its opponents eventually die: "Eine neue wissenschaftliche Wahrheit pflegt sich nicht in der Weise durchzusetzen, daß ihre Gegner überzeugt werden und sich als belehrt erklären, sondern vielmehr dadurch, daß ihre Gegner allmählich aussterben und daß die heranwachsende Generation von vornherein mit der Wahrheit vertraut gemacht ist." Wissenschaftliche Selbstbiographie. Mit einem Bildnis und der von Max von Laue gehaltenen Traueransprache." Johann Ambrosius Barth Verlag: Leipzig, 1948, p. 22.

27. The idea of several paradigms of economics contradicts Kuhn's definition of a paradigm as one dominant theory but is in line with how the concept is normally used. Economics might, perhaps, more accurately be describable in Kuhnian terms as an ongoing crisis in search of hegemonic theory.

28. Fukuyama, *Our Posthuman Future*, 66.

29. "Changing Attitudes to Gay Marriage," Pew Research Center, June 26, 2017.

30. Drew DeSilver, "The Politics of American Generations, How Age Affect Attitudes and Voting Patterns," *Pew Research Center*, Washington, DC, 2014.

31. Robert H. Binstock, "Older People and Voting Participation: Past and Future," *The Gerontologist* 40, no. 1 (March 2000): 18–31.

32. Pew Research Center, "Youth and War," 2006, https://www.pewresearch.org /2006/02/21/youth-and-war/

33. Fukuyama, *Our Posthuman Future*, 65.

34. Yuval Noah Harari, *Homo Deus* (New York: Harper, 2017), 29.

35. John K. Davies, *The New Methuselahs: The Ethics of Life Extension*. Cambridge, MA: MIT Press, 2018, 134.

36. Brad Partridge, Jayne Lucke, Helen Bartlett, and Wayne Hall, "Public Attitudes Towards Life Extension by Intervening in Ageing," *Journal of Aging Studies* (2010): 73–83.

37. John Rawls is the most influential philosopher of left liberalism and his theory seems to offer support for an equal distribution of life-extending treatments. Rawls takes the idea of the free and rational person as his starting point. A just society would allow each person to express this freedom, unencumbered by unfair and discriminatory social arrangements, and empowered with the necessary tools to pursue a freely chosen life plan. A liberal society will therefore secure freedom of speech, freedom of religion, and have laws that treat each individual as a free and equal citizen. This much all liberals agree on. Rawls goes further in a more egalitarian direction when he argues that in addition to classic liberal rights, we should also have the right to certain goods that would enable us to take advantage of these rights. These are goods that we would want regardless of our particular life goals. For example, we would want to have access to education because without it would be difficult to pursue our conception of the good life, no matter what this conception is. A good society would therefore be one where everyone can get a good education. The Rawlsian argument in favor of an equal distribution of life extension treatments would run as follows: being healthy and alive is good, no matter what particular life plan we have. No matter if our life is about making money, being with friends and family, or gaining knowledge or spiritual enlightenment, or playing tennis, or all of it, more healthy years would help. Rawls also has a principle of distribution, the Difference Principle, that tells us how to distribute goods when for practical reasons they cannot be equally distributed: inequality is justified when it works to the benefit of the worst off. If we apply this principle to life extension in the scenario where only the rich can afford it, it would allow them (like Musk in our example) to purchase it, if this arrangement is to the advantage to us who cannot afford it. As argued above, an argument can be made that it is, since the rich give money to the company that can make it profitable and hence capable of attracting investors and enable them to cover their research and development and continue their work until the treatment can be made more readily available. John Rawls, *A Theory of Justice*, (Cambridge, MA: Belknap Press, 1971).

38. Audrey R. Chapman, "The Social and Justice Implications of Extending the Human Life Span," in *The Fountain of Youth: Cultural, Scientific and Ethical Perspectives*

on a Biomedical Goal, ed. Stephen Post and Robert H. Binstock (New York: Oxford University Press, 2004), 352.

39. Leon Kass, "Preventing Brave New World," *The New Republic,* June 21, 2001.

Chapter 12

1. Nick Dragojlovic, "Canadians' Support for Radical Life Extension Resulting from Advances in Regenerative Medicine," *Journal of Aging Studies* 27, no 2 (2013): 151–158.

Bibliography

Adams, Mark B. "The Quest for Immortality: Visions and Presentiments in Science and Literature." In *The Fountain of Youth: Cultural, Scientific, and Ethical Perspectives on a Biomedical Goal*, edited by Stephen G. Post and Robert H. Binstock. Oxford: Oxford University Press, 2004.

Allen, Woody. *Without Feathers*. New York: Ballantine Books, 1986.

Alvarez, Allan, Lumberto Mendoza, and Peter Danielson, "Mixed Views About Radical Life Extension." *Etikk i praksis, Nordic Journal of Applied Ethics* 9, no. 1 (2015): 87–110.

Ariès, Philippe. *Western Attitudes toward Death: From the Middle Ages to the Present*. Baltimore, MD: Johns Hopkins University Press, 1974.

Arking, Robert. "Extending Human Longevity: A Biological Perspective." In *The Fountain of Youth, Cultural, Scientific and Ethical Perspectives on a Biomedical Goal*, edited by Stephen Post and Robert H. Binstock. New York: Oxford University Press, 2004.

Arnold, Edward. *From Religion to Philosophy: A Study in the Origins of Western Speculation*. London: Edward Arnold, 1912.

Arrison, Sonia. *100+*. New York: Basic Books, 2013.

Augustine. *The City of God*. Translated by Henry Bettenson. New York: Penguin Books, 1972.

Aurelius, Marcus. *The Meditations*. Translated by George Long. Cambridge, MA: MIT Classics Internet Library. http://classics.mit.edu/Antoninus/meditations.html.

Bacon, Francis. *The Philosophical Works of Francis Bacon*. Translated and edited by R. L. Ellis J. Spedding and J.M Robertson. London: Routledge, 1905.

Benatar, David. *Better Never to Have Been: The Harm of Coming into Existence*. Oxford: Oxford University Press, 2006.

Berlyne, D. E. "Curiosity and Exploration." *Science* 153 (1966): 25–33.

Binstock, Robert H. "Older People and Voting Participation: Past and Future." *The Gerontologist* 40, no. 1 (March 2000): 18–31.

Borges, Jorge Luis. "The Immortal." In *Labyrinths: Selected Stories and Other Writings*, edited by Donald A. Yates and James E. Irby. New York: New Directions, 2007.

Borges, Jorge Luis. "Three Essays: The Last Voyage of Ulysses / Flaubert and His Exemplary Destiny / Immortality." Translated by Eliot Weinberger and Esther Allen. *New England Review* 20, no. 3 (Summer 1999): 11–16.

Bostrom, Nick. "Existential Risk: Analyzing Human Extinction Scenarios and Related Scenarios." *Journal of Evolution and Technology* 9 (March 2002).

Bostrom, Nick. "A History of Transhumanism." *Journal of Evolution and Technology* 14, no. 1 (April 2005): 1–25.

Bostrom, Nick. "Why I Want to Be Posthuman When I Grow Up." In *Medical Enhancement and Posthumanity*, edited by Bert Gordijn and Ruth Chadwick, 107–137. New York: Springer, 2008.

de Botton, Alain. *The Munk Debates*. Toronto: House of Anansi Press, November 6, 2015.

Bradley, Ben. "When Is Death Bad for the One Who Dies?" *Noûs* 38, no. 1 (March 2004): 1–28.

Brink, David. *Moral Realism and the Foundations of Ethics*. Cambridge: Cambridge University Press, 1989.

Bulterijs, Sven, et al. "It Is Time to Classify Biological Aging as a Disease." *Frontiers in Genetics* 6, no. 205 (June 2015). https://doi.org/10.3389/fgene.2015.00205.

Burley, Mikel. "'The End of Immortality!' Eternal Life and the Makropulos Debate." *The Journal of Ethics* 19, no. 3/4, Special Issue: Immortality (September 2015): 305–321.

Callahan, Daniel. *False Hopes: Why America's Quest for Perfect Health is a Recipe for Failure*. New York: Simon & Schuster, 1998.

Callahan, Daniel. *Setting Limits, Medical Goals in an Aging Society*. New York: Simon & Schuster, 1987.

Callicot, J. Baird. *In Defense of Land Ethics*. Albany: State University of New York, 1989.

Calvin, John. *Institutes of the Christian Religion*. Vol. 2. Translated by Henry Beveridge (Edinburgh: T & T Clark, 1860).

Capek, Karel. *The Makropulos Case, in Four Plays*. Translated by Peter Majer and Cathy Porter. London: Methuen, 1999.

Capelli, Peter. *Managing the Older Worker: How to Prepare for the New Organizational Order*. Cambridge, MA: Harvard Business Review Press, 2010.

Carrington, P. D. "Paul Ehrlich: 'Collapse of Civilization Is a Near Certainty Within Decades.'" *The Guardian*, March 22, 2018.

Cathcart, Thomas, and Daniel Klein. *Heidegger and a Hippo Walk Through Those Pearly Gates: Using Philosophy (and Jokes!) to Explore Life, Death, the Afterlife, and Everything in Between*. New York: Viking, 2009.

Chamie, Joseph. "The Number of Workers per Retiree Declines Worldwide." *Yale Global Online*, December 22, 2015. http://yaleglobal.yale.edu/content/number -workers-retiree-declines-worldwide.

Chapman, Audrey R. "The Social and Justice Implications of Extending the Human Life Span." In *The Fountain of Youth, Cultural, Scientific and Ethical Perspectives on a Biomedical Goal*, edited by Stephen Post and Robert H. Binstock, 340–361. New York: Oxford University Press, 2004.

Charlesworth, B. "Fisher, Medawar, Hamilton, and the Evolution of Aging." *Genetics* 156, no. 3 (November 2000): 927–931.

Chesterton, G. K. *Saint Thomas Aquinas*. Mineola, NY: Dover Publications, 2009.

Clark, William R. *Sex and the Origins of Death*. New York: Oxford University Press, 1996.

Cloutier, J., T. F. Heatherton, P. J. Whalen, and W. M. Kelley. "Are Attractive People Rewarding? Sex Differences in the Neural Substrates of Facial Attractiveness." *Journal of Cognitive Science* 20, no. 6 (June 2008): 941–951.

Collier, Peter. "The Road to Extinction." *Mademoiselle*, April 1970.

Colman, Ricki J., T. Mark Beasley, Joseph W. Kemnitz, Sterling C. Johnson, Richard Weindruch, and Rozalyn M. Anderson. "Caloric Restriction Reduces Age-related and All-cause Mortality in Rhesus Monkeys." *Nature Communications* 3557, April 1, 2014. https://www.ncbi.nlm.nih.gov/pmc/articles/PMC3988801/.

Corbyn, Zoe. "Experience Counts for Nobel Laureates." *Nature, International Weekly Journal of Science*, November 7, 2011. https://www.nature.com/news/2011/111107 /full/news.2011.632.html.

Cornford, F. M. *From Religion to Philosophy: A Study in the Origins of Western Speculation*. Mineola, NY: Dover Publications, 2004.

Curry, Patrick. *Ecological Ethics: An Introduction*. London: Polity Press, 2011.

Davies, John K. *The New Methuselahs: The Ethics of Life Extension.* Cambridge, MA: MIT Press, 2018.

De Gray, Aubrey. "Strategies for Engineered Negligible Senescence: Why Genuine Control of Aging May Be Foreseeable." *Annals of the New York Academy of Sciences* 1019, no. 1, xv–xvi (June 2004): 1–592.

De Gray, Aubrey, and Michael Rae. *Ending Aging: The Rejuvenation Breakthroughs That Could Reverse Human Aging in Our Lifetime.* New York: St. Martin Griffin, 2008.

DeSilver, Drew. "The Politics of American Generations, How Age Affects Attitudes and Voting Patterns." *Pew Research Center*, Washington, DC, July 9, 2014. https://www.pewresearch.org/fact-tank/2014/07/09/the-politics-of-american-generations-how-age-affects-attitudes-and-voting-behavior/.

Dettling, Lisa, and Melisa S. Kearney. "House Prices and Birth Rates: The Impact of the Real Estate Market on the Decision to Have a Baby." *Journal of Public Economics* 110, (February 2014): 1–166.

Devall, Bill, and George Sessions. *Deep Ecology: Living as if Nature Mattered.* Salt Lake City, UT: Peregrine Smith Books, 1985.

Dreher, Rod. "Old Age Is a Humiliation." *The American Conservative*, November 30, 2014.

Dollimore, Jonathan. *Death, Desire, and Loss in Western Culture.* New York: Routledge, 1998.

Dragojlovic, N. "Canadians' Support for Radical Life Extension Resulting from Advances in Regenerative Medicine." *Journal of Aging Studies* 27, no. 2 (2013): 151–158.

Duncan, David Ewing. *When I'm 164: The New Science of Radical Life Extension, and What Happens If It Succeeds.* New York: TED Conferences, 2012.

Durant, Will. *The Story of Philosophy: The Lives and Opinions of the World's Greatest Philosophers from Plato to John Dewey.* New York: Simon & Schuster, 2006.

Dutton, Denis. "Aesthetics and Evolutionary Psychology." In *The Oxford Handbook of Aesthetics*, edited by Jerrold Levinson. Oxford: Oxford University Press, 2005.

Ebner, Natalie C., and Håkan Fischer. "Emotion and Aging: Evidence from Brain and Behavior." *Frontiers of Psychology*, September 9, 2014. https://doi.org/10.3389/fpsyg.2014.00996.

Ehrlich, Paul. "Paul Ehrlich: 'Collapse of Civilization Is a Near Certainty Within Decades.'" Interview with P. D. Carrington. *The Guardian*, March 22, 2018.

Ehrlich, Paul. *The Population Bomb.* New York: Ballantine Books, 1968.

Epictetus. *Discourses.* Translated by Elisabeth Carter. Cambridge, MA: The Internet Classics Archive. http://classics.mit.edu/Epictetus/discourses.1.one.html.

Epictetus. *Enchiridion*. Translated by Elisabeth Carter. Cambridge, MA: The Internet Classics Archive. http://classics.mit.edu/Epictetus/epicench.html.

Epictetus, *Golden Sayings*. Translated by Hastings Crossly. New York: Gutenberg Project, 2006. https://www.gutenberg.org/files/871/871-h/871-h.htm.

Epicurus. "Letter to Menoeceus." Translated by Robert Drew Hicks. The Internet Classics Archive. http://classics.mit.edu/Epicurus/menoec.html.

ESPN. "Roger Federer Pays Emotional Tribute to Rafael Nadal at Laurus Awards." *ESPN Online*, February 28, 2018. http://www.espn.com/tennis/story/_/id/22598117/roger-federer-pays-emotional-tribute-rival-rafael-nadal-laureus-awards.

Ezrati, Milton. "The Demographic Time Bomb Crippling Japan's Economy." National Interest, March 25, 2015.

Feldman, Fred. "Death." In *Routledge Encyclopedia of Philosophy*. London: Routledge, 1998.

Ferry, Luc. *The New Ecological Order*. Translated by Carol Volk. Chicago: University of Chicago Press, 1995.

Fink, B., and I. Penton-Voak. *Evolutionary Psychology of Facial Attractiveness. Current Directions in Psychological Science* 11 (2002): 154–158.

Fisher, Max. "Japan's Sexual Apathy Is Endangering the Global Economy." *Washington Post*, October 22, 2014.

Fleming, Pat A. *"I Still Matter,"* September 2017. http://www.familyfriendpoems.com/poem/i-still-matter.

Frankl, Victor. *The Doctor and the Soul*. New York: Alfred A. Knopf, 1957.

Freud, Sigmund. *Reflections on War and Death*. Translated by A. A. Brill and Alfred B. Kuttner. New York: Yard & Co., 1918.

Fukuyama, Francis. *Our Posthuman Future: Consequences of the Biotechnology Revolution*. New York: Picador 2002.

Gavrilov, Leonid A., and Natalia S. Gavrilova. "Demographic Consequences of Defeating Aging." *Rejuvenation Research* 13, no. 2–3 (April 2010): 329–334.

Gems, David. "Tragedy and Delight: The Ethics of Decelerated Ageing." *Philosophical Transactions of the Royal Society* B 366 (2011): 108–112.

Goklany, I. M. "Deaths and Death Rates from Extreme Weather Events: 1900–2008." *Journal of American Physicians and Surgeons* 14, no. 4 (2009): 102–109.

Gour, H. Singh. *The Spirit of Buddhism*. Whitefish, MT: Kessinger Publishing 2005.

Grabow, Colin. "If You Think Communism Is Bad for People Check Out What It Did to The Environment." *The Federalist*, 2018.

Greenstone, Michael. "Four Years After Declaring War on Pollution, China Is Winning." *New York Times*, March 12, 2018.

Gruman, Gerald Joseph. *A History of Ideas About the Prolongation of Life*. New York: Springer, 2003.

Haidt, Jonathan. *The Righteous Mind: Why Good People Are Divided by Politics and Religion*. New York: Vintage, 2013.

Harari, Yuval Noah. *Homo Deus*.New York: Harper, 2017.

Harari, Yuval Noah. *Sapiens: A Brief History of Mankind*. New York: Harper, 2011.

Hardwig, John. *Is There a Duty to Die? And Other Essays in Medical Ethics*. New York: Routledge, 2000.

Harrington, Anne. *Reenchanted Science: Holism in German Culture from Wilhelm II to Hitler*. Princeton, NJ: Princeton University Press, 1996.

Hassell, Joe, and Max Roser. "Famines." *Our World in Data*, December 7, 2017. https://ourworldindata.org/famines/.

Hayflick, Leonard. *How and Why We Age* New York: Ballantine Books, 1994.

Heiphetz, Larisa. "The Role of Moral Beliefs, Memories, and Preferences in Representation of Identity." *Cognitive Science* 40, no. 7 (2016): 744–767.

Hitchens, Christopher. *God Is Not Great: How Religion Poisons Everything*. New York: Hachette Book Group, 2007.

Hitler, Adolph. *Mein Kampf*. Translated by Ralph Manheim. New York: Houghton Mifflin Company, 1998.

Hobbes, Thomas. *Leviathan*. Edited by C. B. MacPherson. 4th ed. New York: Penguin Classics, 1982.

Homer. *Iliad*. New York: Penguin Classics, 1998.

Hume, David. "On the Standards of Taste." In *David Hume: Selected Essays*. Oxford: Oxford World's Classics, 2008.

Jackson, Peter. *The Lord of the Rings: The Fellowship of the Ring*. Special extended DVD edition. New Line Home Entertainment, 2001.

Kagan, Shelley. *Death*. New Haven, CT: Yale University Press, 2012.

Kant, Immanuel. "An Answer to the Question: What is Enlightenment?" Originally published as "Beantwortung der Frage: Was ist Aufklarung?" *Berlinische Monatsschrift* 4 (1784): 481–494.

Kass, Leon. *Life, Liberty, and the Defense of Dignity: The Challenge for Bioethics*. San Francisco: Encounter Books, 2002.

Kass, Leon. "Preventing Brave New World." *The New Republic Online*, June 21, 2001.

Katsimpari, Lida, et al. "Vascular and Neurogenic Rejuvenation of the Aging Mouse Brain by Young Systemic Factors." *Science* 344, no. 6184 (May 2014): 630–634.

Kazez, Jean. *The Weight of Things: Philosophy and the Good Life*. Hoboken, NJ: Wiley–Blackwell, 2007.

Kennedy, Pagan. "To Be a Genius, Think Like a 94-Year-Old." *The New York Times, Sunday Review*, April 7, 2017.

Kidd, Celeste, et al. "The Psychology and Neuroscience of Curiosity." *Neuron* 88, no. 3 (2015): 449–460.

Kirkwood, T. *Time of Our Lives*. New York: Oxford University Press, 1999.

Kripke, Saul. *Naming and Necessity*. Cambridge, MA: Harvard University Press, 1980.

Kuhn, Thomas. *The Structure of Scientific Revolutions*. Chicago: University of Chicago Press, 1970.

Kuran, Timur. *Private Truths, Public Lies*. Cambridge, MA: Harvard University Press, 1997.

Kurzweil, Raymond. *The Age of Spiritual Machines*. New York: Viking Press, 1999.

Laaksonen, S. J. "A Research Note: Happiness by Age Is More Complex Than U-Shaped." *Happiness Studies* 19 (2018): 471–482.

Larissa, Nina Strohminger, and Liane L. Young. "The Role of Moral Beliefs, Memories, and Preferences in Representations of Identity." *Cognitive Science*, vol. 40, no.7, (2017): 744–767.

Larkin, Phillip. "Aubade." In *The Broadview Anthology of British Literature*. Vol. 6. Edited by Joseph Black, Leonard Conolly, Kate Flint, Isobel Grundy, Don LePan, Roy Liuzza, Jerome J. McGann, Anne Lake Prescott, Barry V. Qualls and Claire Waters. New York: Broadview Press, 2004.

Leclerc, Emilie, et al. "The Effect of Caloric Restriction on Working Memory in Healthy Non-Obese Adults." *CNS Spectrum* 25, no. 1 (February 2020): 2–8.

Lieber, F. *Das Stufenalter des Mannes*, print published by Gustav May Söhne, Frankfurt, 1900.

Lorenzo, G. L., J. C. Biesanz, and L. J. Human. "What Is Beautiful Is Good and More Accurately Understood: Physical Attractiveness and Accuracy in First Impressions of Personality." *Psychological Science* 21 (2010): 1777–1782.

Lucas, George. *Star Wars Episode III: Revenge of the Sith*. Los Angeles: Lucasfilm Ltd., 2005.

Lucretius. *De Rerum Natura*. Translated by Cyril Bailey. Oxford: Clarendon Press, 1910.

Lucretius (Titus Lucretius Carus). *On the Nature of Things: De Rerum Natura*. Translated by Anthony M. Esolen. San Francisco: Cengage Learning, 1995.

Lukács, Georg. *The Destruction of Reason*. London: Merlin, 1954.

Luper, Stephen. "Annihilation." *Philosophical Quarterly* 37, no. 148 (1987): 233–252.

Mainwood, Paul. "Einstein Believed in a Theory of Space Time That Can Help People Cope with Loss." *Forbes*, December 28, 2016.

Malthus, Thomas Robert. *An Essay on the Principle of Population*. New York: Electronic Scholarly Publishing Project, 1998.

Marx, Karl. *Capital: A Critique of Political Economy*. Translated by Ernest Untermann from the 4th German edition. New York: The Modern Library, 1906.

Maslow, A. H. *Psychological Review* 50, no. 4 (1943): 370–396.

Matthews, Chris. "Forget Greece, Japan Is the World's Real Economic Time Bomb." *Fortune*, February 26, 2015.

Medawar, Peter B. "An Unsolved Problem in Biology." In P. B. Medawar, *The Uniqueness of the Individual*. New York: Dover Publications, 1981.

Meilaender, Gilbert. *Should We Live Forever: The Ethical Ambiguities of Aging*. Grand Rapids, MI: Eerdmans, 2013.

Mendoza L., A. Alvarez, and P. Danielson. "Mixed Views about Radical Life Extension." *Etikk i praksis, Nordic Journal of Applied Ethics* 9, no. 1 (2015): 87–110.

Mhaske, R. "Happiness and Aging." *Journal of Psychosocial Research* 12, no. 1 (2017): 71–79.

Mill, John Stuart. *On Liberty*. Mineola, NY: Dover, 2002.

Millwar, David. "Eric Clapton Struggling to Play Guitar Because of Damage to His Nervous System." *The Telegraph*, June 12, 2016.

Mirandola, Giovanni Pico della. *Oration on the Dignity of Man*. Chicago: Gateway Edition, 1956.

Momeyer, Richard. *Confronting Death*. Bloomington: Indiana University Press, 1988.

Montaigne, Michel de. "That to Philosophize Is to Learn to Die." In *The Complete Essays of Montaigne*, edited by Donald M. Frame. Stanford, CA: Stanford University Press, 1958.

"Muggles' Guide to Harry Potter/Characters/Voldemort," Wikibooks. Accessed January 31, 2019. https://en.wikibooks.org/wiki/Muggles%27_Guide_to_Harry_Potter /Characters/Lord_Voldemort.

Murphy, Kevin M., and Robert H. Topel. "The Value of Health and Longevity." *Journal of Political Philosophy* 114 (2006): 871–904.

Myrskyla, M., H.-P Kohler, and F. C. Billari. "Advances in Development Reverse Fertility Declines." *Nature* 6 (August 2009).

Naam, Ramez. *More Than Human: Embracing the Promise of Biological Enhancement.* New York: Random House, 2005.

Nagel, Thomas. "Death." *Nous* 4, no. 1 (1970): 73–80.

Nagel, Thomas. *Mortal Questions.* New York: Cambridge University Press, 1979.

Nietzsche, Friedrich. *The Birth of Tragedy.* Translated by Walter Kaufmann. New York: Vintage, 1967.

Nietzsche, Friedrich. *Twilight of the Idols*, Thought 14: Anti-Darwin. Indianapolis, IN: Hackett, 1989 [1889].

Nozick, R. 1981. *Philosophical Explanations.* Cambridge, MA: Belknap Press.

Nuland, Sherwin B. *How We Die: Reflections on Life's Final Chapter.* New York: Knopf, 1993.

Nussbaum, Martha C. *The Therapy of Desire: Theory and Practice in Hellenistic Ethics.* Princeton, NJ: Princeton University Press, 1994.

OFDA/CRED. International Disaster Database, 2011, Université Catholique de Louvain, Brussels, Belgium. https://www.emdat.be/.

Ohlsson, Eric. "The Epicurean Death." *Journal of Ethics* 17, no. 1–2 (2013): 65–78.

Olshansky, Jay. Testimony of December 12, 2002, to President's Council on Bioethics Hearing on "Adding Years to Life: Current Knowledge and Future Prospects," Session 1. https://bioethicsarchive.georgetown.edu/pcbe/transcripts/dec02/session2.html.

Olshansky, S. Jay, Leonard Hayflick, and Bruce A. Carnes. "Position Statement on Aging," *The Journals of Gerontology: Series A,* 57, no. 8 (August 2002): 292–297.

Orwell, George. *1984.* New York: Signet Classics, 1961.

Osborne, Michael A., and Carl Benedikt. "The Future of Employment: How Susceptible Are Jobs to Computerization?" *Oxford University Department of Engineering Science* (September 2013): 1–72.

Overall, Christine. *Aging, Death and Human Longevity.* Berkeley: University of California Press, 2005.

Parfit, Derek. *Reasons and Persons.* Oxford: Oxford University Press, 1986.

Partridge, Brad, Jayne Lucke, Helen Bartlett, and Wayne Hall. "Ethical Concerns in the Community about Technologies to Extend Human Life Span." *American Journal of Bioethics* 9, no. 12 (2009): 68–76.

Partridge, Brad, Jayne Lucke, Helen Bartlett, and Wayne Hall. "Ethical, Social, and Personal Implications of Extended Human Lifespan Identified by Members of the Public." *Rejuvenation Research* 12, no. 5 (2009): 351–357.

Partridge, Brad, Jayne Lucke, Helen Bartlett, and Wayne Hall. "Public Attitudes Towards Life Extension by Intervening in Ageing." *Journal of Aging Studies* (2010): 73–83.

Paul, Alexandra. "Overpopulation Facts—The Problem No One Will Discuss: Alexandra Paul at TEDxTopanga." Topanga, CA: 2013 presentation. https://www.youtube .com/watch?v=fNxctzyNxC0.

Penn, Ivan. "California Invested Heavily in Solar Power: Now There's So Much That Other States Are Sometimes Paid to Take It." *Los Angeles Times*, June 22, 2017.

Petersen, Peter. *Gray Dawn: How the Coming Age Wave Will Transform America and the World*. New York: Times Books, 1999.

Pew Research Center. "Survey of Aging and Longevity, Living to 120 and Beyond: Americans' Views on Aging, Medical Advances and Radical Life Extension," August 6, 2013. http://www.pewforum.org/dataset/survey-of-aging-and-longevity/.

Pew Research Center. "Youth and War." 2006. https://www.pewresearch.org/2006 /02/21/youth-and-war/.

Pinker, Steven. *The Better Angels of Our Nature: Why Violence Has Been Declining*. New York: Viking, 2011.

Pinker, Steven. *The Blank Slate: The Modern Denial of Human Nature*. New York: Viking, 2002.

Plato. *The Dialogues of Plato* Translated by Benjamin Jowett. 3rd edition. Oxford: Oxford University Press, 1892.

Plato. *The Republic*. Translated by Benjamin Jowett. The Internet Classics Archive. http://classics.mit.edu/Plato/republic.2.i.html

Plotinus. *The Enneads*. Translated by Stephen MacKenna. London: Penguin Books, 1991.

Post, Stephen, and Robert H. Binstock. *The Fountain of Youth: Cultural, Scientific, and Ethical Perspectives on a Biomedical Goal*. Oxford: Oxford University Press, 2004.

Quine, Willard van Orman. *Word and Object*. Cambridge, MA: MIT Press, 2013.

Raush, Jonathan. *The Happiness Curve: Why Life Gets Better after Midlife*. London: Bloomsbury, 2018.

Rawls, John. *A Theory of Justice*. Cambridge, MA: Belknap Press, 1971.

Redman, Leanne, Steven R. Smith, Jeffrey H. Burton, Corby K. Martin, Dora Il'yasova, and Eric Ravussin. "Metabolic Slowing and Reduced Oxidative Damage with Sustained Caloric Restriction Support the Rate of Living and Oxidative Damage Theories of Aging." *Cell Metabolism* 27, no. 4 (2018): 805–815.

Roser, Max. "Land Use in Agriculture." Our World in Data, 2016. https://ourworld indata.org/land-use.

Roser, Max, and Hannah Ritchie. "Food Per Person." Our World in Data, 2017. https://ourworldindata.org/food-per-person.

Russell, Bertrand. "A Free Man's Worship." In *Mysticism and Logic*. London: Routledge, 1976 (1903).

Saltus, Richard. "Partial Reversal of Aging Achieved in Mice." *Harvard Gazette*, November 28, 2011. https://news.harvard.edu/gazette/story/2010/11/partial-reversal-of-aging-achieved-in-mice/.

Sandel, Michael J. "The Case Against Perfection." *The Atlantic*, April 2004.

Sartre, Jean Paul. *Existentialism Is a Humanism*. Translated by Carol Macomber. New Haven, CT: Yale University Press, 2007.

Schopenhauer, Arthur. *The Essays of Arthur Schopenhauer: Studies in Pessimism*. Translated by T. Bailey Saunders. New York: CreateSpace Independent Publishing Platform, 2015.

Schopenhauer, Arthur. *The World as Will and Idea*. Translated by E. F. J. Payne. Mineola, NY: Dover Publications, 1966.

Sebert, Kesha Rose. "Crazy Kids," track 5 on *Warrior*, RCA, 2012 CD and LP.

Seneca, *Epistles, Volume I: Epistles 1–65*. Translated by Richard M. Gummere. Loeb Classical Library 75. Cambridge, MA: Harvard University Press, 1971.

Seneca. "On the Shortness of Life," "On Taking One's Own Life," and "On Tranquility." In *The Stoic Philosophy of Seneca: Essays and Letters*, translated by Moses Hadas. New York: Doubleday, 1958.

Sinsheimer, Robert. "The Presumptions of Science." *Daedalus* 107, no. 2 (Spring 1978): 23–36.

Slaughter, Ann Marie. "The Failure of the Phrase 'Work-Life Balance.'" *The Atlantic*, December 16, 2015.

Slaughter, Ann Marie. "Why Women Still Can't Have It All." *Atlantic Monthly*, August 2002.

Smuts, Aaron. "Immortality and Significance." *Philosophy and Literature* 35, no. 1 (April 2011): 134–149.

Sophocles. *Oedipus at Colonus: The Tragedies of Sophocles*. Translated by Richard C. Jebbs. Cambridge: Cambridge University Press, 1904.

Tabor, Abby. "Human Activity in China and India Dominates the Greening of Earth, NASA Study Shows." NASA, February 11, 2019. https://www.nasa.gov/feature/ames/human-activity-in-china-and-india-dominates-the-greening-of-earth-nasa-study-shows.

Taleb, Nassem Nicholas. *Antifragile: Things That Gain from Disorder*. New York, Random House, 2012.

Umwält Bundesamt. (The German Environmental Protection Agency website.) "Data on the State of the Environment in Germany: A Mixed Picture." https://www.umweltbundesamt.de/en/topics/data-on-the-state-of-the-environment-in-germany-a.

United Nations Children's Fund. "Levels and Trends in Child Mortality, Report 2017." *UN Inter-agency Group for Child Mortality Estimation*, 2017. http://www.childmortality.org/2017/files_v21/download/IGME%20report%202017%20child%20mortality%20final.pdf.

United Nations Department of Economic and Social Affairs, Population Division. "World Population Prospects, Key Findings and Advance Tables: 2017 Revision." https://esa.un.org/unpd/wpp/publications/files/wpp2017_keyfindings.pdf.

United Nations Department of Economic and Social Affairs, Population Division. "World Population to 2300." New York: United Nations, 2004. http://www.un.org/en/development/desa/population/publications/pdf/trends/WorldPop2300final.pdf.

United States Environmental Protection Agency. "EPA's Report on the Environment." 2017. https://cfpub.epa.gov/roe/.

United States Social Security Administration. "History of Social Security, Life Expectancy for Social Security," September 2019. https://www.ssa.gov/history/lifeexpect.html.

Wargo, Eric. "Beauty is in the Mind of the Beholder." *Association of Psychological Science: Observer*, April 2011. https://www.psychologicalscience.org/observer/beauty-is-in-the-mind-of-the-beholder.

Wells, H. G., and Aldous Huxley. *The Science of Life* (New York: The Literary Guild, 1934).

Wendler, David. "Understanding the Conservative View of Abortion." *Bioethics* 13, no. 1 (1999): 32–56.

Wheelock, John Hall. "Song on Reaching Seventy." *In Songs of Experience: An Anthology of Literature on Growing Old*, edited by Margaret Fowler and Priscilla McCutcheon. New York: Ballantine Books, 1991.

Whitehead, Alfred North. *Process and Reality*. New York: Free Press, 1979.

Whitman, Walt. *Leaves of Grass*. Mineola, NY: Dover Publications, 2007.

WHO/UNICEF Joint Monitoring Program (JMP) for Water Supply and Sanitation. Accessed on May 18, 2017. https://www.unwater.org/publication_categories/whou nicef-joint-monitoring-programme-for-water-supply-sanitation-hygiene-jmp /#:~:text=JMP%20is%20the%20only%20drinking,SDG%20targets%206.1%20 and%206.2).

Williams, Bernard. "The Makropulos Case: Reflections on the Tedium of Immortality." In *Moral Problems: A Collection of Philosophical Essays*, edited by James Rachels. New York: Harper & Row, 1979.

Wise, Hadrian. "Death Is Good for You." *Fortnight*, no. 436 (June–August 2005).

Wittgenstein, Ludwig. *Tractatus Logico-Philosophicus*. Translated by C. K. Ogden. Mineola, NY: Dover Publications, 1999.

Woodcox, Adam. "Aristotle's Theory of Aging." *Cahiers des Etudes Anciennes* 55 (2018): 65–78.

Index

Acceptance
  of aging, 26, 30
  of death, 1, 6–14, 18–20, 138
Adaptive preferences. *See* Sour grapes
Afterlife, 4–6, 12–14, 19–20, 94, 136
  Buddhist views of, 67–68
  Epicurean view of, 39
  Plato's view of, 39
  rewards in, 73
Aging
  case against, 24–37 passim
  definition of, 23
  as a disease, 34–36
  symptoms of, 24–25
Alzheimer's disease, 2, 19, 25, 34, 167,
    191, 194, 199
Annihilation, 6, 19–20, 43, 67
Antiaging
  interventions, 26, 35, 155–156, 182
  as preventative medicine, 35–36, 194,
    200
  products, 12
  research, 19, 172, 176, 199
  resistance to, 34–36, 201, 207
  and worries about access, 191–192,
    194–195
Antinatalism, 63–64. *See also* Benatar,
    David
Apologism, 6–7, 9, 89, 200
Aquinas, Thomas, 79
Ariès, Phillipe, 89–90

Aristotle, 35, 70, 78–79, 126
Arrison, Sonya, 178
Aurelius, Marcus, 6, 54, 77, 81, 85
Autonomy, 16–17, 20, 37, 200

Bacon, Francis, 90–91
Beauty, 96, 133, 139–147
  creation of, 143
  theories of, 140–141
Benatar, David, 61–64. *See also*
    Antinatalism
Bioconservative(s), 15, 17, 19, 28, 93,
    101–102, 110, 168, 197
Boredom, 62, 105–106, 109, 118, 201
  pill against, 109–110
Borges, Jorge Luis, 106, 121–122,
    124–126, 196
Bostrom, Nick, 213n38
Bradley, Ben, 44
Brink, David, 213n32
Buddhism, 67–68

Callahan, Daniel, 10, 15, 17, 82, 89, 100
Callicot, J. Baird, 83
Caloric restriction, 3, 179
  mimetic, 3
Camus, Albert, 66, 74
Cephalus, 28, 30
Chapman, Audrey R., 194–195
Clapton, Eric, 30
Clark, William R., 134, 146

Climate change. *See* Global warming
Collectivism, 86
Compressed morbidity, 33
Conservatism, 28, 33, 100, 181, 183–184
Courage
  death as a condition for, 109,
    133–134, 145
  in the face of death, 13, 18
  to use your own intelligence, 92
Curry, Patrick, 83

Davies, John K., 155–156, 190–191
Deadline, 105, 114, 121, 127, 202–203
Declaration of Geneva, 35
Demographic
  challenges, 60, 173, 176
  projections, 157
Deprivation account, 40–43, 45–46, 96
Devall, Bill, 83
Distress, 190–191. *See also* Davies,
  John K.
Distribution of life extension. *See* Life
  extension: access to
Drugs
  antiaging, (*see* Caloric restriction:
    mimetics)
  psychotropic, 110, 148, 196, (*see also*
    Boredom: pill against)
Duncan, David Ewing, 5

Ecclesiastes, 60, 71, 131
Egalitarian, 194
Egalitarianism, 91
Ehrlich, Paul, 150–151, 157, 159–160,
  168
Einstein, Albert, 78, 124, 217n9.
  See also Eternalism
Enhancement, 16–17, 21–22, 36, 110,
  172
Epictetus, 82, 231n11
Epicurean, 18, 106. *See also* Lucretius
  atomism, 39, 52
  death cannot harm us, 39–47

indifference to death, 47–50, 70, 84
  therapeutic philosophy, 54–56
  (*see also* Nussbaum, Martha)
Equality, 88
  vs. freedom, 126
  of human souls, 91
  for women, 154
  worries about, 95 (*see also* Inequality;
    Life extension: access to)
Eternalism, 44, 217n9
Euthanasia, 50
Evolution, theory of, 127–128
  and aesthetics, 140–141
  and aging, 2, 4, 26, 86
  and holism, 87, 205
  and love, 143

Fallacies, 140, 145
Falsified preferences, 26, 36–37. *See also*
  Kuran, Timur
Family, 27, 190
  vs. career, 129–130
  enjoying, 146, 189
  losing, 47–49, 74, 82, 106, 202 (*see also*
    Epicurean: indifference to death)
  member with dementia, 45 (*see also*
    Alzheimer's disease)
  need to care for, 103
  relationship, 124, 147
  shrinking, 175, 188
Fertility rate, 150–157, 167, 171, 173,
  175–178, 187–188, 207
Forced choice, 156. *See also* Davies,
  John K.
Frankl, Victor, 113
Freud, Sigmund, 115, 223n19
Fukuyama, Francis, 9, 168, 178–180,
  186–189, 236n26

Gems, David, 26, 34
Geroprotective medicine. *See* Antiaging:
  as preventative medicine
Global warming, 151, 163–165

Graying of society, 171, 173, 176, 183.
    See also Life expectancy; Graying of
    society; Fertility rate
Gruman, Gerald J., 7

Haidt, Jonathan, 134–135, 147
Haldane, J.B.S, 8
Harari, Yoval Noah, 190
Hardwig, John, 82, 119
Hayflick, Leonard, 23, 25
Hedonism, 48, 55
Hierarchies, 172, 179–180
Hitchens, Christopher, 13, 40
Hobbes, Thomas, 91, 134–135
Holism, 80, 83, 85–86
Homer, 80, 84, 121, 123, 133–134
Hubris, 7, 8, 9, 11, 56, 66, 201
Human condition, 7, 13, 18, 59, 147,
    197, 206
Human nature, 17, 78, 93–95, 140,
    172
Hume, David, 135, 140, 222n2, 226n16
Huxley, Aldous, 87, 110–111
Huxley, Julian, 8, 87

Immortality
    absolute, 20, 96–97, 145
    in animals, 2
    contingent, 20, 97, 109, 122, 145–148
    definition of, 20
    Epicurus on, 40
    in Greek myth, 7–8, 66
    holist notions of, 83–84
    in modern fiction, 8–10
    transhuman, 4
    Wise View on, 10–11, 14
Imperial perspective, 168, 172
Impossible projects, 126. *See also* Smuts,
    Aaron
Indifference
    toward death, 49–50, 56
    toward life, 70, 105–106
Individualism, 14, 89–91, 93, 154

Inequality, 87, 190, 192, 195, 201
    causing distress, 190
    of health, 195
    justification of, 237n37 (*see also* Rawls,
        John: Difference Principle)

Japan
    demography, 153, 168
    economy, 173–176, 178, 182, 188,
        193, 207

Kagan, Shelley, 46, 107–108, 136
Kant, Immanuel, 91–92, 205,
    212–213n32
Kantianism. *See* Kant, Immanuel
Kass, Leon, 9, 15, 89, 147–148, 197
    on aging, 33
    and bioconservatism, 15, 17–18
    on death and beauty, 139–144
    death and boredom, 95–99
    on death and meaning, 113–117, 122
    on death and virtue, 133–137
    fallacies of, 145–148
Kazez, Jean, 118
Kenyon, Cynthia, 28
Kübler-Ross, Elisabeth, 10
Kuran, Timur, 212n27
Kurzweil, Raymond, 4, 21

Larkin, Phillip, 13, 42–44, 46
Lewis, C. S., 8–9
Liberalism, 15, 17, 88, 91–92, 193
    vs. conservatism, 184
    and economics, 181, 193
    vs. holism, 89–93, 102
    left-, 193, 237n37 (*see also* Rawls,
        John)
    vs. Nazism, 88
    and prolongevism, 14–17, 20, 200
    rights, 172
Life expectancy
    average increase over time, 1–2, 4, 28
    and boredom, 148

Life expectancy (cont.)
  and the economy, 172–178
  and overpopulation, 150, 152–157,
    168–169
  and procrastination, 115, 127, 129,
    148
  and societal progress, 182–183,
    186–188, 195, 205–207
Life extension
  access to, 16, 189–196
  bioconservative view of, 16
  and boredom, 95, 97, 99, 102, 108
  fallacies in reasoning about, 114, 122,
    145–146
  indefinite, 12
  liberal view of, 16–17
  as medicine. See Medicine
  and nature, 93
  and overpopulation, 149, 155–156,
    169, 172
  public attitudes toward, 5, 201,
    211n22
  radical, 17, 21, 35, 60, 97, 114, 155,
    172, 189, 196, 200, 207
  and religion, 12
  research, 2, 4
  social consequences-based worries
    about, 60, 149. See also Tragedy of
    the commons
  in stories, 8
  and transhumanism, 21
Locke, John, 8, 16, 91, 186
Longevity. See Life expectancy; Life
    extension
Lucretius, 6, 47, 50, 149, 171
  death in the big scheme of things,
    80
  diminishing the time we do not exist,
    53–54
  fear of death, 55
  hopeless desires, 66–67
  mirror argument, 50–53
  summary of arguments, 6

Makropulos Case, The, 104–105.
    See also Williams, Bernard
Malthus, Thomas, 150, 162, 173
Marx, Karl, 159, 176, 181
Medicine
  antiaging, 5, 10, 102, 201
  distribution of antiaging, 156,
    190–194
  increasing the average life span, 4,
    153, 167
  meaning and purpose of, 10, 23,
    34–37, 89, 93, 110–111
  preventative, 35–36, 194
Meilaender, Gilbert, 27, 33
Methuselah, 86
Mill, J. S., 91–92
Mirror argument, 50, 53
Modernity, 88, 90, 92, 165, 188, 197
  as a cause of decreased fertility,
    153–154
Momeyer, Richard, 12
Montaigne, Michel de, 6, 32–33

Nagel, Thomas, 11, 45–47, 85, 115
Nihilism, 49, 82, 109
Nonexistence, 48, 50–53, 67
  posthumous, 50–51
  prevital, 50–51
Nuland, Sherwin B., 86
Nussbaum, Martha, 117–118

Opportunity cost, 9, 34, 41. See also
    Deprivation account
Overall, Christine, 53, 100
Overpopulation, 133, 149–153,
    156–157, 159, 161, 163, 165,
    167–169, 175–176, 201

Personal identity, 51–53, 106–107,
    109, 136. See also Kagan,
    Shelley
Pessimism
  about extending life, 4

about life, 57–64, 67–70 (see also Schopenhauer, Arthur)
about overpopulation, 151, 157, 162,
167–169
PEW Research Center, 5, 11–12, 25
Plato, 6, 79, 84
on aging, 28, 30
on beauty, 140–141
on death as liberation from the body,
64–68, 84
on fearing death, 39
on justice, 135
on knowledge, 125–126
Population pyramid, 172, 207
Presentism, 3 (see also Einstein, Albert)
President's Council of Bioethics, 9, 82
Priorities, 19, 107, 189, 194
Procrastination, 114–115, 129, 132
Prolongevism, 6, 12, 15, 19
Prolongevist, 4, 100, 194
Prometheus, 96, 134
PSR (potential support ratio), 173–175

Rawls, John, 92, 237n37
Difference Principle, 237n37
Rebel, 10, 12–14, 17, 56, 68, 77, 88
Reiss, Steven, 103
Religion, 7, 12–13, 90, 108, 153
Resignation, 32, 70
Russell, Bertrand, 73

Sandel, Michael J., 15–17
Sartre, Jean-Paul, 74
Schopenhauer, Arthur, 59, 61–64,
67–68, 71, 127
Seneca, 40, 82, 84, 129, 203–204
Sessions, George, 83
Sisyphus, the myth of, 66
Skepticism, 109
Slaughter, Anne-Marie, 129–130
Smuts, Aaron, 121
Social consequences, 145, 149, 171, 189
Social hierarchies, 172, 179–180

Socrates, 6, 28, 65, 68–70
Sophocles, 29, 62
Sour grapes, 14, 63, 199
Stagnation, 153, 179, 200
Stapleton, Olaf, 8
Stoicism, 6, 40, 56, 81–82, 84, 106, 144
Superhuman, 56, 84, 144, 196

Taleb, Nassem Nicholas, 164
Terror
of dying, 40
management, 30, 55
Thanatophobia, 10
Tithonus, 7, 134
Tolerance of death, 49
Tolkien, J. R. R., 8–9
Tragedy, 10, 13–14, 60, 68, 77, 84, 131,
142, 186, 188, 191
Tragedy of the commons, 60
Transhumanism, 21–22, 74, 172

Underdetermination, 114–115, 136
United Nations, 2
access to water, 158
International Panel on Climate
Change (IPCC), 163
population division, 152–153,
171–172, 176
Utilitarianism, 91, 126

Value(s)
aesthetic, 140
of aging, 23, 26, 28
changing, 107, 182
common, 37, 85
death as a condition of, 95–97, 132,
144, 146
economic, 174, 176, 178
happiness as a, 91
liberal, 14–16, 92, 182, 183, 189
of life, 44, 46, 57
medical, 19 (see also Medicine)
moral, 135–137

Value(s) (cont.)
  and opportunity cost, 118, 129, 130
  of persons, 84 (*see also* Kant,
    Immanuel)
  and place in time, 51
  and politics, 184
  subjective vs. objective, 17–18, 91–92,
    212–213n32
  tension between, 126

Wells, H. G., 1939, 87
Wendler, David, 82–83
Wheelock, John Hall, 142
Whitman, Walt, 83
Williams, Bernard, 104, 105–109, 122,
    226n16
Wise View, 77, 137, 145, 147–148, 168,
    195, 200–201, 206–207
  of aging, 23, 25, 37
  argument against, summarized, 18–22,
    210n10
  defined, 6, 10–11, 77
  fallacies of, 145, 147
  hindering antiaging research, 195, 207
  as incongruent with our liberal values,
    14
  internalized, 206
  on its way out, 200–201
  as morally and intellectually superior,
    11, 137
  and the need to avoid tragedy, 13, 148
  pessimism as a, 168
  and public opinion, 11–14, 201,
    211n22
Wittgenstein, Ludwig, 119–120